Ethelred L. (Ethelred Luke) Taunton

The English black monks of St. Benedict

A sketch of their history from the coming of St. Augustine to the present day

Ethelred L. (Ethelred Luke) Taunton
The English black monks of St. Benedict
A sketch of their history from the coming of St. Augustine to the present day

ISBN/EAN: 9783742861160

Manufactured in Europe, USA, Canada, Australia, Japa

Cover: Foto ©ninafisch / pixelio.de

Manufactured and distributed by brebook publishing software (www.brebook.com)

Ethelred L. (Ethelred Luke) Taunton

The English black monks of St. Benedict

THE ENGLISH BLACK MONKS OF ST. BENEDICT

VOLUME THE FIRST

THE
ENGLISH BLACK MONKS
OF ST. BENEDICT

A SKETCH OF THEIR HISTORY FROM THE
COMING OF ST. AUGUSTINE TO
THE PRESENT DAY

BY THE
REV. ETHELRED L. TAUNTON

IN TWO VOLUMES
VOLUME THE FIRST

LONDON
JOHN C. NIMMO
NEW YORK: LONGMANS, GREEN, & CO.
MDCCCXCVII

Printed by BALLANTYNE, HANSON & CO.
At the Ballantyne Press

TO

MY DEAR FATHER,

IN REMEMBRANCE OF

THE COMMON SORROW

OF

FEBRUARY 13, 1897.

INTRODUCTION

IN these two volumes I venture to bring before the notice of English readers the history of the English benedictines, or "black monks," as they were called in the olden times. To the student the names are well known of men who have devoted large and costly books to the past glories of the monks of this country. These works, however, are difficult of access; and from their very multiplicity of detail, require a mastery of the subject (to be gained only by long and patient study), before a just and general idea of the history as a whole can be obtained. Besides, such works as the *Monasticon* of Dugdale, and others of the school of antiquaries connected with his labours, professedly deal only with the black monks, among other orders, up to the dissolution of the monasteries under Henry VIII. Their subsequent history, known but to a very few even of their descendants, has in course of time become obscured by a legendary growth which does not bear the test of research. It is as an attempt at completing in broad lines the picture of English benedictine history, both ancient and modern, that these pages have been written. The vastness and importance of the subject would require many volumes to treat it adequately, and would be a task beyond my present purpose. But here for the first time is given a definite account of the history, for the last thirteen hundred years, of men who have played no mean part in the making of England, and whose names have ever been revered and cherished.

Writers on the later history, whether in manuscript or otherwise, have drawn their information mainly from the Chronicles of Dom Weldon, a choir brother of St. Edmund's, Paris. That he was often misinformed and also did not understand the nature of the documents he had in hand is a conclusion one is bound to arrive at when his statements are brought to the test. In the present work, I have contented myself (with two most important exceptions noted below) with going to the first-hand evidence contained in the wealth of printed and manuscript material at the disposal of the public; and I feel sure that any further light to be obtained from private sources will only go to illustrate, not to alter, the lines here given. Every statement has been verified, and every reference has been given.

My grateful thanks are due to the many friends who have helped me in what has been a work of love. It is also a tribute of the affection and esteem which I, an outsider, have for the English monks. But I cannot let these pages go forth without a special acknowledgment of my sincere gratitude to the Very Rev. Dom Anselm Burge, O.S.B., prior of St. Laurence's monastery, Ampleforth, for giving me full access to Dom Allanson's voluminous manuscripts; and to Mr. Edmund Bishop for allowing me the free use of his manuscript collections relating to the English benedictines of the middle ages. From these latter I have selected, as most proper for my purpose, the consuetudinary of St. Augustine's, Canterbury, contained in the Cotton MS. *Faustina* C. xii., the transcript of which (completed, as the date tells me, just five-and-twenty years ago) has served me for the appendix to the present volume. This document has the further recommendation of having been hitherto practically overlooked by the ecclesiastical antiquaries.

E. L. T.

LONDON, *August* 6, 1897.

CONTENTS

VOLUME THE FIRST

CHAPTER I

THE COMING OF THE MONKS

PAGES

The vision of St. Benedict—He destined to be "The Father of many Nations"—The growth and influence of the benedictine monks and what England owes to them—The landing of Augustine and his companions—His instructions from Gregory the Great—His institutions—The attitude of the remnants of the British church to him—The acknowledgment of his plan by Irish and Scottish monks—The growth of monastic institutions in England—Wilfrid and Benet Biscop—Bede the Venerable—The Danish invasion and destruction of the Saxon abbeys—The restoration of religious houses and of civilisation by the monks—Archbishop Dunstan and bishops Ethelwold and Oswald: their work as restorers and their institutions—The daily life of the monks under the *Concordia Regularis* of Ethelwold 1-17

CHAPTER II

THE NORMAN LANFRANC

The growth of the Anglo-Saxon church: its second devastation—The Norman invasion—Lay abbats and the disorders they provoked—The confederation of Cluni and the character and growth of the cluniacs—The Italian Lanfranc; he becomes prior of Bec—William of Malmesbury's account of the Christ Church monks in the eleventh century—The Norman attitude

CONTENTS

to the Saxon monasteries and how far it was justifiable—Lanfranc as archbishop of Canterbury : his reforms and statutes : the spread of his changes and their unwelcomeness to the Saxon monks—The incoming of the cluniacs and their settlements in England—The growth of monasticism coeval with the growth of chivalry—Bishop William of St. Carileph and his foundations—The development of constitutional organisation . . 18–30

CHAPTER III

THE BENEDICTINE CONSTITUTION

The nature of the benedictine constitution : the absence from it of the forms of government and special objects peculiar to other orders : its aims and vows : the resemblance of its basis to the family basis of society—Lanfranc's definition of St. Benedict's Rule—The autonomy of the individual houses and their mutual confederation—The embodiment of this principle in the twelfth decree of the Fourth General Council of Lateran—Instances of the observance of the decree in England—The decree enforced by a bull of Benedict XII.—The observance of the bull in England and the holding of chapters—Clement VI.'s modifications of the bull of Benedict XII.—The secession of Christ Church, Canterbury, from the general chapter—The bishop's jurisdiction over the abbats of his diocese—English abbeys which were exempt from episcopal control—The internal government of the abbeys—The benedictine's freedom from peculiar outside work and his consequent power to take up any work 31–48

CHAPTER IV

THE MONK IN THE WORLD

The monk's readiness to labour in the world : his social status and his relation to agricultural industries—The means of livelihood afforded to artisans by the monastic institutions—The monk as an educationalist—The benedictine school foundations—The relief of the poor at the religious houses and the manner in which they were relieved—The spiritual supervision of the people by the monks—The monks the originators of the present parochial system—The origin of vicars—The impropriation and appropriation of benefices in England and the proportion of income reserved to the vicar: English legislation in the matter—The position of the secular clergy—The monasteries as schools for the sons of the nobility—The admission of the greatest of the land to confraternity with the monks—The privileges of the confrater and the ceremony of admission—Kings and princes as confratres—The disadvantages of the monasteries being shelters for the rich as well as poor—Enforced endowments to scholars nominated by the king—The possessions of the monks weighed against their responsibilities 49–64

CHAPTER V

THE MONK IN HIS MONASTERY

The private life of the monks: its calmness and freedom from incident—The combination of the broad outlines of mediæval English life necessary to form a picture of the inner life of the monks—The true history of a monk of the thirteenth century presented in the imaginary history of John Weston of Lynminster—His parentage and education—His dedication to God and his preparation for the monastic life—The attention paid to his physical development—The awakening of his soul—His admission as a novice and his training in the spiritual life—His trial and duties in the year of his novitiate—He becomes a monk—The devotions of the day—The day's meals and what they consisted of—The day's studies—The day's work—The sleeping-house and its arrangement—The monk's recreation and exercise—The foundation of Gloucester Hall, Oxford, by John Gifford, and its incentive to the higher education of the monks—The building of chambers by the abbeys for their own students—John Weston goes to Oxford—His daily life there—His return to Lynminster and his ordination—He teaches the novices—The internal government of the abbey—He becomes prior—He takes the plague—His death and burial 65–96

CHAPTER VI

WOMEN UNDER THE RULE

PAGES

The uncertainty as to St. Scholastica being a nun—The tradition of St. Benedict founding a community of virgins—The absence of any reference to this in his Rule—The reasons for the supposition—The existence of cloisters of women before St. Benedict's time proved—Reasons for supposing that the early English convents were benedictine—Noble foundresses of Saxon convents, Hilda, Eanswith, Ethelburga, Sexburgh, Mildred—Other Saxon nunneries—Ethelburga's abbey at Barking—Cuthburg's foundation at Wimborne—The destruction of the nunneries during the Danish invasion—The convents which survived the invasion—The privileges of abbesses—The life of the benedictine nuns and their partial freedom from the enclosure restrictions of other orders—The nun in Chaucer—The employments of the nuns in their convents—Study and intellectual pursuits their favourite employment—Needlework also practised—Other pursuits—The convent as a place of retreat for lay women—The influences and tendencies of convent life—The social influence of the nuns . . 97–116

CHAPTER VII

CHRONICLES OF THE CONGREGATION. I

The state of the monasteries before their fall—The influence of the abbats compared with that of the bishops—Their mutual relations—An instance of the disputes between monastic chapters and their bishops—St. Edmund and the monks of Christ Church, Canterbury—The character of Edmund—The appeal of the monks to pope Gregory IX.—The papal judges—Intervention of the king—Edmund gives way—Other disputes—Edmund goes to Rome and his dispute with the Canterbury monks is renewed—His return to England—He excommunicates the Canterbury chapter—The reforms of the Lateran Council—The legate Otho and the black monks—His legislation—The alien priories and their origination—The revenues

CONTENTS

estreated by King John—Seizure of the priories by Edward I.: legislation affecting them: their total suppression by Henry V.—The "Black Death" of 1348-49: the terrible effects of the visitation: was mainly responsible for the break-up of the feudal system: its effect upon the monasteries—The conference of Henry V. with the abbats and other prelates in 1422—The king's address—The deliberations of the conference—The nature of its decrees—Their effects—The state of benedictinism on the continent before the dissolution—The cause of the decline there attributable to the system of *commendam*—The system arrested by the reforms of Barbo of Padua—Their spread and efficacy. 117-142

CHAPTER VIII

THE DOWNFALL

The dissolution of the monasteries—The outcome of the trend of events prior to the reign of Henry VIII.—The unpopularity of the monasteries with the court—Henry's accession and Wolsey's rise to power—The pope's authorisations to Wolsey as legate—He suppresses thirty monasteries—The cardinal's agents—Allen and Thomas Cromwell—The fall of Wolsey and the elevation of Thomas Cromwell—Henry's avarice aroused: his want of money—Cromwell authorised to visit the monasteries—The nature of the oath tendered by his commissioners—Royal commission instituted: its powers and object—The worthlessness of the commissioners' reports: their endorsement by the king—The act of dissolution passed by Parliament—The monasteries given to the king in trust only: the enactments relating to this—The people reconciled by public declarations—Appointment of the "court of Augmentations"—The houses suppressed and the value of their lands and personal goods—The exception of some houses and the founding of two new ones by the king—The Lincolnshire risings and the king's merciless suppression of them—Further seizures and surrenderings of houses—Three abbats hanged for high treason—The downfall 143-159

CHAPTER IX

JOHN FECKNAM, ABBAT

PAGES

The state of the monks immediately after the dissolution—The influx of monks to the monastic colleges at the universities—John Fecknam of Evesham—His birth, parentage, and early education—He is sent by the benedictines to Oxford—His return to Oxford after the suppression—Abbat Clement Lichfield of Evesham—Fecknam becomes chaplain to the bishop of Worcester: and to the bishop of London—He is presented to the living of Solihull—His imprisonment in the Tower—The reasons for his committal—He is "borrowed" from prison to hold disputations—Returns to the Tower—Is released and returns to the bishop of London—He becomes rector of Greenford Magna—Is made chaplain and confessor to Mary and dean of St. Paul's—He intercedes for Lady Jane Dudley and for the princess Elizabeth—Assists Mary in her attempt to restore the Catholic Church—The mass restored at Canterbury—The benedictines resume their habits—Renunciation of abbey lands by the queen—Restoration of Westminster abbey—Pole introduces Cassinese ideas—Fecknam appointed abbat—His installation—He receives the mitre—The queen's visit—Fecknam's hospitality—He attends Parliament—His endeavours to restore other monasteries—The petition of the Glastonbury monks—Death of Mary and of cardinal Pole—The accession of Elizabeth—Her political hostility to the catholics—The opening of Parliament and its enactions—The act of the Royal Supremacy passed—The suppression of all religious houses decided upon—The second dissolution of Westminster abbey—The deprivation of the bishops—Fecknam's refusal to take the oath and his ejection—His imprisonment together with the bishops—His life in the Tower—The penalty of death decreed for a second refusal of the oath—Fecknam committed to the care of the bishop of Winchester—Recommitted to the Tower—He justifies his refusal—His treatment in the Tower—Removed to the Marshalsea—Released on parole—He engages in charitable works—Denounced for abusing his parole—Placed under the charge of the bishop of Ely—The regulations for the bishop's treatment of him—His so-called confession—His removal to Wisbeach Castle—His death—Personal appearance—Bequests and surviving MS. works 160–222

CHAPTER X

THE STATE OF ENGLISH CATHOLICS, 1559-1601

PAGES

The deprivations; resulting from the tendering of the oath of supremacy—The state of England after Elizabeth's accession—The conciliatory endeavours of Pius IV. to remedy matters—The succession of Pius V. and his determination to crush the queen—The bull of excommunication and deprivation of sovereign rights—Its effect upon English catholics—Parliamentary counter-enactments to the bull—The establishment of seminaries at Douai and Rome for the English mission—The origin and marvellous development of the jesuits—Their objects—They send two missioners (Parsons and Campion) to England—The characters of the missioners—The objections of the English Catholics overcome—The political intrigues of Parsons—The martyrdom of Campion—Parsons flies to the continent—The failure and ill-advised nature of his intrigues—Other jesuits in England—Parsons' attempt to subjugate the secular clergy to the jesuits—The nature of his tactics and their assistance to Elizabeth—Wisbeach and its miserable dissensions—The arch-priest controversy—The appeal to Rome—Treatment of envoys—Elizabeth favours a deputation of the clergy to the pope—The reception of the deputation and the termination of the contest—The situation on the eve of the return of the benedictines to the mission field 223–255

APPENDIX

THE CONSUETUDINARY OF ST. AUGUSTINE'S, CANTERBURY 257–310

THE ENGLISH BLACK MONKS
OF ST. BENEDICT

CHAPTER I

THE COMING OF THE MONKS

ST. GREGORY the Great (604), in the second Book of Dialogues,[1] tells us that shortly before the death of St. Benedict (542) that great monastic law-giver saw one night in vision the whole world gathered together under one beam of the sun. The eyes of the Saint surely must have rested with a peculiar satisfaction upon one small island, then, save one little corner, all shrouded in pagan darkness. For England was destined within some fifty years after his death to be taken hold of by his children and, once converted, to become the most favoured spot in all his patrimony. For, like Abraham of old, Benedict was destined to be " the Father of many Nations," the harbinger of Truth and Justice and Civilisation to races still wrapped in the darkness of heathendom. And when he had entered into his patrimony, in

[1] Chapter xxxv.

thousands of monasteries, in Europe alone, was he invoked as father; and each of these houses became a centre of Life and Light to all the country round. But nowhere did his sons identify themselves with the land, and link themselves in love with the people, as in England. Here they were racy of the soil; and in English Benedictine hearts love of country existed side by side with love of their state. Up and down the land most of the episcopal sees, those centres of Life to the Church, were founded by them; and in course of time monks formed the chapters. For centuries the Primate of all England wore the habit of St. Benedict, and was elected to his post by the monks of Christ Church cathedral-monastery. And in the social order, the England of to-day owes much to the monks, who founded schools and universities, hospitals and workshops. All the learning there was they possessed, and, with generous hand, freely did they open their stores of knowledge to all comers. The very foundations of English liberty and law and order were laid by benedictines interpreting and living according to their Rule.

"They were all in all to England; its doctors and its lawyers and its councillors; and on every page of the country's annals their names may be found in honour as the champions of the liberties of Church and People."[1]

It is not going too far, but it is the sober truth to

---

[1] *A Sketch of the Life and Mission of St. Benedict*, by a monk of St. Gregory's Priory (Downside, 1880), p. 24.

say, England in great measure is what she is to-day through the work and the influence of St. Benedict's sons. And there has always been deep set in English hearts a love for the Benedictine name, which no time, absence, or calumny could efface.

Sent by Gregory the Great, himself a monk and founder of monasteries, and who himself would have come had not his elevation to the Chair of Peter intervened, Augustine, prior of the monastery of St. Andrew's on the Celian Hill,[1] at Rome, with forty companions, after long journeyings and much discouragement, landed on English soil. Richborough, in the Island of Thanet, is the spot which, if tradition speaks truly, welcomed the monks, and whence they spread gradually over the whole country. No time was lost in preparing for their work. In solemn procession, with silver cross and painted banner borne aloft, they set out, chanting litanies in the grave, majestic Latin tongue; and they called upon God, through the intercession of His saints, to enlighten the Saxons who then sat in darkness, to dispel the shadow of death hanging over the land, and to set this people's feet in the ways of peace.[2] How the glad tidings were received by king and people, and how, in a short hundred years, from that corner in Kent a force went forth which stirred up the hearers to receive the faith, and going beyond the

[1] The Cardinalitial title of *SS. Gregory and Andrew on the Celian Hill* was assigned with peculiar fitness to the late cardinal Manning, and again to his successor, the present archbishop of Westminster.
[2] Bede's *Historia Ecclesiastica Gentis Anglorum*, lib. i. c. xxv.

borders, roused other missioners, monks too, to come and help in the work of evangelising, is well known to all. The impulse and example were Augustine's. The other helpers in the vineyard at length fell in with the plan he received from pope Gregory and the traditions he brought from the Apostolic See.

The foundations of the English Church were set with consummate skill. Both Gregory and Augustine were men full of the Benedictine largeness of mind. In answer to Augustine, Gregory had instructed him to select any of the rites and usages found in the neighbouring churches of Gaul and elsewhere, which he might consider more useful for the newly-formed English Church than those observed in Rome.[1] And so, tended by such men, the Faith of Christ took root in a congenial soil, and in due time grew and took the outward form of beauty, in harmony with the national characteristics.

On his first arrival he built, just outside the city walls, a monastery which he dedicated to SS. Peter and Paul (afterwards known as St. Augustine's), in

---

[1] "You know, my brother, the custom of the Roman Church, in which you remember you were bred up. But it pleases me that if you have found anything either in the Roman or the Gallican, or any other Church which may be more acceptable to Almighty God, you carefully make choice of the same, and sedulously teach the Church of the English, which, as yet, is new in the Faith, whatsoever you can gather from the several Churches. For things are not to be loved for the sake of places, but places for the sake of good things. Choose therefore from every Church those things that are pious, religious, and upright, and when you have, as it were, made them up into one body, let the minds of the English be accustomed thereto."—BEDE, *Histor. Eccl.*, lib. i. cap 27 (Bohn's Translation), pp. 41, 42.

which he chose his last resting-place. But as the centre of his work, Augustine founded, along with his cathedral of Christ Church at Canterbury, a monastery for his monks, thus reproducing in the dedications at Canterbury the two features of Rome, the Lateran and Vatican churches; just as at Rochester, hard by, they recalled by the same means their old home of St. Andrew's on the Celian Hill, and at London St. Paul's, *extra muros*. From his companions he selected Mellitus and Justus to be bishops of the sees he had set up at the neighbouring towns of London and Rochester. Paulinus, too, was sent by him to York, there to lay the foundations of the Church in the kingdom of Northumbria.

Among the remnants of the British Church which had fled for shelter to the mountains of Wales, were many Irish monks whose manner of living was much the same as that of St. Columbanus; and great monasteries, as for instance that of Bangor, still flourished. But they would have nothing to do with the new-comers, who invited them to help in converting their hated oppressors the Saxons. They would not heed the call of Augustine, and on frivolous pretexts refused to acknowledge him. Neither would they bring themselves into line with the rest of the Western Church on changes of discipline which, in their present isolation, were unknown to them. They would not listen, but remained sullen and obstinate in their separation.

Not so, however, with other monks from Ireland and the Scottish isles. They came into the northern parts of England and walked in harmony with the Roman missionaries. But when in some of them, too, the conservative element asserted itself unduly and made them want to remain stationary while the rest of the world moved, these remnants of a past age retired from the scene, and the more vigorous of the Celtic missioners gradually amalgamated with the Roman monks.[1]

Although in parts the Faith for a while was resisted and missionaries had to fly the storm, other monks took their place and toiled on, gathering in the harvest which lay white on all the country round. Soon, too, sprung up monasteries of virgins who served God in the monastic habit. Hilda,[2]

[1] The rule of St. Columbanus professes to be simply a tradition of what he had learnt in Ireland. The code of discipline is marked by much sternness and severity, forming in this a complete contrast to the moderation of St. Benedict. Lashes, even to two hundred in number, were freely bestowed for very trivial faults. Fastings, excommunications, and lengthened periods of enforced silence were also ordinary punishments. This rigidity was bound to give way in time to the more human, and therefore more natural, spirit which came from Monte Cassino.

[2] St. Hilda, from her connection with St. Aidan, evidently at first followed the Scottish rule. But we find her later on sending some of her monks to Canterbury to learn the discipline and rule of the benedictines at Christ Church. Probably after the famous synod of Whitby (664), when she found so many of the columban monks preferring their dead traditions to the living voice, she turned for safety's sake to St. Benedict's rule, which had come to England directly from the Chair of Peter. Lingard says that the benedictine Rule was first introduced into Northumbria in 661; while the West Saxons received it in 675, and the Mercians not until 709. See *History of England* (ed. 1849), vol. i. p. 269, *note*.

Etheldreda, Mildred, Werburgh, Edith, and others, were leaders in a movement which called maidens from the courts of kings to the cloister of the King of kings. Princes, too, put down their crowns and sceptres and put on the humble garb of the monk, and, in the silence of the monastery, won victories more glorious than had been theirs outside the cloister.

So the work sped. Great names such as Wilfrid (709) and Benet Biscop (690) stand out as pre-eminent in the work of introducing the rule of St. Benedict into the North. The first, educated at Lindisfarne, gained his earliest impressions of Benedictine life from Canterbury, whence he journeyed through France to Rome. There he was confirmed in them. The other, who had become a monk at Lerins[1] in 666, came from Rome itself in the train of the great archbishop Theodore, and by him was made abbat of St. Augustine's at Canterbury. After two years, in 671, he, too, went to Northumbria, and built an abbey at Wearmouth and another at Jarrow. These were the men raised up by God to strengthen and establish monastic discipline throughout England after the pattern laid down by St. Benedict. By their travels in France and Italy they were able to gather, here and there, the best features of regular observance, and returning they introduced them into English houses during their frequent journeys up and down the country. Ædde in his life of Wilfrid

---

[1] St. Augustine stayed at Lerins on his way to England.

speaks in the fourteenth chapter of the visits to Canterbury, whence "returning with the Rule of Benedict to his own region (Ripon), with Ædde and Æona, the chanters, and with architects, and with the ministry of almost every kind of art, he right well improved the institutions of the Church."[1] Benet, like Wilfrid, was constant in his journeyings to Rome. But while the one went for Justice, the other was drawn abroad in the interests of his monasteries of Wearmouth and Jarrow. He collected a large library, and introduced into England new arts and industries, notably those of building in stone and the glazier's craft. He brought back ancient manuscripts, rich paintings and vestments, and great stores of relics of saints and martyrs. In one of these monasteries (Jarrow) dwelt Bede the Venerable, the type of the monk; a student and a scholar, who loved to impart his knowledge to others. Passing from childhood to old age in the faithful observance of the Religious Life, he is the flower of the monastic schools, such as were started by Aidan and Aldhelm. He, too, is the father of English history.

About a hundred years after Benet Biscop had lived and worked, the storm of Danish invasion swept down upon the coast, and the northern monasteries felt to the full the effects of the disastrous times.

---

[1] Gale, *Rerum Anglicarum Scriptores*, vol. iii. p. 58.

But long before destruction thus fell upon them at home, Saxon benedictine monks had turned their faces towards the still heathen tribes of Germany. Winfrid, Willibald, and Willibrord, with a host of others, including nuns who went to do Woman's work in evangelising, became the apostles and teachers of other countries, and by toil and blood founded Churches fruitful in saints.

When the fierceness of the invaders passed, the Saxon monks set themselves manfully to repair the disaster, and rebuild the broken walls of the houses destroyed by the Danes.[1] How they restored civilisation Cardinal Newman shall tell us; for the picture he draws of St. Benedict's Mission to Europe in general is perfect in detail as regards England in old Saxon days.

"He (St. Benedict) found the world, physical and social, in ruins, and his mission was to restore it in the way—not of science, but of nature; not as if setting about to do it; not professing to do it by any set time, or by any series of strokes; but so quietly, patiently, gradually, that often till the work was done, it was not known to be doing. It

[1] The nunneries in the northern parts of England, the most exposed to the Danish invasion, never recovered themselves as the monasteries did. It was not until after the Conquest that convents for women were again established in these parts. The southern parts were more fortunate in some instances. This will also account for the fact that there were so few houses for women that were abbeys. The Saxon houses were invariably abbatial; but of the Norman foundation three only attained that dignity; to wit, Godstowe, Malling, and Elstowe.

was a restoration rather than a visitation, correction, or conversion. The new world he helped to create was a growth rather than a structure. Silent men were observed about the country, or discovered in the forest digging, cleaning, and building; and other silent men, not seen, were sitting in the cold cloister tiring their eyes and keeping their attention on the stretch, while they painfully deciphered, then copied and recopied, the manuscripts which they had saved. There was no one that *contended or cried out*, or drew attention to what was going on; but by degrees the woody swamp became a hermitage, a religious house, a farm, an abbey, a village, a seminary, a school of learning, and a city. Roads and villages connected it with other abbeys and cities which had similarly grown up; and what the haughty Alaric or fierce Attila had broken to pieces these patient meditative men have brought together and made to live again. And then, when they had in the course of many years gained their peaceful victories, perhaps some new invaders came, and with fire and sword undid their slow and persevering toil in an hour. . . . Down in the dust lay the labour and civilisation of centuries — churches, colleges, cloisters, libraries—and nothing was left to them but to begin all over again; but this they did without grudging, so promptly, cheerfully, and tranquilly, as if it were by some law of nature that the restoration came; and they were like the flowers and shrubs and great trees which they reared, and which, when ill-treated, do not take vengeance or remember evil, but give forth fresh branches, leaves, and blossoms, perhaps in greater profusion or with richer quality, for the very reason that the old were rudely broken off."[1]

Thus did the monks live and work after the eighth century had expired amid the flames the Danes had enkindled. Foremost in the work of restoration was Dunstan, whose name is writ large over the history of his times. To him and to his fellow-worker Ethelwold and to Oswald must be given the success of the revival. Of the former, Cardinal Newman says:—

"As a religious he shows himself in the simple character of a benedictine. He had a taste for the arts generally, especially music. He painted and embroidered; his skill in smith's work is recorded in the well-known legend of his combat with the evil one. And, as the monks of Hilarion joined gardening with psalmody, and Bernard and his cistercians joined field-work with meditation, so did St. Dunstan use music and painting as directly expressive or suggestive of devotion. 'He excelled in writing, painting, moulding in wax, carving in wood and bone, and in work in gold, silver, iron, and brass,' says the author of his life in Surius, 'and he used his skill in musical instruments to charm away from himself and others their secular annoyances,

[1] *Historical Sketches*: "The Mission of St. Benedict," vol. iii. pp. 410, 411.

and to raise them to the theme of heavenly harmony, both by the sweet words with which he accompanied his airs and by the concord of the airs themselves.'"[1]

Abbat of Glastonbury, and looking forward to no other occupation than that of training the vine committed to him, Dunstan, by one of those noteworthy exceptions, was called from the peace of the cloister into the turmoil of political life.

"It must be a serious emergency, a particular inspiration, a sovereign command, which brings the monk into political life; and he will be sure to make a great figure in it, else why should he have been torn from his cloister at all? . . . The work (he) had to do, as far as it was political, was such as none could have done but a monk with his superhuman single-mindedness and his pertinacity of purpose."[2]

Made successively bishop of Worcester and of London, and then archbishop of Canterbury, he was able by his influence to bring about a general restoration of monasticism in England. Beyond a peremptory and somewhat overweening assertion of a Winchester monk writing at the end of the tenth century, there seems to be no contemporary proof of the often asserted proposition that monasticism had almost ceased in England. The fact seems to be the reverse, for the documentary evidence at hand points to the existence of houses other than Glaston and

---

[1] *Ibid.* pp. 415, 416.   [2] *Ibid.* pp. 381, 382.

Abingdon. It was the northern monasteries that principally felt the effects of the Danish invasion, while those of the south escaped. But doubtlessly learning and observance had greatly fallen in the surviving monasteries, and it was from the restored vigour of Glaston, Abingdon, and Winchester that English benedictines renewed their spirit. Together with the new life came an outburst of intellectual activity. A religious and artistic development took place, which is the crowning glory of the Anglo-Saxon Church.

Dunstan found a powerful support in the pious King Edgar, who seconded all his efforts with the resources of the temporal power. Ethelwold, bishop of Winchester, and one of the monks of his own monastery of Glaston, carried out in detail the plan conceived in the master mind of the great primate. At Worcester, too, bishop Oswald was working to the same end, on lines he had learnt at Fleury, where he had become a monk. Under these bishops, monks were introduced into the cathedral churches of Winchester and Worcester.

The king and a thane, Alfreth, gave Ethelwold the manor of Southborne, on the condition he translated the Rule of St. Benedict into Anglo-Saxon, so that those who did not know Latin might learn the monastic life.[1] This the bishop did, and to him is also due the redaction of the *Concordia Regularis*,

[1] This is very possibly the very translation which has been lately edited on a collation of the MSS. by Professor Schröer.

a body of rules to be observed by English monks and nuns.[1] This was also translated into the native tongue.[2]

Under the care of Dunstan and Ethelwold and Oswald, in a few years more than forty monasteries rose from their ruins, and God's praises were sung throughout the land once more by Benedictine lips. Piety and learning[3] again flourished.

The author of the *Concordia Regularis* states that he has allowed himself the same freedom Gregory gave to Augustine, of choosing the best things he could find, and that he had taken whatever he considered useful[4] in the two nearest great centres of Benedictine life, Fleury[5] and Ghent, in the abbeys

---

[1] For the *Concordia Regularis* see Reyner's *Apostolatus Benedictinorum in Anglia*, iii. pp. 77-94.

[2] See "Anglia" of Halle, vol. xiii. p. 365.

[3] The feast of the Conception of Our Lady seems to have originated in England, and can be traced to the monks of Winchester. It was prevalent and firmly established before the Conquest, when, like so many English customs, it suffered a temporary eclipse. Its revival was mainly due to the younger Anselm, abbat of St. Edmundsbury, in the latter half of Henry I., and was formally sanctioned by a council held in London, 1129. The story of Helin of Ramsey is in the highest degree doubtful. See *Downside Review*, vol. v. p. 107.

[4] See *Prœmium* of the *Concordia Regularis*.

[5] Ethelwold, as soon as he became abbat of Abingdon, besides getting chanters from Corbie (*Chron. de Ab.*, vol. i. p. 129), sent Osgar "to Fleury to be further instructed in the observance of St. Benedict's Rule." See "Saxon Leechdoms," vol. iii. p. 409, in *Roll Series*. Mr. Cockayne is mistaken when he adds "and to fetch home a copy"; this is not the meaning of the original texts. As a fact, the earliest known copy of St. Benedict's Rule, and embodying the primitive text, is an English manuscript of a date more than two centuries earlier than Ethelwold.

of which latter city Dunstan, during his exile under Edwi (956), had found shelter.

But while the author of the *Concordia*, who evidently writes under the influence of the master-mind of Dunstan, was quick enough to recognise and use all that was good in foreign interpretations of the Rule, he was too wise to establish wholesale such of their provisions as were unsuitable to Englishmen. There was no rough upheaval of past traditions; neither were these treated with contempt and set aside as useless. He particularly lays down that: "We have determined in no ways to cast aside the worthy customs of this country pertaining to the (service of the) Lord, which we have learnt from the practice of those who went before us; but (on the contrary) altogether to give them new force and vigour."[1] A wise provision; for in a rule so wide and elastic as St. Benedict's, and in which so much is left to the discretion of local superiors, it is but common sense to suppose that Englishmen will be the best interpreters of what is useful for the men with whom they have to deal, and of what is most in keeping with the national character.

The daily life of monks under the *Concordia Regularis* was on the following plan, with local variations no doubt. The monks rose at 2 A.M., and spent a long day in the office and work appointed till 8 P.M., when they went to bed. The constitutions go into many interesting details both

[1] *Proœmium to the Concordia Regularis.*

of liturgical and domestic interest. For instance, the little hours took place at the normal times of 6 for prime, 9 for tierce, which was followed by the mass, 12 for sext, 2 or 3 for none, 4 or 6 for vespers, and 7 for compline. After prime, or before in summer, the monks put off the habits they had slept in, and washed and shod themselves for the day. From Easter till Holy Cross, in September, they dined after sext, and then had a *siesta*. The intervals were filled up with reading; and it is evident from their remains that the time was well spent. From Holy Cross till Lent, the time of the monastic fast, they dined after none. But in Lent they did not break their fast till vespers had been sung. Before compline they put off their day-clothes, and, on Saturdays, washed their feet. In the winter, " from the Kalends of November till the beginning of Lent," a fire was provided in the common-room, to which all might go for warmth. They had only one full meal a day, together with a collation out of Lenten time.[1] Such was the re-

---

[1] Here it will be useful to gain a true view of the question, How far did the law of perpetual abstinence enjoined by St. Benedict in his Rule [*Cap.* 39] obtain in English monasteries? Prescinding from the discretion he leaves to superiors, who are the best judges of the present needs of their monks, we stand on solid ground when we listen to the teaching of history on this point—and its teaching is clear and precise. In the most flourishing time of English monasticism the use of flesh meat was allowed. The use of poultry did not come under the prohibition which forbids the *carnes quadrupedum*. Then, the example of St. Ethelwold, on whom fell the practical work of refounding English observance, is instructive. Whilst he himself, as a rule, never eat meat, yet twice at least we find him going beyond his ordinary

newed Benedictine life which Dunstan, Ethelwold, and Oswald built up again in England, and which went on until an almost greater upheaval took place when the Norman mastered the land, and for a time foreigners were set to rule in abbeys and priories. But, as we shall see, English monasticism was of too sturdy a character to lose its own individuality. Once more it quietly absorbed all the good there was in the new element, and then reasserted itself on its old lines, only more strong and more comely than ever.

custom. Once, during a space of three months, when sick, he eat meat by the express command of St. Dunstan, his former abbat and spiritual guide, and then again during his last illness (See the original life of the saint in *Chron. de Ab.*, vol. ii. p. 263). But while severe to himself, he was lenient to others in this matter. At Abingdon, his first and most special foundation, he showed his estimate of the common need by permitting in the refectory a dish of stew mixed with meat, *ferculum carne mixtum;* and on certain feast-days, meat puddings, *artocreæ* (*Chron. de Ab.*, vol. ii. p. 279). It is hardly to be doubted that what was established at Abingdon represented the custom Ethelwold had learnt at Glaston from Dunstan himself, and found its counterpart in the other monasteries existing and restored at this time. "He established monasteries in Abingdon, Hyde, Ely, Burgh, and Thorney, and in all (introduced) the customs which prevailed in the monastery of Abingdon" (*Chron. de Ab.*, vol. i. pp. 345-348; ii. p. 279). Of course, from the practice of St. Ethelwold, it cannot be necessarily inferred that the custom obtained in every English monastery. But the *Concordia*, which was drawn up for all, seems to provide for and recognise the custom as generally existing. *Pinguedo* (pork fat) is here allowed up to Septuagesima (*Apostolatus*, iii. p. 85). Thus far we get light upon a subject about which there has been much misapprehension, and find what was the custom, as a matter of fact, in houses the most fervent and most affected by the great revival under St. Dunstan.

CHAPTER II

THE NORMAN LANFRANC

THE Church of the Anglo-Saxon, the work mainly of monks, spread over all the land. Its growth in holiness, in civilisation, in learning of all kinds, is witnessed by the memories of a Bede, a Wulstan, a Paulinus, an Erkonwald and Aldhelm, and many others whose names are sweet in English ears; and the sons of St. Benedict were regarded with loving reverence as the benefactors of their country. But all this fair province of God's Church was once more to be devastated but not destroyed, changed but not altered. Not this time by pagan Dane, but by Christian Northmen, men who to their native simplicity and bravery had added the culture of the Franks, whom they had conquered, and among whom they had settled.

But the changes about to be wrought in England did not come solely from the fact that the Saxons had to recognise Normans as masters by right of conquest. The invaders were the means by which a movement already greatly developed abroad made its power felt in English monasteries.

The changes then going on in society at large

brought into relief, more strongly than at other times, a feature in Benedictine government which might, under force of exterior circumstances, degenerate from its primitive institution. Each abbey, being alone and separated from other houses, was obviously less capable of resisting external attacks than when united with others for common defence. It was not an unknown thing, for instance, for some lay nobleman, through royal influence and favours, to be appointed abbat of a monastery in his neighbourhood. Taking up his residence in the abbey, he would bring with him a train of servants and his family to boot. All this was to the grave detriment both of the property of the abbey, and was fatal to its welfare and discipline. These disorders, to appear under another guise later on, were prevalent in the districts of Burgundy and the western parts of Germany. In 927 Odo of Tours began at Cluni, of which he became abbat, to cope with the difficulty. He met it on two sides—by ordaining a confederation of houses, over which the abbat of Cluni should preside, and by periodical chapters of the abbats of the Order to be held at the head-house. Before long this naturally resulted in subjection; the abbat of Cluni became lord and master of all. Together with these constitutional changes were others regarding the daily life of those who joined the reform. The cluniacs, for so the new Order was called, claimed to live in strict accord with the spirit of the Rule of St. Benedict, and certainly in the matter of the Divine Office, "the Work of God" as the Law-giver calls it, they let nothing be preferred before it. Their ritual observances were marked by a great wealth of splendour and a grandeur and majesty hitherto not realised.[1] It was the marked feature of their life and work. Cluni was fortunate in having at its start many remarkable men, who, gifted with wise energy, stirred up an enthusiasm which carried on the reform, or rather the new Order, to a successful issue. Its houses spread far and wide, and the influence of Cluni made itself felt in quarters where its ideals, as a whole, did not find favour. But it attained its success at the loss of a vital principle. The family tie, so essential a feature in Benedictine life, was lost; for the cluniacs, in whichever of their hundred of houses they might happen to live, were counted members of this great abbey. We need not carry on the history of the Order. Enough has been said to illustrate the character of the changes that awaited the black monks of England.

The chief agent in bringing about the consoli-

---

[1] Some of the other peculiarities of the cluniac Order may here be noted. Two high masses were celebrated every day, and on all greater solemnities the deacon used to be communicated with a part of the priest's host. They were employed more apparently in manual labour, in which all had to take a share, than in study; for as a matter of fact, in view of their enormous extension, the books they wrote are comparatively few. At the chapter each monk was bound to publicly accuse his brethren of any faults he had seen in them. There was great charity to the poor.

dation of the Norman-Saxon Church, was the illustrious Lanfranc, archbishop of Canterbury and *ex officio* abbat of the cathedral-monastery of Christ Church.

Born at Pavia (1005), he became renowned as a teacher, and was in the height of his fame when suddenly the vocation came. Hurrying off to Normandy, he hid himself about the year 1042 in the abbey of Bec, under the abbat Herluin. It was then but a poor monastery, consisting of mud hovels; yet under its holy superior it was growing rich in virtue and the gifts of the spiritual life. Here the light of Lanfranc's learning and piety could not be hid; and his brethren found in the humble brother the famous professor whose loss the learned world was then bewailing. Soon his retreat was discovered, and many of his old scholars flocked to Bec and implored him to help them. The abbat ordered him to resume his lectures; and at once, from being an unknown monastery, Bec became one of the most famous centres of learning in Europe. Lanfranc had by that time become prior of Bec, and Herluin's chief adviser. The large ideas and the sense of beauty in ecclesiastical art he had brought from Italy, joined with the new ideas of liturgical splendour emanating from Cluni, seized upon the prior, and he determined to make of "white-robed Bec"[1] a model of monastic observance. The idea of magnificence

[1] The monks of Bec till 1626 wore a whitish-coloured habit. *Cf.* Leland's *Antiquarii Collectanea*, ed. alt. vol. iv. p. 13.

had, by that time, taken possession of the Normans and was showing itself in stately buildings, magnificent apparel, and a personal grandeur which had become marked features of the age. Hence the time was propitious for the prior's project. The abbat built a church which surpassed in splendour anything known in those parts, and for its use a consuetudinary, "the Use of Bec,"[1] was drawn up in which were reflected the ideas of great stateliness and beauty of worship.

And how did Lanfranc find his cathedral-monastery of Canterbury? If William of Malmesbury, who wrote the *Gesta Pontificum* in 1125, is to be relied upon, "The monks of Canterbury, like all then in England, were hardly different from seculars, except that they were careful on the score of chastity. They amused themselves with hunting, with falconry, with horse-racing; they loved to rattle the dice; they indulged in drink; they wore fine clothes, studied personal appearance, disdained a frugal and quiet life, and had such a retinue of servants, that they were more like secular nobles than monks."[2]

But it will be well to remember that the Normans

---

[1] "The Use of Bec" was adapted in other abbeys, with such changes as various surroundings and traditions demanded. In 1063 Lanfranc was made abbat of Caen, a monastery built by William Duke of Normandy on a scale of princely splendour. In 1067 he refused the archbishopric of Rouen. This was the man who, in 1070, was chosen by William the Conqueror as archbishop of Canterbury.

[2] Malm., *De Gestis Pontif.* (Roll Series), p. 70.

treated the Saxons as a conquered people, and looked upon everything they found as barbarous and needing reformation. The monasteries, being in the minds of the new masters hotbeds of conservatism in which the old Saxon spirit was deeply engrained, they must be taken severely in hand and purged of all such tendencies. Hence it was with a prejudiced eye that writers, such as William of Malmesbury, looked upon the native monk. His account must therefore be taken for what it is worth. Besides, be it remembered, by his express testimony morality was kept in repute, and this hardly seems likely if the picture he draws is to be taken as an accurate one. Where drinking, gaming, and feasting are, there chastity is not likely to remain long: and yet they are expressly exempted from such a charge by the historian. His account does not tally with experience. That the rigour of discipline had fallen off since the days when their cathedral and monastery had been burnt by the Danes, and their archbishop Elphege (1011) murdered might well have been. But there must have been "grit" in them; for by 1020 they had repaired their church and resumed their life after the simple earnest ways of their forefathers. Their number, however, was small; and where numbers are small, observance is difficult.

Whatever their state may have been at Canterbury at the time of the Conquest, one thing is certain, it did not satisfy the more magnificent ideas of Lanfranc. The simplicity of Saxon ritual did not accord with the splendour of worship which had been borrowed from Cluni for Bec and then for his own abbey at Caen. Canterbury must be brought up to the level of the new ideas, and a favourable opportunity offered itself. The cathedral church of Christ Church, the mother-church of the land, had been burnt down on St. Nicholas' day 1067, and although it had been repaired, its condition but ill sorted with its dignity. Lanfranc lent himself manfully to the task. In a short time, but seven years, a new church arose, or rather a new choir (1070) more commensurate with his dignified ideas. Built in the Norman style of the period, the few remains, such as they are, still delight us. The monastery itself was rebuilt, and soon one hundred and fifty monks were gathered together and sang God's praises. For them Lanfranc compiled his famous " statutes," a code of observation largely liturgical. It is in reality in most points but little else than the " Use of Bec." When he sent them to Henry, prior of Christ Church, he enclosed a letter in which he says :—

"We send to you written customs of our Order which we have gathered from the customs of those monasteries which nowadays are of the greatest weight in the monastic Order. We have also added a very few things and changed also a little, especially as regards the celebration of the festivals, deeming they ought to be kept with greater excellence in our Church on account of its having the primatial chair. In which things, however, we do not wish in any way to hamper either ourselves or those who come after us, so that we cannot either add to or take away from, or change them if we think that these matters can be improved on either as the result of our own experience or by the example of others. For however far advanced a man may think himself to be, he is woefully deficient if he thinks that he cannot improve. For a greater or less number of brethren, a varying income, circumstances, differences of personal appreciation, often call for changes. So that hardly any Church can imitate its neighbour in all things."[1]

Lanfranc's changes were the work of time, spreading over many years; for, to quote William of Malmesbury again:—

"Lanfranc was most skilful in the art of arts, the government of souls, and knowing well that habit is second nature, though bent on reforming, he did his work with prudence, and plucking up the weeds little by little, sowed good seed in their place."[2]

His nephew, Paul, who had been set over the abbey of St. Alban's, took Lanfranc's constitutions bodily and introduced them into his house, and adopted his uncle's prudent methods also.[3] What the local influence and example of Lanfranc achieved at Canterbury and at St. Albans, was done on similar lines at other abbeys, where new rulers

[1] *Apostolatus*, iii. p. 211.
[2] Malm., *De Gestis Pontif.* (Roll Series), p. 71.
[3] Walsingam, *Gesta abbatum monasterii S. Albani* (Roll Series), vol. i. p. 52.

would naturally introduce such changes as they themselves had been accustomed to in the Norman abbeys wherein they had learnt the monastic life. A general similarity would mark the movement, but local influence would of course have had full play; for whether we visited Glaston, St. Albans, York, or Chester, we should have found these local peculiarities which must grow round anything that is worthy of the name of "home."

These changes were sore indeed to the Saxon monks, and were sometimes brought about only after great difficulty; for it was not every abbat who, at a time when race antipathies were strong, had Lanfranc's discretion. For instance, when Thurstan, a monk of Caen, was appointed as abbat of Glaston, one of his first steps was to introduce the fashion of chanting to which he had been used. This was the signal for trouble; for, to quote the words of Ordericius :—

"When the violent (*protervus*) abbat tried to force the Glastonians to give up the chant the English had learnt from the disciples of blessed Gregory, the pope, and learn from these Flemings or Normans another chant quite unknown or unheard of before, so fierce a strife arose, which was soon followed by the disgrace of the holy Order. For while the monks would not receive these new regulations, and by their contumacy the stubbornness of their master continuing, lay-men, by the authority of their lord, fell upon the luckless monks in choir with arrows, and some of them were cruelly hurt, and (so it is said) even mortally wounded."[1]

A similar story is told of Malmesbury abbey. In the case of Glaston, the result was in favour of the monks. Thurstan was removed by the King, and a more prudent man set in his place.

In the wake of the Normans, the monks of Cluni entered England and brought with them the idea of monasteries ruled by superiors, the mere nominees at will of an abbat of the house beyond the seas which counted them all her subjects. At the suggestion of Lanfranc, it appears, William, Earl of Surrey, the Conqueror's son-in-law, first brought over in 1077 the cluniacs and settled them at Lewes. In a few years, before William Rufus began his reign, they had secured other houses in England and thence spread. The houses of Bermondsey, Northampton, Thetford, Wenlock, Lenton, Montacute, and Castleacre, are some of their better known foundations, and we may note that altogether there were some thirty-eight houses of this Order in England, besides three hospitals in London and two manors depending on the abbey of Cluni itself. Although the number of their houses was thus considerable and many were large, their peculiar form of government did not find favour with Englishmen, and their Order never became racy of the soil. And even when some cluniacs were appointed over English abbeys, this did not affect the inde-

[1] *Historia Ecclesiastica*, ed. Migne, p. 335.

pendence of these houses. Even those great English abbeys which at times were ruled by cluniacs, kept themselves aloof from any relations with Cluni itself, except that their revenues — as, for instance, at Glaston and Winchester—were used to free Cluni from debt, and seem for four years practically to have supported that house.[1]

This century was the golden age for monasticism. Abbeys and priories sprung up on every side. The burst of new life which the Conquest gave to England, and the tone of mind induced by the growth of chivalry, turned men's minds strongly to the high and noble ideal of the monastic state. The monk was the "Knight of God," and his victories over sin and self appealed to ardent hearts which consumed themselves in the task of accomplishing deeds of valour and heroism. Hence to this period we owe many of our greatest foundations, *e.g.* Durham, where the bishop, William of St. Carileph, formerly abbat of St. Vincent's at Mans, accomplished what his predecessor had vainly tried to do. He gave the secular canons, who possessed the church he designed for his cathedral, the choice of either remaining as monks or of else departing. All, except the dean, elected to go; and for them the bishop, by command of the Pope, instituted the collegiate churches of Aukland, Darlington, and Norton, and provided them with suitable pensions.[2]

[1] *Cf.* Sir G. F. Duckett's *Charters and Records of Cluny*, p. 79.
[2] *Simeonis Dunelmensis Historia de Dunel. Ecclesia.*, lib. iv. cap. 2 et 3.

The monks from the old abbeys of Wearmouth and Jarrow were translated to Durham in 1083; and these houses thenceforth became merely cells dependent on the cathedral-monastery. St. Mary's, York, Battle Abbey, Colchester, Reading, Pershore, and Gloucester are some of the many foundations of this period, to say nothing of the new Order of the white monks of Citeaux, and the black or augustinian canons, and the white canons of Premontré.[1]

In the midst of all this activity, one side of the peculiar movement, which resulted in the new Orders of Cluni and Citeaux, began to tell upon the black monks here and elsewhere. We refer to the constitutional organisation which now began to develop itself. In France, for instance, the abbats of St. Amand, Lobbes, Liesse, Anchin, Rebais, Lagny, and others, all belonging to the ecclesiastical province of Rheims, agreed, about the year 1132, to hold annual meetings for the maintenance of discipline.[2]

An assembly in the year 1152 of the abbats of Upper Lorraine at Metz, under the presidency of

[1] The origin and aims of the cistercians were briefly these: In 1098 Robert, abbat of Molesme, with Stephen Harding and some companions, left his monastery in order to carry out the Rule of St. Benedict to the letter. They found a shelter at Citeaux. The cistercians had a halo of glory cast over them by the great St. Bernard, abbat of the house of Clairvaux. In opposition to the cluniacs, they rejected liturgical pomp. They turned their attention to husbandry and agriculture.

[2] See *Introduction to Monks of the West*, by Dom F. A. Gasquet, ed. Nimmo, vol. i. p. 39; and *Downside Review*, vol. v. p. 59.

Jordan, cardinal-priest, may have had a similar object. These meetings are interesting, for they show that in the immediate neighbourhood of Cluni the idea of some form of association was beginning to work its way among monks who had preserved their own independence. It was being slowly generated, and the time and opportunity for putting it into practice upon strictly Benedictine lines was close at hand.

Innocent III. in the year 1215 held a general council at Rome (the Fourth Lateran) which was attended by 412 bishops and nearly 1000 abbats and priors, and there decreed, among other legislation, a system of union for black monks. What this system was, and how well it meets both the acknowledged want and the requirements of the Benedictine ideal, will be seen in the following chapter.

CHAPTER III

THE BENEDICTINE CONSTITUTION

THERE are no such things, properly speaking, as benedictine constitutions in the sense the word is used in other orders. The benedictines do not form one large body with a general at their head; for St. Benedict did not legislate for a world-wide corporation but for a state of life. Such a form of government as obtains, for instance, in the franciscan or dominican orders would be entirely foreign to the spirit of the holy Rule. Each of the modern orders has some special work in view, to which all their life is directed. They have to find their salvation through the various works of charity for which they were formed, or which they have taken up as an integral portion of their work. Not so with the benedictine. He has no external work peculiar to his order. St. Benedict's ideal is that of the common Christian life of the "Counsels" practised to a higher degree than can be in the world. It is simply the Gospel put into practice. The vows, for instance, of Poverty and Chastity are not explicit as to other orders; for when the Christian life is drawn out to its perfection on the plain, broad Gospel lines, the spirit of poverty must be cultivated and the body kept in subjection.

The vows the benedictine makes are three in number: Stability, that is, to remain attached to his monastery and not wander at will; Conversion of life, that is, until death to labour after attaining the perfection of the state to which he is called; and lastly, Obedience to the abbat. The first two vows concern mainly his interior life, the last his external relation to his superiors. Obedience understood, then, by a benedictine does away with the necessity of laying down minute laws and tracing carefully the lines in which a superior and a subject respectively may move. Constitutions of this kind would cut away entirely at the Benedictine idea of the "home," which we may venture to describe as of this kind.

As God made Society to rest on the basis of the Family, so St. Benedict saw that the spiritual family is the surest basis for the sanctification of the souls of his monks. The monastery therefore is to him what the "home" is to lay-folk. It is a self-contained family, having friendly relations indeed with others, but in no wise losing its own independence and individuality. It has its own peculiar way of looking at things, its own ideals and its own kind of work, which it has spontaneously undertaken, or which has come to it unsought, and which it always manages to stamp with its own peculiar mark. Of this family the abbat is the father; the monks are his sons. The whole spirit is "homely." The monks trust their abbat whom they have freely elected. He loves them and has confidence in them, and in no way can he effectually act except through them. In the benedictine abbey which has grasped the idea of its lawgiver, there will be order and rule, for no family can exist without them: but the yoke will be sweet and the burden light. Largeness and breadth will be the spirit of every house; while from the fact that the influence of any one monastery must necessarily be circumscribed to its own immediate neighbourhood, there will be less chance of friction between one house and another. When each is independent and works out its fortune in its own way, it is an easy matter so to steer the course as to keep clear out of the way of others. From this family idea comes another result: the very fact that St. Benedict did not found an Order but only gave a Rule, cuts away all possibility of that narrowing *esprit de corps* which comes so easily to a widespread and highly organised body.

Lanfranc in the above-mentioned letter to Henry, prior of Christ Church, says: "One point is most carefully to be attended to, namely, that these things without which there is no salvation are to be thoroughly observed: I mean, faith, contempt of the world, charity, chastity, lowliness, patience, obedience, sorrow for past sins, lowly confession of sin, frequent prayers, a fitting silence, and many other things of this kind. Where these are observed, there truly may the Rule of Holy Benet be said to be followed, and there the monastic order kept. No matter how different other things may be; for there are points which have obtained differently in different monasteries by the opinions of different people."[1]

This, then, being the idea, any form of government which destroys the autonomy of each house, or which tends to break up the family, is foreign to the very first principles of benedictine life, and can only be tolerated for a time under the plea of some very great necessity. Confederation of houses for mutual support and advice, on the other hand, is in keeping with the family idea; and for the general good each family may give up some of its rights, as is done in the State. But it must be so arranged that the essential rights are preserved intact, otherwise it is Socialism in its baldest form. There had been, as we have seen, for some time past a movement towards some kind of union among black monks. The vitality which existed in each house is enough to account for such a movement seeking to share its principle of life with others; and we need go no further to seek for the cause. We have also seen how the first steps towards such an end had resulted in specifically distinct orders like those of Cluni and Citeaux. The obvious plan was for the heads of neighbouring houses to meet together, bringing some of their monks, and discuss such

[1] *Apostolatus*, iii. p. 211.

matters as were of general interest. This was the
plan the Church adopted and has expressed in the
Fourth General Council of Lateran. The twelfth
decree, the only one which concerns the monastic
order, in substance is as follows:—

In each province or kingdom let all the abbats
and priors of houses which are not abbeys meet
together (saving all episcopal rights) every three
years in some convenient monastery, and there hold
a chapter, to which all not lawfully excused are
bound to come. Let them, while new to the business, invite, for advice as to procedure, two of the
neighbouring cistercian abbats as being accustomed
to such meetings;[1] and to these must be elected
other two of their own, and the four shall preside
over the assembly. But let these presidents take
heed lest they claim any superiority; for if it is
found expedient they may, after due deliberation, be
changed. The chapter must last for several days,
after the manner of the cistercians; and it is to treat
of such things as the reformation of the order and
of regular observance. Whatever is decided and is
approved of by the four presidents is to be held
as binding upon all. Before the chapter closes,
the date of the next one must be fixed. Those who
attend must lead the common life, and bear proportionately their share of the expenses. If room
cannot be found for them all in one house, then

[1] The first cistercian chapter was held by St. Stephen Harding at Citeaux, 1116.

several together are to lodge elsewhere. Certain men of religious circumspection are to be chosen by the chapter as visitors of every abbey in the province or kingdom. They are to visit in the pope's name both monks and nuns; and correct and reform what they find amiss. If on visitation they find it necessary that any abbat or prior should be deposed, they are to denounce him to his own bishop that he may remove him. If the bishop will not do so, then the case is to be referred to the judgment of the See Apostolic. Any difficulty that may arise in the application of this decree has also to be referred to the pope. This decree also is to be applied to all canons regular, each according to their order. Moreover the bishops have to take such heed to the state of the monasteries in their dioceses, that when the capitular visitors come, they may rather find matter for commendation than correction. The bishops are also to take care that their monasteries are not over-taxed by the visitors, for while the Holy See desires to guard all rights of superiors, she has no wish to injure the subjects. The pope also distinctly orders both bishops and presidents of chapters, under pain of censure, to compel all lay-folk to desist from wronging the monks in person or property; and offenders are to be compelled to make due satisfaction, so that the divine service may go on with all freedom and peace.

Nowhere was the decree so loyally observed, both

in letter and spirit, as in England. Our monks put it at once into force on the lines of the partition of the ecclesiastical provinces of Canterbury and York. No acts of the chapters held in the northern province have come down to us, or, at least, have as yet been printed.[1] In the *Apostolatus* we have collected decrees of a number held in the southern province.[2] These meetings went on, at least, to 1516, when there was a general chapter held in Coventry.[3]

Three years after the Lateran Council, the prelates of the province of Canterbury were holding a chapter in September 1218 at Oxford. The sessions were put off until the 14th of September 1219, when it again met at St. Albans. Its presidents were the abbats of Evesham and St. Augustine's, Canterbury, both of whom had assisted at the Lateran Council. The southern province does not seem to have availed itself of the help of any cistercian abbats. Perhaps the two presidents, fresh from Rome, felt quite capable of conducting the business of chapter without any outside help. From 1218 to 1300 we have traces of no less than twenty-four of these provincial chapters. Oxford and its neigh-

---

[1] The acts of one chapter of the northern province seemed to have been in the hands of Dom Baker: "et aliud (Capitulum) Eboraci circa annum 1266 cujus acta habentur et exordium eorum authenticé discriptum ad tendere possumus" (*Apostolatus*, ii. 39). This chapter is mentioned in *Hist. Dunelm. Scriptor. tres* (Surtees Society), p. 48, in terms which imply a standing institute.

[2] See also *Downside Review*, vol. v. p. 59.

[3] See the Statutes in the Appendix to vol. iii. of *Historia et Cartularium Monasterii Sti. Petri, Gloucestriæ* (Roll Series), pp. 298, 299.

bourhood seems to have been the usual place of meeting, though Glastonbury, Evesham, London, and Northampton were favoured, as well as St. Albans and Reading. In 1236-37 a general chapter, seemingly of all, was held in London preparatory to the opening of the legatine Council of Otho. At this council the legate passed a decree (No. 19) concerning the use of flesh meat. The Italian was judging of the state of English monasticism by what he had been accustomed to in his own warmer land. He says he had gladly heard that the abbats of the order throughout England had lately held a chapter in which they enforced perpetual abstinence according to the Rule of St. Benedict;[1] which decree he now confirms. This change, however, was soon found impracticable; and in the provincial chapter held in 1300 at Oxford, under the presidency of the abbat of Westminster, a decree was passed to dispense with it, as impossible to be kept under the circumstances. This chapter also did away with the number of extra vocal prayers which had been accumulating since the days of St. Dunstan. The meeting at Oxford, 21st September 1253, seems to have been one of both provinces.[2]

It was not long, however, before the benedictine provinces of Canterbury and York were united into one general chapter of a Congregation, coextensive

---

[1] And, it appears, in accordance with the legate's wishes.
[2] *Annales de Theokesberia*, ed. Luard, p. 153; *Annales de Wintonia*, ed. Luard, p. 94.

with the country. The Lateran decree had been only fully carried out in England, and nowhere else. Therefore in 1334 Benedict XII. issued from Avignon on June 20th the famous bull called the *Benedictina*, which enforced the Lateran decree and extended its scope. The abbats of St. Albans and of St. Mary's, York, one for each province, were charged by the Holy See to execute the bull in England. It is a long document, and consists of thirty-nine chapters. As it is one of the most important pieces of legislation for the Order ever issued by the Holy See, it will be well to give here a brief *résumé* of its more important clauses.

After having re-enforced the decree of the Lateran Council about triennial chapters, which affects all superiors, abbats Cathedral and other conventual priors, the pope orders those who cannot attend personally to send proxies, otherwise they are to be fined a double amount of the usual tax levied for chapter expenses. The power of the presidents is to last from chapter to chapter. The two provinces of Canterbury and York are to unite and form only one chapter. (I.) Visitors are only to stay two days at any house when on visitations; and on such occasions there are to be no feastings; neither is money allowed to be received or offered excepting for the bare expenses. Penalties are inflicted against those who infringe this law. (II.) Besides the general chapter; every year a chapter of each particular house has to be held. (III.) The general chapter has power of taxation for general purposes. (IV.) In every house in which there are at least six monks, the daily conventual chapter is to held. (V.) In every house a properly paid teacher is to be appointed to instruct the monks in Grammar, Logic, and Philosophy. Seculars are not to be taught with the monks. (VI.) One monk in twenty must be sent to the universities for higher studies, and he is to have a fixed allowance. Superiors, under penalties, have to seek advice as to whom they send to the university. (VII.) Pensions are to be paid to students according to their rank, out of which they must find food, clothes, books, &c. A prior of the home of studies is to be appointed by the presidents. Each monk-student has once a month to send in his list of belongings. (VIII.) Then, after chapters on the general management of monastic houses regarding business matters (IX. to XXV.), come these laws. Every Wednesday and Saturday, and every day in Advent and from Septuagesima to Easter are days when flesh meat is forbidden to monks unless superiors judged well to dispense in individual cases. All are to sleep in one dormitory, separate cells being strictly forbidden except for students who can use them for purposes of study but not for sleeping. (XXVI.) In monasteries all priests are to celebrate at least twice or thrice a week. Those who are not priests confess at least once a week and communicate once a month.¹ (XXVII.) The rest of the decrees concern benefices and other ecclesiastical injunctions of no general interest.²

This bull was duly announced by the two abbats by letters dated March 10, 1337, and a chapter appointed to be held at Northampton, at the cluniac monastery of St. Andrew, on the following June 10th for the publication of the bull. Northampton was chosen as being most accessible; and the pope allowed the holding of chapters, if more convenient, in houses belonging to another Order.

On June 10, 1338 (Wilkins gives this date), the first united chapter was held as arranged.³ The abbat of York said the mass, and afterwards he of St. Albans preached in Latin *prout decuit*. As soon as the chapter had begun its session, a royal messenger, one Master Philip, a cleric of London, was announced. He brought letters from the king forbidding the fathers to do aught contrary to the royal prerogative or to the laws of the land. The

---

¹ The old rule laid down in the *Concordia Regularis* was daily Communion; even on Good Friday; and the reason was given in the words of St. Augustine: "Because in the Lord's Prayer we do not ask for our yearly but for our daily bread. . . . So live as to be worthy to receive every day; for he who is not worthy to receive daily is not worthy to receive once a year" (*Lib. de Verbis Domini*). It must be remembered that the wording of the *Benedictina* was made to apply to all countries, the names of Canterbury and York being only inserted in the copy sent to England. Hence the regulation in Chapter XXVII. does not go to prove that in England, at least, monks had fallen off from their old practice.

² Wilkins, *Concilia*, vol. ii. pp. 585-613.

³ *Ibid.* p. 626.

session was prorogued for two days to consult how to satisfy the king and obey the pope's commands; which they were able to do by showing the meeting to be concerned only with their own internal affairs. After this they proceeded to business, and the abbats of Westminster, Gloucester, and Bardney were chosen presidents. The bull was formally read, and was ordered to be kept at Westminster, as the most secure place of deposit. Visitors were nominated for the whole of England, and a commission was appointed, now that the two provinces were united, to overlook the decrees of the former provincial chapters and decide what was to be kept as binding upon the whole Congregation.

These chapters, held then at fixed intervals until the Dissolution, were regularly representative bodies, consisting not only of the heads of the houses, but also of ordinary monks deputed by their fellow-religious to attend. The records of some of these chapters still exist, and are full of interest, showing as they do the practical working of the system. For instance, at the third provincial chapter of the year 1343 some modifications by Clement VI. of the bull of Benedict XII. were read.[1] A demand was made to chapter by the cardinals who had brought out the bull, for payment of 300 crowns as their expenses, and threats were used in case of non-payment. The king took the matter into his own hands and forbade any such payments. An important decree was

[1] Wilkins, *Concilia*, vol. ii. pp. 713-15.

passed, to the effect that all provisions of former chapters were to be considered as revoked unless reaffirmed by each succeeding chapter. In another (1422), a stop was put to excessive cavalcades on the part of those who came to the meeting. No one, however dignified, was to have a train of more than twenty horses.[1]

Abbats were ordered to look after their monks and to live among them, especially on feast days. They were not to be absent from the monastery more than three months in the year; and were to be careful to spend Easter with their brethren. The abbats agree once a year to make a full statement to their monks of everything which concerns the abbey. Their power of alienation was checked. From September 15th to Lent no supper was to be allowed except to the aged, sick, and those below twenty years of age. A decree allowing of eating meat was also passed, for the reason that doctors and experience both teach that a total abstinence from flesh is contrary to nature and hurtful to the system: so were monks to be confined to such diet alone, they would become weak and suffer, a thing the rule neither orders nor desires."

The visitations ordered by chapter were realities and no merely formal visits. The reports were read at the succeeding chapter. For instance, the abbat of St. Albans, who had been appointed visitor of

[1] *Ibid.* vol. iii. p. 419.

St. Augustine's, Canterbury, reports to the fathers assembled, in 1426,[1] that he was grieved to have found something there needing correction, about which he would later on confer with them more fully. The abbat of Cerne, on the same occasion, reports well of all the houses he had to visit, with the exception of Abingdon, about which he too had something to report privately to the president. At Shrewsbury, too, he says, there were strifes and a want of concord. We do not find any account of capitular visitation of nunneries; and are thereby led to conclude that the houses of women were not considered (although the Lateran decrees gave the power of visitation) as being formally part of the Congregation at all.

The general chapter was for some time exercised as to the repeated contumacy of the monks of Christ Church, Canterbury, who refused to appear when summoned.[2] They were warned and threatened with fines and excommunication again and again. But with no effect. The monks of Christ Church protested that, as being the mother-house of all benedictines in England and, *sede vacante*, holding the primatial jurisdiction, it beseemed not their dignity to be summoned to any general chapter. If general chapter there need be, theirs it was to summon it, and to preside over its deliberation. In 1360 they wrote, in the name of the king, to the pope ex-

---

[1] Wilkins, *Concilia*, vol. iii. p. 464.
[2] *Literæ Cantuarienses*, vol. ii. pp. 224, 398, 400, 448, 510.

posing their woes and claiming exemption; and in 1363 appointed proctors in Rome to carry on the appeal. But in 1373 the chapter still persisted in its claim and began to threaten the monks of Christ Church with further grave penalties, of which the prior bitterly complains in a letter to the archbishop. Five years later, Urban VI. writes to archbishop Simon of Sudbury, and gives full exemption to the monks of his cathedral-monastery.

While the general chapter was exercising jurisdiction and sending visitors to the different abbeys in the pope's name, we must not forget that these same abbeys and other houses were also subjected to the visitations of the bishops of the diocese. The bishop was the ordinary of the whole diocese, and had to correct whatever was amiss in his flock.[1] He could, if necessary, even dispose an abbat whom he found unworthy, and thus obviate any difficulties

[1] In the Constitutions of Giles of Sarum (1256), the bishop lays down this decree for his monasteries: "Since by the rule of the holy fathers, religious men are bound to know by heart the psalms, hymns, and certain other things to be read or sung according to their own observance, both in the night and day offices, we order that no one who has entered now or at any future time a monastery in our diocese, should he not know his office by heart, be promoted to any obedience (*i.e.* any post of trust) unless it be a case of invincible ignorance. In case of contravention of this law, both the appointer and the appointed are suspended" (Wilkins, *Concilia*, vol. i. p. 718). The visitations held in the diocese of Norwich, and published by the Camden Society, show how strict and searching the visitations were; and how much indeed, up to the time of the Dissolution, depended upon the bishop.

which might arise from life appointments. His
leave was necessary for an election, and he was
called upon to confirm the choice of the monks.
It was the bishop of the diocese who had to bless
the newly appointed abbat, and who had to keep
his eye upon him and see he did his duty. There
were in England only five abbeys exempt from
episcopal control, viz., St. Albans, Canterbury, St.
Augustine's, Westminster, Evesham, St. Edmund's
Bury. In these abbeys, although there was freedom
from the bishop's visitation, they were under the
capitular jurisdiction. Their elections depended on
the pope for confirmation, and they had to pay
heavily for the privilege.[1] They had to go to Rome
in person or by proxy for confirmation; and there
the chancery fees were enormous. In 1308 the cost
of papal confirmation for the election of Richard de
Sudbury, as abbat of Westminster, was no less than
8000 florins. Towards the end of the fifteenth
century they got dispensation from going or sending
to Rome, and had, instead, to pay a yearly tax of
200 florins to the papal collector.

Now to go back to the abbey in itself. As becomes a father of the family, the abbat held his post
for life. It was only for some grave reason that he
could be deposed. Religious orders, and congre-

---

[1] They also had to pay heavy sums to the king for leave to elect.
In 1235 the monks of St. Albans had to pay the king 300 marks
(nearly £4000 of present money) for the privilege.—*Gesta Abb. Sti. Alb.*
(Roll Series), vol. i. p. 306.

gations not belonging to the monastic state, find in frequent changes of superiors advantages which would by no means be such to monks. A dominican, a franciscan, or a jesuit, has no *home* in any one house of his order more than another. He is here to-day and gone to-morrow. But "home" is the very idea of a benedictine monastery; and "home" means oneness of surroundings and traditions, oneness of rule, of love and way of looking at things. Around the monastery cling all those natural feelings and sentiments which are the mainstay of the family life. Here the monk is content to live and die. Here will he dwell for ever, because he has chosen it. Once more, "home" means one father.[1]

Another point to which we have referred. The benedictine has no outside work peculiar to himself. He can therefore, when called by obedience, take up all or any. He may follow the contemplative life or the active ministry of the Apostolic mission. He may teach or may write books. He may plant trees and till the soil, or he may follow Art in any of its many branches. He may convert

[1] The learned benedictine bishop Hedley of Newport thus writes on this subject : "Every benedictine monastery is, and ought to be, a home; whatever the external work to which a monk may find himself called, the normal thing must always be, to live in his own monastery. It would be a mistake to encourage any one to profess himself a benedictine unless he could look forward with pleasure to live "for better for worse" till death itself in the home of his profession, under the Rule, and in the daily work of the choir."—*Ampleforth Journal*, April 1896, p. 248.

the heathen or preside over the welfare of the universal church from the Chair of Peter. Any work a Christian may do, he may do. Whether he takes up one form of work or changes to some other, it is all one to him. He is still a benedictine. He works for work's sake; for the discipline it gives to the soul; for the avoiding of idleness; and for his own support; for then, says St. Benedict, "we are true monks when we live by the works of our hands."[1] Hence the wideness of his spirit and the elasticity of his rule, which adapts itself to any work required by the circumstances and the time. In a word, the benedictine life is not so much that of an Order as it is a State of Life, the life of the Evangelical Counsels.[2]

[1] *Regula S. Benedicti, cap.* xlviii.
[2] When we use the term "order," as applied to benedictines, it must be remembered it has quite a different meaning to what it does when used of the later religious bodies. In the benedictine meaning it is the same as the term "*state*" in the "monastic state," and is analogous to the term "order" as when we speak of the clerical "order."

CHAPTER IV

THE MONK IN THE WORLD

PROFESSING as he does to follow the ordinary Gospel teaching, the monk cannot be unmindful of the words, "*Bear ye one another's burdens.*"[1] Filled with the strength and the peace which has entered his soul since his "conversion,"[2] he is always ready, when his abbat gives the word, to labour for those left exposed to the cares and dangers he has escaped. He is no misanthrope, but is wise enough to know that the welfare of the body is a great means towards securing the welfare of the soul. For human misery, want, and poverty are all so many obstacles in the way of Grace working the change unto Life Eternal. Little is the use of preaching to starving men, especially if the preacher be himself well fed. Feed, clothe, and house them; and then will they be able to understand that "*Life is more than meat, and their bodies more than raiment.*"[3] This common sense, human way of looking at things, judging of others

---

[1] Gal. vi. 2.
[2] See the *Conversio morum suorum* of the monastic vows.
[3] St. Matthew vi. 25.

by the practical knowledge a man has gained of himself, taught the monk to make his monastery a centre for reaching the people among whom he lived; for an abbey was often possessed of vast estates which afforded occupation and work to thousands. The black monks were good landlords, who lived in the midst of their tenantry and knew the profit of keeping their people on the ground. The personal welfare of their tenants, their comfort and convenience, was as much a consideration to the monks as were their own, and they were as well looked after. Even with all the changes brought about in land-holding as the result of the Black Death, and the civil wars so impoverishing to any country, the black monks, in spite of their genuine distress, were but slow and sparing imitators of those who had found it so profitable to inclose their lands for pasturage.[1]

"As agriculturists and judicious managers of property the monks of a benedictine house had no equals. They were business-like, exact, and prompt in their dealings. They required from their tenants and servants a just and faithful performance of their different services and tasks; but whilst they did so they were not hard or ungrateful masters. . . . The constitutions and regulations contained in the Gloucester Cartulary . . . are, as I firmly believe, the

---

[1] The cistercians were famous as wool-growers, and at one time seemed to have had almost a monopoly of the wool trade. Hence pasturage was more important to them than agriculture.

production not of a parcel of drunken and besotted monks, but of intelligent landlords and agriculturists who had a due care for the stewardship of the things committed to their care. Agriculture was one of the leading features of the Benedictine Order, and in this the monks achieved a great success."[1]

Wherever there are great buildings, there work will always be found for many. The bare keeping in repair of places like Canterbury or Ely or Peterborough must have meant a livelihood for generations of artisans, and trained artisans too, men whose artistic tastes were carefully cultivated. There were also in the working of a great abbey an example given of careful agriculture, of management, of thrift, and of a higher ideal than could be found elsewhere. All these must have tended to elevate the tone of the people who dwelt near, and been a means of culture which would infallibly tell in the long run.

But these are indirect ways of helping one's neighbours which perhaps are more efficacious as not interfering with the spirit of sturdy independence so important to a nation. There is a difference between doing a thing for people, and showing them how to do it for themselves; and this was the policy the monks followed. But children and the sick are cases which are helpless, and this was fully recognised. The monks became the great

[1] Mr. Hart's Introduction: *Historia Monasterii Gloucestris* (Roll Series), vol. iii. p. xciii.

educationalists of the day, and did not confine their work to men of their own rank, but spread the blessings of learning far and wide. For instance, as early as the year 1198 the abbat (Sampson) of St. Edmundsbury built and endowed a public school; while in the twelfth century the school of St. Albans, successively under Neckham and Master Warin, was of such fame that Matthew of Paris says: "There was hardly a school in all England at that time more fruitful or more famous either for the number or the proficiency of its scholars."[1]

It is interesting to note that Master Warin, a secular, was nephew both to the abbat and the prior; and was "so like his uncles in dignified demeanour, worshipful life, and in learning, that he truly deserved to be called the nephew of such men, or rather their brother."[2]

The abbats of Evesham paid yearly £10[3] and "borde and tabelying frely in the monasterie to one scholemaster for the keeping of a free schole in the said town of Evesham."[4]

Westminster, Glaston, and all the great houses kept free schools in their own towns and on the various properties they held up and down the country.[5]

---

[1] *Memoirs of St. Edmund's Abbey* (Roll Series), vol. i. p. 296. There was also a school at Beccles kept up by the same convent (*ibid.* vol. iii. p. 182).

[2] *Gesta Abbatum*, vol. i. pp. 195–6.

[3] Equal to about £120 of our money.

[4] H. Cole, *King Henry the Eighth's Scheme of Bishoprics*, p. 117.

[5] For instance, the royal monastery at Westminster had possessions in 97 towns, 17 hamlets, besides 216 manors.

The claims of the sick, of the really poor, and of the wayfarer were looked to. Where was the natural resource for all in need or distress, but at the great abbey? Food and shelter would be freely found at God's house for those who wanted; and the dole would not pauperise the receivers. Day by day at stated hours were the poor fed at every religious house; and guest-rooms were built to shelter those who wanted to stay. For two days and nights were travellers made welcome; and during that time, if their health allowed, they followed, as at Abingdon, the spiritual exercises of the convent.[1] They fared the same as did the monks. When their time was up, they were bidden god-speed and went on their journey, sure of finding the same hospitality in the next religious house at which they stopped. The neighbouring poor had their daily dole; and from the monastic dispensaries the sick could always have the medicines and attendance they required. In fact, "the myth of the fine old English gentleman, who had a large estate and provided every day for the poor at his gate, was (as the late Professor J. S. Brewer said) realised in the case of the monks, and in their case only."[2]

Not in bodily help only did they provide for the people, but they looked also after their spiritual profit. For dependent on the abbey were also many tracts of land up and down the country, left as alms

---

[1] MS. Cott., Claud., B. VI. f. 206.
[2] *Geraldi Cambr. Opera*, ed. J. S. Brewer, IV. p. xxxvi.

to the monks.[1] These lands, while sources of income, also brought responsibilities. For the monks became not only the temporal landlords but also the spiritual pastors, and were obliged to look after the souls of their people. But as the very idea of an abbey is, as we have said, that of a home, it would not be in

[1] Archdeacon W. Hale, writing on the question of patronage and tithes, says: "It is a prevalent idea that we owe our parochial system to the centralised operation of bodies of clergy united under a bishop at the cathedral who went forth to preach, and who planted churches throughout the diocese, the mother-church being their parent as well as their head. Whatever truth there may be in this opinion, we regret to observe that it derives little support or confirmation from those notices respecting patronage and tithes which are scattered throughout this volume. If the bishops and their clergy were the original cause of churches being built, the churches themselves appear very soon to have become possessions of the laity, and, together with lands and manors, to have passed as patrimony from father to son. It is a remarkable fact that there is not a single church mentioned in this volume the patronage of which, in the times before the Conquest, did not accrue to the monastery of Worcester from gifts made by laymen. . . . But though all the rights of patronage which the monastery of Worcester possessed were in the earliest times derived from the laity, it is worthy of remark that, as respects the receipt of tithes from churches of which the monastery were patrons, there is a marked difference in the case of churches received before the Conquest and after that event. From the churches of the former period tithes as well as pensions were generally received; from the churches of the later period pensions alone. It would seem, too, from the fact of the Prior, the Sacristan, or the Almoner receiving portions of the great tithes of the churches given to the monastery in the earlier period, that the appropriation of tithes to religious houses and the establishment of vicarages have a much earlier origin than is commonly supposed."—Introduction to the *Registrum Prioratus B.M. Wigorniensis*, pp. xxvi., xxvii. (Camden Society, 1865). This raises the question whether the prevalent ideas are not theories based on fancy, and whether the origin of so many parish churches is really not due to the monks. The whole matter requires reconsideration on the basis of an investigation into facts.

keeping to send monks out away from their cloister for any length of time to do the work of parochial clergy.[1] Sometimes it was so done, according to Kennet; but the result was not satisfactory; and from an early date, in many monasteries, they began to look about for secular priests to do this duty for them. Hence rose the present system of Vicars. Difficulties of administration came, and there were cases in which the monks did not always act fairly to their vicars. For when a church was appropriated or impropriated[2] it was always stipulated that a certain proportion of the income was to go to the priest who did the work. For instance, when in 1170 the living of Lamberton was appropriated to Tavistock abbey by Bartholomew, bishop of Exeter, he declared in the deed of gift that the monks " should

[1] There was a marked difference in the position of the black monks and the white monks respecting this question of monastic vicars. The policy of the cistercians was to overcrowd their houses; and when there came a time of agricultural depression, they had to cast about how to live. From the very nature of their organisation a sort of general policy ensued. With the benedictines, on the contrary, the policy was to restrict the community to the number the foundation would support. With the independence of each house, difficulties were met according to local views and circumstances.

[2] *Impropriation* is the alienation of titles to laymen. *Appropriation* is the assignment of them to clerical corporations, which thus became responsible for the performance of the duties. It is calculated that within 300 years of the Conquest about one-third of the benefices in England had fallen by appropriation into the hands of the religious orders, sees, colleges, &c. That abuses came from this is natural; for corporations are never as active in the discharge of duties as individuals are. On the whole question see Kennet's *Case of Impropriations* and Sheldon *On Tithes*.

hold it on the terms expressed in that donation, viz., one half to the abbat and monks, and the other moiety to the vicar."[1]

The general rule seems to have been for the monastery to receive two thirds, and the vicar one.[2] This at first seems an unfair division; but when we consider that the monks undertook the repairs of the church, which in many cases they themselves had built at their own cost, and also held themselves responsible for all the poor of the parish, it is pretty clear that Master Vicar, who got his one-third clear, a house free of rent, and all his stole fees and dues, was by no means in so unfavourable a position as some modern writers make out.

But often, it appears, the monks did not keep to their bargains, especially when the churches were far away from the abbey. The vicars began to complain, and complained so loudly that it reached the Court. Richard II. passed a law securing a proper maintenance to the priest who served the

---

[1] Kennet's *Case of Impropriations*, p. 40. Spelman, *The Larger Treatise concerning Tithes* (1647), p. 151.

[2] This was on the lines of the old canonical division: one third for the support of the Church, or, as it was called, for God; one third for the Poor; and one third for the Priest. St. Gregory, in his letter to St. Augustine (Bede, Book I. chapter 27), speaks of and recommends the custom of a fourfold division, a share for the bishop being included. It is difficult to say the exact proportions that obtained in England, but the principle was there; the burthen and the profits were divided between patrons and priests. See also Lingard's *Antiquities of the Anglo-Saxon Church*, p. 83.

churches the monks either had built or had received together with the land at the time of gift.[1]

Henry IV. went further, and altogether forbade the monks to act as parochial clergy, and ordered them to institute to the livings members of the secular clergy.[2]

The monks, as patrons, retained however the rights of presentation, as we find expressed in the Privileges of St. Alban's abbey (1257):—

"Item that we may make choice of priests for them, and present them to the diocesan of the place, and assign to them their portions; the which priests shall be answerable to the ordinaries of the place in spirituals[3] and to us in temporals."

The bishop was obliged to institute their nominee unless there was some canonical objection. The vicars, who were either for life or removable at will, had to swear fidelity to the abbat and convent, and pay each year certain sums as rectorial first-fruits. These payments were often assigned to divers officers of the abbey, *obedientiaries* as they were called, for the discharge of their office. For instance, the profits of a certain set of vicarages would go to the Sacristan or to the Precentor, or

[1] *e.g.* Glaston had no less than seventy-one churches dependent upon it.

[2] Dixon's *History of the Church of England*, vol. i. p. 89.

[3] Sometimes, as at St. Albans or Evesham, the abbat was ordinary of the place, and had the rights of archdeacons. There is a curious verse containing sixteen "reserved cases" in the jurisdiction of St. Albans. See Rev. P. Newcome's *The History of the Abbey of St. Albans*, p. 221.

to the Infirmarian. Sometimes in the deed of gift the land or church was left for a specified purpose; even (as there were cases) for providing a better brew of beer for the brethren, or an extra pitance on the anniversary day of the donor.[1] In other cases it was the abbat who allotted the means of revenue for each department. There were often charges, too, upon the gift which materially lessened the value to the monks, in the shape of *corrodies*[2] to different friends or relatives of the donor. These charges went on sometimes for generations.

The system of vicars in churches appropriated to benedictines, may seem to have put the secular clergy into an undue state of dependence. But a

[1] A pitance, from *pietas*, was an extra dish over and above the monastic commons, and was given out on special days—such as feast days, anniversaries. It might take the form of dessert, or of eggs, or of an extra amount of fish or even meat. St. Benedict provides for it in his Rule (*Ch.* XXXIX.): "If, however, their work chance to have been hard, it shall be in the abbat's power, if he think fit, to make some addition" (*to their usual allowance*), "avoiding above everything all surfeiting, that the monks be not overtaken by indigestion." A practical warning when men ate generally only once a day.

[2] A corrody was a monk's portion of food and drink. One given by the abbat of Tavistock to John Amadas in the time of Henry VIII. consisted of "one white loaf, another loaf called 'Trequarter;' a dish called 'General,' another dish of flesh or fish called 'Pitance'; three potells of beer or three silver halfpence daily; also a furred robe at Christmas yearly, of the same kind as those of our esquires, or the sum of 20s." Whenever John chanced to be at the abbey, he was to have a proper chamber, with firing and three candles called "Paris candells"; and also stabling for his horse. When the abbey was dissolved, the king ordered the corrody to be commuted into a yearly pension for the lucky John of an annuity of £5 in lieu of all these daily comforts and perquisites. See Preface to Oliver's *Monasticon Dioceris Exoniensis*, p. vi.

consideration will show if there were dependence it would also be that begotten of gratitude. For it must be remembered it was from the free schools kept by the monks that most of the clergy got their education, and thence the very means of entering the priesthood. For, by the common law of the Church which then obtained, no cleric could be ordained unless he had a "title"; or in other words some one to fall back upon, who undertook in case of need to be responsible for his support: and these titles had to be obtained from those who had them and were willing to present. In a note attached to his work on *Henry VIII. and the English Monasteries*, Dom F. A. Gasquet points out that in the diocese of York, between the years 1501 and 1539, there were 6190 priests ordained. Of this number 1415 were religious of various kinds; 4698 were seculars presented on titles furnished by a monastery or college, and only 77 on a title provided elsewhere. The yearly average of ordinations was over 158. When the troubles began for the monasteries these numbers fell at once. In 1536, 92 only were ordained priests; in 1537 no ordinations are recorded; in 1538 only 20; and in 1539 only 8.[1] So that, were it not for the monasteries, secular priests would have hardly had any means of living.

It was not only the civil law which looked after the interests of the vicars. The Church was provident also. At that time the usual stipend for a

[1] Vol. i. p. xxx.

chaplain was 5 marks (about £40) a year, and this was advanced to 6, 8, and 10 marks, which latter sum equals about £80.[1]

But provincial constitutions settled that the portion allowed to vicars should never be less than 12 marks a year; that is to say, close upon £100,[2] an income considerably better than Goldsmith's Vicar, who was "passing rich on forty pounds a year," and who had a wife and family to boot.

The monasteries were also schools for the nobility. Under the care of the abbat were youths often of the highest rank, who were to be brought up in the courtesy and polite education which made the monasteries far better schools for Christian gentlemen than the Court. For the abbey had its friends throughout the country; and the abbat of the greatest houses, being generally a peer of the realm, had his seat in Parliament and entered into the council of kings. So he and his monastery were well known to the great. Besides, there were other ties. Many members of noble and gentle families were monks themselves, and to these the benedictine, whatever his birth, was akin through the discipline of his life, his circumstances and his surroundings, and through that tone and bearing which come to him who lives habitually in God's sight. Many of the great ones of the land wished to be united in some kind of spiritual bonds with

---

[1] Kennet, *ibid.* pp. 57, 58.
[2] Lyndewood's *Provinciale* (ed. Oxford, 1679), *De officio Vicarii*, p. 64.

an abbey where they had relatives or friends; and we find them suing for admission to friendship or confraternity with the monks. The effects of this confraternity were that they became real members of the house and shared in all its good works and merits. The Confrater was sometimes allowed an honorary seat in the chapter. Special prayers were offered for him at his death, and his anniversaries were kept with Dirge and Requiem. He, on his side, promised always to befriend the abbey and to help and protect it to the best of his abilities. The petitioner for confraternity would present himself in the chapter-house before the assembled monks, and there prostrate himself until the abbat asked, "What asketh thou?" to which he answered, "I ask through God's mercy and yours, and that of all the elders, the brotherhood and goodwill of this monastery." The abbat then said, "May the Almighty Lord grant thee what thou seekest, and may He give thee a fellowship with His elect." The petitioner then knelt at the abbat's feet who gave him the book of the Rule, and, both putting their hands on the sacred text, said: "We admit thee into fellowship and into brotherhood. Now as thou art henceforth for ever a sharer even as one of ourselves in the masses, hours, prayers, watches, disciplines, fasts, alms, and other spiritual good deeds that are done in this church, let us also be made partakers in thy good works." He was then received to the kiss of peace by all the convent, and was entered in the chart as a confrater. Kings and princes considered it an honour to become *confratres* of abbeys. William the Conqueror was a confrater of Cluni and also of Battle abbey, which he had founded. In 1460 Henry VI. coming to Croyland, and being delighted with the religious life of the monks, stayed three days and begged to be admitted into their brotherhood; which being granted him, he, in return, gave them his charter whereby their liberties[1] were confirmed.

High ecclesiastics, like Wolsey at Evesham in 1516, sought for fellowship; or great officers of State, as Blessed Thomas More,[2] "Lord Chancellor of this most flourishing kingdom of England," at Christ Church, Canterbury, where he had been a boy at school. The neighbouring nobility and gentry were eager to be on good terms with the monks, and their names, still extant on some of the registers which have come down to us, show that the privilege was highly prized.

But this connection with the great was not without its disadvantages too; for monasteries became not only the shelter for the poor, but also for the rich. They were the hotels of the day. Kings and nobles put up with the monks, and often over-stayed their welcome, filling the place with their retinues and disturbing the peace of the cloister. A favourite time for the royal visitors to spend some weeks at

---

[1] Steven's *Additions to Dugdale*, vol. i. p. 374.
[2] See *Report of Historical MSS. Com.*, vol. i. p. 121.

an abbey were the holiday seasons of Christmas, of Easter, of Whitsuntide. He would add the majesty of his presence and of all his train to some function in the Church, and the splendour of the celebration of such or such a feast would remain long in the memories of monk and people to whom the Church's ceremonies were living realities. The monasteries also afforded asylums to honourable families in reduced circumstances. Dom Gasquet produces a letter from the son of the duke of Buckingham to Henry VIII. in which the writer says that he "hath no dwelling place meet for him to inhabit (and he was) fain to live poorly at board in an abbey this four years day, with his wife and seven children."[1]

They were also often called upon to provide pensions and grants to favourites, and thus vicariously pay for services done to their royal patrons.

"In some case the abbats were bound to give endowments to scholars of the king's nomination or provide them with competent benefices, pensions; and corrodies were granted under the privy seal to yeomen ushers of the wardrobe and the chamber, to clerks of the kitchen, servers, secretaries, and gentlemen of the chapel royal; and these were strictly enforced, whatever might be the other encumbrances of the house."[2] The monks, although themselves men of peace, had to provide their quota of knights and men-at-arms for the royal service, and in the civil

---
[1] D. Gasquet, "*Henry VIII. and the English Monasteries,*" vol. i. p. 34.
[2] *Ibid.* vol. i. pp. 28, 29.

wars so frequent in England soldiers were quartered upon them.

Hence we may conclude, if the monks had vast possessions they also had vast responsibilities, and responsibilities to which they nobly rose. They looked upon their wealth as so much entrusted to them for the welfare of others. And if in times of prosperity they knew how to spend lavishly, it was more in the service of their neighbour than for themselves. Their vast hospitalities, the exactions of kings, social changes and disasters such as fires and diseases,[1] often crippled them and reduced them to the verge of destruction, but they never forgot the saying of the Lord: "*It is more blessed to give than to receive.*"[2] They went on their beneficent way as long as their homes stood, "*Doing good to all, but especially to those of the household of the faith.*"[3]

---

[1] During the plague known as "the Black Death" (1348-49), the monks, as well as the rest of the clergy, suffered severely. It is calculated that about two-thirds of the clergy died. It is very likely that the monastic orders would in proportion suffer more severely than the parochial clergy, for the chance of infection is always greater when there are a number together. At Westminster the abbat and twenty-six monks died, and found a common grave in the southern cloister. So it was all round, wherever the plague raged.

[2] Acts xx. 35. [3] Gal. vi. 10.

CHAPTER V

THE MONK IN HIS MONASTERY

THE question now arises: What was the private life of those monks who thus spent themselves in the service of God and their neighbours? What was the secret of their life, the spring from which they got their strength? In this chapter we will endeavour to give a sketch of the life of a monk in his monastery, and note the sort of effect on his character of his vows.

But it is not possible for us to take an example from any one particular house as typical of the rest. First of all because we have but few references to the inner life of any one monastery. Where all went on calmly and regularly, what need to record the conditions of a life all knew and experienced daily? It is only on occasion of some important event that, as it were by accident, the veil is lifted and for a moment we catch a glimpse of cloister life. Even had we a full and detailed account of some one house, it would not necessarily tell us about the particulars of the life in others.

But scattered here and there in our numerous records are indications of what was done in various houses, so that a picture, true in its details, as finding a counterpart in real life, may be pieced together and a sufficiently vivid picture given of the general outlines of the life of an English monk in the later mediæval times. Whatever the local variations might be (and in every house with a vigorous life of its own, there would always be its own peculiar way of looking at things and its own development, based on conditions obtaining there and not elsewhere), still, from the intrinsic power of the Rule and a living tradition, there would be necessarily in every house certain features which would find themselves repeated in all benedictine monasteries. There would be that peculiar tone amid all sorts of variations which clearly marks off the benedictine from other religious, and which finds its root in the distinguishing feature of St. Benedict's Rule, the ample discretion allowed in interpretation.

But in order to give a picture to the reader of the inner life of a monk, we are obliged to combine in one whole such details, gleaned from all parts, which may be fairly considered as truly representative, in the broad outlines, of life as it really existed throughout England. Without dwelling unduly upon local customs, save as far as they go to prove the existence of a principle which would find its counterpart elsewhere, we will throw into the form of an imaginary biographical sketch what may be useful for our present purpose. The facts are true; but the reader must bear in mind that the setting is imaginary.

John Weston was a monk of Lynminster, an abbey with a history counted by centuries. The son of a knight, at an early age his widowed mother had placed him in the claustral school at this, the most famous abbey in the neighbourhood. Here his father and uncles had also received such education as had fallen to their lot. To this abbey he had been offered by his mother, according to the old ceremony. One day at mass, after the gospel, the chalice was put into his hands and the priest wrapped up the child's hands in the altar-cloth [1] as a sign that he was, if found worthy, to be dedicated to the service of God. From his earliest days—he was but seven—he was kept under strict discipline; [2] and wore in the monastery a form of the monk's dress, and had his head shaven in the form of a crown. He was taught along with other boys, perhaps in the free school or in the singing-school, which most of the great abbeys supported for the services of their minsters. He had a sweet voice and some talent in singing; so it is likely he found a place in the singing-school. The treatment was kind but severe. If he became a monk, it were well he should know from his earliest days that a monk had to work and not live an idle life; and if he returned to the world, what better lesson could he take out than the great law of labour? John was taught among other things

---

[1] Rule of St. Benedict, Ch. LIX.
[2] "The children are to be kept under discipline at all times and by every one" (Rule, Ch. LXIII.).

reading, writing, his Latin grammar, some simple elements of the art of reckoning, his prayers and faith, the laws of politeness, and the great art of holding his tongue. Singing would not be forgotten. Plainsong and prick-song had mysteries the knowledge of which was highly considered; and beside John, with all his companions, had to attend in the great minster every day and sing at the solemn mass and vespers.

While there was a good deal of solid instruction going on, and a good deal of knowledge was being instilled into him, the boy's mind was being educated and its powers developed. He was quietly and unconsciously drinking in the influence of the place. His character was forming itself to habits of industry, self-restraint, thrift, charity in his dealings with others; and he was gaining a sense of the reality of life. All he saw in the lives of those with whom he passed his days; their earnestness and diligence, their prompt obedience to the abbat, and their frequent little practices of humility, and above all the solemn chanting of the office and the daily sacrifice, acts not of this earth, all these must have had their effect on the boy. The more so as it was the outcome of what he saw and observed for himself, more than anything said or preached at him. For at Lynminster there was little of that sort of thing. Monks after St. Benedict's mind are not what the world thinks them to be. Religion being the very atmosphere in which they live, God's side of every question comes so natural to them, so much a matter of course, that there is no trying to be always "improving the occasion" nor striking attitudes, mental or otherwise, which are foreign to their simple idea of what He requires. The monks preferred, if God was calling the boy, to let Him do His own work in His own way. They dared not force or hurry on what they knew was in wiser hands than theirs.

John was a boy, merry of heart and full of life and fun, as all healthy English boys are; and though these qualities have to be regulated like everything else, yet, as they are most valuable, his teachers were careful not to repress them too much. He, no doubt, was mischievous as others are, and had his fling of boyish spirits. Nor was he without his share in all the sports and manly excitements suitable to his age and condition. These were all useful to make him what he ought to be—a reasonable being, giving a reasonable service to his Maker. There is one thing abhorrent to all benedictine ideas of education, and that is the formation of the prig. So we may be sure the result in the case of John Weston was not that.

For some time, since his fourteenth year, there had been going on a gradual awakening of the boy's soul; and he was beginning to question himself. The old problems we have all had, doubtlessly, presented themselves over and over again: "What is the meaning of Life? Why was I made?" Sometimes in the midst of his play or of his study, maybe when singing the *Credo* at high mass or the *Magnificat* at vespers, a seriousness and awe would fall upon him; and something ('twas the Voice of God, but, at first, he knew it not) whispered to him: "God made you for Himself." The truth sank deeper and deeper in his soul, and he began to realise it was a personal and entire service God asked of him. And day by day the example he saw began to tell more and more on the lad. "The monks are serving God. That is why they are here. How peaceful and happy they are." Such thoughts as these flashed across his mind; and the high ideal of life which the monastic state aims at began to attract him.

Then came one day, never to be forgotten; a great light dawned upon his soul. God spoke to him clearly and distinctly in one of the many ways He speaks to His creatures. Maybe it was some sudden sorrow, the death of his mother or of some other loved friend; or perhaps some sudden inrush of joy at a realisation of God's Fatherhood; or some word of the daily-heard office which suddenly broke upon him with a new meaning and struck home; or maybe some sin into which he had fallen and which mercifully revealed to him his own weakness: I must give myself to God; and "*Here* will I dwell for ever."[1] With heart full of emotion and joy at his call, he told his master the hope he dared hardly express. But the monk, skilled in the art of counsel, while

[1] Ps. xxiii. 6.

giving him encouragement also set before him in grave words the hardness of the life to which he aspired, and the sacrifices he would have to make. He spoke, doubtlessly, too of the sweetness there is for them whom God calls to serve Him. So he wisely bids the lad pray, and wait a while, and try himself, lest the desire may come from human motives rather than from God. If the good monk knew that the lot of those who have entered the cloister to follow God is sweet beyond words, on the other hand he knew full well that those who come into the fold not by the door of Vocation, may expect nothing but unhappiness and bitterness.

After much prayer and trial, John, now in his nineteenth year, has persevered, and in the chapter-room has been admitted by the abbat, and clothed as a novice.[1] No longer a mere school-boy, he

---

[1] "The Book of Ely," f. 106 [Lambeth MSS., No. 448], contains the outfit required in that cathedral-monastery by a novice.

Necessaria noviciis noviter ad religionem venientibus providenda.

Imprimis i matras (matrass).
Item ii par blankettys.
Item ii par straglys (quilts).
Item ii couverlytes.
Item i furrypane.
Item i blewbed de sago (bed-curtains of serge).
Item i cuculla cum froco (cowl and frock).
Item i tunica nigra furra (black furred tunic).
Item i tunica nigra simplex (for summer wear).
Item ii tunica alba.
Item i amita simplex (amuce).
Item i zona, cum i powch, cultela, tabula et pectine, filo et acu in les powch.
Item i parva zona pro noctibus.

wears the habit, and is given into the charge of the novice master, whose duty it will be to train him in the spiritual life. In the noviciate the real work was one more of education than instruction. Dom or "Dan"[1] John, as he was now called, was shown, as it were, two mirrors. One reflected the image of what God intended him to be; and the other what he really was, with all his faults and weakness. He was a true novice; he read the pictures aright. St. Benedict has given his monks seventy-two "instruments" by which they are to

- *Item* iii par stamainorum (woollen under-garments).
- *Item* iiii par bracarum (breeches), cum brygerdel (a kind of belt) et poyntes (garters).
- *Item* ii par caligarum (shoes).
- *Item* iiii par de le sokke.
- *Item* ii par botarum pro diebus.
- *Item* i par botarum pro noctibus.
- *Item* i pylche (a pilche, a fur garment = *toga pellicea*).
- *Item* iii par flammeole (kerchief? *v.* Du Cange).
- *Item* iii pulvonaria (pillows or cushions).
- *Item* i pileo albo pro noctibus (nightcap).
- *Item* ii manutergia (towels).
- *Item* i pokett pro vestibus lavandis (soiled clothes-bag).
- *Item* i schavyn cloth.
- *Item* i crater a bowl (lamp? *v.* Du Cange).
- *Item* i ciphus murreus (a mazer goblet, generally of valuable materials).
- *Item* i coclear argent (silver spoon).

The above is interesting as showing that the English benedictine cultivated a certain amount of dignified manner of life. Everything was good, simple, and plain. The cold moist climate of Ely, and in most other English monasteries, made the use of fur in winter-time a necessity.

[1] In old Catholic England monks kept their baptismal names, and were known also by their surname, or the name of the place whence they came. In the old lists that have come down to us most of the names are territorial; names, too, generally of places in the immediate neigh-

work out their salvation. These were carefully studied and their meaning and use examined; and with them Dom John, diligently and soberly, set to work to make the two pictures correspond. He was not expected in his novitiate to become suddenly perfect. But he was expected to see his faults and to show his determination to labour at their correction.[1]

Now there was one of his companions, Dom Gilbert of London, a youth whom all loved; one kindly and thoughtful for all, devout at his prayer and diligent at his books. But when he looked at himself in the second mirror, he forgot what manner of man he was, and sighed and gave up the attempt at self-correction. He was wanting in the manliness and determination needed for a monk. So he went his way out into the great world; and Dom Gilbert was heard of no more. This failure was of use to our Dom John. It made him humbler, and steadied him down to a slower and surer growth. Perhaps

bourhood. As a monk used to be called either by his family or territorial name, sometimes by one and sometimes by another, it is often difficult to identify a name we come across. The practice of giving new names, generally those of some saint, seems to have been introduced at some places just before the dissolution occurred. It came from abroad. We find them at Glaston under abbat Bere (1524), who probably introduced the custom from Italy; the names adopted were generally "house" names, of saints to whom there was a special local veneration. See also list of Bath monks in the *Monasticon*, vol. ii. p. 271. In 1500 Richard Kidderminster, abbat of Winchcombe, went to Rome on the affairs of his order and was there a year. "He informed himself in learning, and improved himself in several useful regulations belonging to a monastic life" (Dodd's *Church History*, vol. i. p. 229). He also may have introduced the custom.

[1] Rule, Ch. IV.

he had begun to run before he could walk, as novices often try to do.

Besides thus setting his feet in the way of perfection, the master taught him the psalms and hymns and responsories which had to be learnt off by heart, since most of them would have to be sung at matins, and at that early hour (midnight) there would be but little light to read by. The books he loved to watch the monks copying and illuminating, were too precious for such as he. He must make a copy for his own use from which to learn them. Then there were the ceremonies to be got up both for church and elsewhere. Conduct had to be regulated according to a fixed method, which was based upon a sense of the Presence of God, and was no empty form. He would have to learn also the language of signs, which was commonly used in all religious homes, not as a means of conversation, but of expressing one's wants without disturbing others. Then, no doubt to try him, at times he would be put to do menial work, such as the house servants did.[1] For in those days in English benedictine monasteries there were no lay-brothers, but servants were kept to do the household work.

After his trial, generally a year, during which the convent watched him narrowly to see whether they would care to admit him into their family as a life-long companion, and he, on his side, whether he

[1] Rule, Ch. LVIII.

could live until death with them (for the profession of a novice is a serious thing to those admitting as well as to those admitted); and after the Rule according to the injunctions of St. Benedict had been read to him several times, together with the warning, "Behold the law under which thou desirest to fight. If thou canst observe it, enter in; if thou canst not, depart freely;"[1] the abbat took counsel with his monks, and they agreed to admit him to profession. Then one morning the abbat sang solemn mass, and during the solemnity Dom John was led forward to the altar, and in the hearing of all vowed Stability, Conversion of his Life, and Obedience. Then, with arms outstretched, three times did he sing the verse: "*Uphold me, O Lord, according to Thy Word, and I shall live; and let me not be frustrated of my hope;*"[2] and the whole community repeated it as many times, adding thereunto the *Gloria Patri*. Then, clothed in the full monastic garb, the newly-received brother cast himself at the feet of all, begging them to pray for him and receive him to the kiss of fraternal love. Dom John Weston was now a monk.

What was his life, now that he had reached the goal of his desires?

He rose a little before two o'clock [3] and was down

---

[1] Rule, Ch. LVIII.   [2] Ps. cxix. 116.
[3] The hour for matins varied in each house. Some, as at Durham, rose at midnight, while others, as at Westminster, got up at 2 P.M. In all cases they went back to bed for the time between matins and lauds. This was one of the changes Lanfranc introduced. According to the

in his stall ready to begin matins, the longest office of all, which lasted from one hour and a half to two or more hours. In the darkness of the night, while the rest of the world was sleeping, Dom John took his place among his cowled brethren and worshipped God with psalm, and hymn, and canticle. Sometimes, he listened to reading of Holy Writ or to one of the fathers of the Church, and anon joined in some soul-lifting responsory. The organ, too,[1] added its solemn strains to the voices and helped to lift his soul up to Him Who dwelt there in sacramental presence over the altar.[2] This time of matins was one of the happiest hours in his day; for then he was fulfilling one of his greatest privileges, "the work of God." This, the liturgical prayer, was the source of his strength. There lay the whole secret of his spiritual life. For to a benedictine the liturgical spirit is all

Rule, monks are to rise for the night office at the eighth hour, a varying period, which in winter would be, in the latitude of Rome, about 3 A.M., and earlier in the summer, when the hours were shorter.

[1] "The monks, when they were at their matins and service at midnight, then one of the said monks did play on the organs themselves and no other."—*Rites of Durham* (Surtees Society), p. 54.

[2] In monastic churches, as in all others at that time, it was an unheard of thing to banish Our Lord to a side chapel. The Gospel idea of prayer is that He is in our midst when we pray. The whole value of our prayer (and the divine office is the prayer *par excellence*) is that it is made with, by, and in Him who is the one Mediator between God and man. The Church recognises this: and orders in monastic churches the Blessed Sacrament to be kept at the high altar (*S. C. Epis.*, 10th *Feb.* 1579 *and* 29th *Nov.* 1594). Abbey churches are not cathedrals; and a custom warranted by the requirement of the latter is no reason why, against all rule, such a practice should obtain elsewhere.

in all.¹ He wants nothing more than the common prayer of the Church. Every other devotion he considers as nothing compared with its might and ineffable dignity. It is "the Work of God" in its fullest sense; for the Divine Head of the Church uses man as an instrument whereby He, the Incarnate Word, praises the Eternal Father. Hence it is that to a benedictine, brought up as Dom John was, the office is the foundation of all his spiritual life.²

The long midnight office with its concluding lauds being sung, back to bed goes Dom John, tired indeed, but at peace.

At five o'clock, he again rose, this time for prime, which was duly followed by chapter, at which he

[1] "It is with this voice of the divine office the monk speaks not only to his Creator, but to his fellow-men as well. The perpetual round of prayer and praise is something more than an intercessory power. It, rightly understood, is the medium of intercourse between the monastic body and the people in the midst of which it dwells. No one is so dull that he cannot understand the faith in the unseen, the hope of another world and burning love of God which are manifested in the perennial sacrifice and song of praise in the monastic choir. Through the individual preaching of the monk, through his works, through his words of counsel and of comfort, through his hospitality, through his dealings with his fellow-men in all the varied relations of life, he exercises some portion of his apostolate; but the choir of the monastery is the monk's real pulpit, and the daily office his most efficient sermon."—From Dom Gasquet's Introduction to *The Monks of the West*, p. xvii.

[2] The monk's private prayer is affective or contemplative. Long and formal meditations were not known in those days. St. Benedict prescribes (Ch. XX.) that prayer be short and pure; except it be perchance prolonged by the inspiration of Divine Grace. "But," he adds, "let prayer made in common always be short: and at the signal given by the one presiding let all rise together."

had to make public confession of his breaches of the Rule and do penance.[1] Here also he had to listen to words of spiritual instruction from his abbat, and, perhaps, receive directions about the work of the day. After prime in winter, and before in summer, he changed his night-habit for his day one and washed.

At six the short chapter mass, generally of "Our Lady Saint Mary," was sung, at which he assisted. He then studied in the cloister till near to nine, when the bell summoned him to choir again for the holy hour of terce. This was followed by the central act of the day, the sacrifice of the mass, celebrated with all the wealth of ceremonial at the disposal of the abbey. If it were a high feast day, the abbat would pontificate, and wear his mitre;[2] and Dom

---

[1] The benedictine makes use of corporal austerities as a means of keeping his body in subjection: according to St. Paul's words, "*I chastise my body*" (1 Cor. ix. 27). But his life is more ascetic than austere. The discipline, besides that administered in punishment, used to be taken publicly in chapter by all as a mortification. This, which had hitherto been a private act, was introduced by St. Peter Damian, and in all the convents he founded it was taken every Friday. The custom soon spread, and we find traces of it at Evesham, Croyland, and Christ Church, Canterbury. It probably became universal in the later mediæval ages. In the list of "Instruments of good works" (Ch. IV.), St. Benedict, without specifying the particular means, gives "To chastise the body" as a principle; also "To fear the Day of Judgment," and "To be in dread of hell." These are quite enough to account for the growth of the practice of self-flagellation and other usages of the ascetic life.

[2] The first abbat in Christendom to get the rights of *pontificalia* was the abbat of St. Augustine's abbey, Canterbury. The grant was made by Pope Alexander II. in 1063, but Lanfranc would not allow it to be used (*Hist. Monast. S. August. Cantuar.*, Roll Series, p. 27).

John might assist in the sanctuary and carry the abbat's crosier unless he was wanted in the choir. The sacrifice of the mass was the centre of all his life, and the light of his day. To it, either as preparation or thanksgiving, were directed all his prayers. It was the mass that gave the meaning to his office, and was the jewel of rare price which was set in the gold of the psalter. At the altar, too, did he often kneel and receive the bread of life and become more and more united with Him his soul loved. The mass was followed by the office of sext.

Then about eleven he had his first meal, if it were not a fasting day, in which case he would break his fast after nones or after vespers according as it was a fast day of the Rule or the stricter fast of the Church. The meal was eaten in silence. Dom John sat with others at a table; and a portion of food was set in a dish between so many. A curious account has been left of the food at Christ Church, Canterbury, on a fish day. In this document we read :—

"To every two monks, when they had soles, there

It was again renewed in 1179, and a like privilege was granted to most of the other abbeys. Most cathedral-monasteries seem to have obtained the same privilege before the end of the fifteenth century, but the priors seem to have been confined to the use of a knobbed staff instead of the ordinary episcopal stave affected by the abbats. The right of singing mass pontifically, of giving the solemn blessings and singing vespers, was much prized by the abbats, and gave a dignity and grandeur to the great festivals hitherto known only in cathedrals when the bishop officiated. As a rule, the abbat only sang mass pontifically seven or eight times a year. He had the right, too, of using his *pontificalia* in any house or church belonging to his abbey.

were 4 soles in a dish; when they had plaice, 2 plaice; when they had herring, 8 herrings; when they had whiting, 8 whiting; when they had mackrell, 2 mackrell; when they had eggs, 10 eggs. If they had anything more allowed them beyond this ordinary fare, it was either cheese or fruit or the like."[1]

Canterbury is near the sea, so fish was abundant. It must be remembered in estimating the allowance that it was the only meal in the day, and the monks had been up and at work nearly ten hours. Besides, it is perfectly evident that in those days people ate much more largely than we do. Bread was of course allowed; so much and no more. And St. Benedict, in his fatherly thoughtfulness, orders that two dishes should be prepared, so that the monks may have a choice of dish and every one be satisfied. At dinner Dom John drank cider or ale, which was sometimes a very poor creature, should the home have a procurator or cellarer too careful, not to say stingy, with his malt. This would sometimes happen. Or he might have wine, especially on feast days; for some of the monasteries cultivated the grape, and had vineyards of their own, either here or in more favoured France.[2]

If he had meat it would be three or four days in

---

[1] Quoted from a *Reg. Eccl. Cant.* by Battely in his continuation of *The Antiquities of Canterbury* (Somner), Part II. p. 96.

[2] Christ Church, Canterbury, had vineyards at Triel and St. Brice. See *Literæ Cantuarienses* (Roll Series), vol. i. p. 211.

the week, and never during Advent or Lent. In his turn, he took his share of waiting on his brethren or of reading to them during the meal from the high pulpit in the refectory. He would read to them from Holy Writ or from some other book comfortable to their souls. Dinner over, he went in procession, for such was the custom in some houses, with the rest of the monks to the cloister-garth where the dead were buried. There all bareheaded the brethren stood "a certain long space, praying among the tombs and 'throwghes' for their brethren's souls, being buried there. And when they had done their prayers they returned to the cloister and there did study their book."[1]

The cloister was the scene of their daily work, and where all the life of the monastery was carried on. It was generally situated on the southern side of the church, thus getting what sunshine might be. The western side of the cloister was the part which Dom John at first frequented, for there was held the school for the younger monks. Sitting at desks one behind the other, they studied the *trivium* (grammar, rhetoric, and dialectics) and *quadrivium* (music, arithmetic, geometry, and astronomy), under which all knowledge was then summed. "Their master had a pretty seat of wainscot adjoining . . . over against the stall where they sat."[2] Let us hope that sometimes, when youthful spirits found vent in tricks upon one another, the discreet master was not always looking.

[1] *Durham Rites*, p. 74.   [2] *Ibid.* p. 70.

The northern side of the cloister was reserved for the elder brethren, where they pursued their studies, commonly in little oaken carrels, three to each window—each one separate, and containing "a desk to lie their books on." These little studies were handsomely wainscoted, "all but the fore part, which had carved work which gave light in at their carrell door . . . and over against the carrels against the church wall did stand certain great cupboards of wainscot all full of books, with a great store of ancient manuscripts to help them in their study, wherein did lie as well the old ancient written Doctors of the Church, as other profane authors, with divers other holy men's works, so that every one did study what doctor pleased them the best, having the library at all times to go study in besides their carrels."[1] On the south side, or near the chapter-house, sat the abbat and the elders; and there the business was done, and there also would Dom John go on Sundays after prime to be shriven. The windows in the cloister were glazed; and in the winter-time straw or hay was spread on the ground for warmth's sake. In one side of the cloister, often the south, and close to the refectory door was the lavatory,[2]

---

[1] *Durham Rites*, pp. 70, 71.

[2] "Within the cloister-garth, over against the Frater house door, was a fair Laver or Conduit for the monks to wash their hands and faces at, being made in form round, covered with lead, and all of marble saving the very outer walls (and with) many little conduits or spouts of brass with xxiiii Cocks of brass . . . having the closets or almeries . . . kept always with sweet and clean towels, as is aforesaid, to dry their hands" (*Durham Rites*, p. 70).

where the monks would wash their hands before dinner; for cleanliness is a virtue as well as a necessity in a monastery.

A cloister in the days of Dom John would be a very different sight from what they are nowadays. Then they were the workshops of the monastery. But a strange workshop it was, in truth; for the workmen were all silent, and no busy hum of worldly work was heard. Recollection reigned over all the place; no hurry, no bustle. These men worked for eternity, not for time; and knew that God rewards not the amount done but the love with which it is wrought. This is the secret of the success of the work and the spirituality of the art of the old days. This also explains the reason why modern work, done in all the turmoil of life, so often fails in grasping the spirit of repose and strength which characterise the work of olden days. Here, then, while some would be busy in study, others would be writing, others illuminating, others designing, others embroidering. Others, again, would be engaged in the details of administration, unless they had separate offices, as was often the case. Place for all pursuits was found; and the debt the world owes to those patient silent workmen of the cloister cannot be measured. On Saturdays it was the scene, too, of the weekly washing of feet.[1] Then,

[1] At stated intervals, the mysteries of the bath were practised and changes of clothes given out. A *dirty* monk would be a nuisance to all around him, and this was guarded against by the ordinary routine.

too, at stated intervals of a week or so, and always before the greater feasts, would the brethren shave one another—a difficult task; for not only the face but the whole head, save a ring or crown of hair, was shaven. But so clumsy were some of the operators that, as at St. Augustine's, Canterbury (1252), laymen were often deputed to shave the brethren. Here also, four or six times a year, was the solemn practice of the *minutio* gone through. This, in other words, was that panacea for all bodily ills, blood-letting. Those who had been bled had for three days extra food and rest to recover themselves. Here also, round the cloister, were made the procession on Sundays and feasts, during which the priest sprinkled with hallowed water the various places.

In this cloister, then, would Dom John after dinner remain at work, or perhaps even napping, until *two*, when nones were sung in the church, after which work again till vesper-time, which was at six. But an hour before vespers the house had been shut up, and no more strangers were admitted. Vespers, the sacrifice of the evening incense, were sung with great solemnity. It was followed, if it were not a fasting day, by a small collation, so called originally from the spiritual reading, generally from Cassian's *Collationes* or Conferences, which were read during the repast. A manchet of bread with a drink of beer or such like was all. Rising from the collation, they went straight into the church for compline, which being over, left them free to be in bed before 8 p.m.[1]

As they had spent the day together, so the night found them in one common dorter, or sleeping-house. This was either one large open-room with uncurtained beds, as more than one constitution ordered, or the room was divided off into cells. "Every monk having a little chamber of wainscott, very close, several, by themselves and their windows towards the cloister . . . the partition between every chamber was close wainscoted one from the other, and in every of their windows a desk to support their books for their study."[2] As a rule the dorter was kept most strictly for sleeping purposes, although at Durham it seems to have been allowed to be used for study as well. Perhaps at the time of the afternoon sleep, often the custom, those who did not want to sleep read. The furniture of the cells was simple. The monks of Christ Church, Canterbury, for instance, had a mat and a hard pillow to lie down upon, and a blanket or rug to keep them warm. They slept in their clothes.[3] At St. Albans the bedsteads were of oak, says Matthew of Paris. Strict silence was always kept in the

---

[1] We have taken the *horarium* mainly from Westminster.

[2] *Durham Rites*, p. 72.

[3] *Reg. Eccl. Cant.* quoted by Battely, *ut supra*. It will be remembered, from the list given in the "Book of Ely" and elsewhere, that the monks had special garments for night wear which correspond to the modern idea.

dorter; and a light, according to St. Benedict's Rule,[1] burnt the whole night.

This was a long and a hard day for Dom John and his fellow-monks. Eight hours were given to choir work, for besides the day's office, there would be also the office of the dead and that of Our Lady to be said as well. Eight hours were given to the body for food, sleep, and recreation; and the other eight to study, or to the administration of such offices as were committed to their charge. We have said nothing, however, about recreation. The bow cannot be kept over-bent, or the result would be to make a very dull monk of Dom John.

There were times and places of recreation duly fixed. There was the "frayter," or common house, where the monks could meet at lawful hours for conversation. It was generally in the afternoons they met here; and merry and bright would it be; for in that monastery was one Dom Edward, a merry wight, full of jokes and stories mirthful. At times of recreation he would amuse the brethren with some droll conceit or merry quip; a certain little gesture of his lent a point to his story, and a twinkle of his eye betrayed the coming jest. But withal, be it remembered, he was a grave doctor, learned in divinity and much looked up to; for had he not been to Rome itself, on business connected with the abbey, and seen its wonders, and had many tales to tell of the monasteries he had visited and

[1] Ch. XXII.

edified? In the "frayter" was also a fire in wintertime, to which the monks could come to warm themselves. The room was hence often called the "Calefactory." Hard by, at Durham for instance, was a garden for pleasaunce, and a bowling alley at the back of the house for the recreation of the younger men when it pleased their master to give them leave.[1] Besides, there would be the whole of the enclosure to take exercise in. These enclosures were sometimes very large. That at Glaston, for instance, was sixty acres in extent. But outside of this the monks were never allowed to go without leave. This was a very strict rule, and its infringement subjected them to severe penalties.

But Dom John was not kept a close prisoner. He could get leave to go out. He would go away at intervals to one of the granges or cells which Lynminster had in various parts of the country. What the sort of life was, during these visits, may perhaps be gathered from a letter of the prior of Durham to the prior of the cell at Finchal, written in 1408. As the cathedral-monastery was

[1] *Durham Rites*, p. 75. There were periods of recreation at the times of the great feasts of the year. Visits of great men, or any extraordinary function in the church would also break the routine of the cloister life. There would be little feasts occasionally, with something extra in the way of cakes, &c. For instance at Durham, in the common house, "the master of it kept his *O Sapientia* once a year, viz. between Martinmas and Christmas, a solemn banquet that the prior and convent did use at that time of the year only, when their banquet was of figs and raisins, ale and cakes, and thereof no superfluity or excess, but a scholastical and moderate congratulation among themselves."—*Durham Rites*, p. 75.

then in difficulties, the recreations which the monks used to have were for a time suspended, and instead the brethren were sent to Finchal, there to have a little relaxation. And in view of this the cathedral prior makes some regulations. Four monks, for three weeks at a time, will be sent from Durham to Finchal to join the little community, then consisting of a prior and four religious. Two of the visitors have to be present daily at matins, mass, and vespers, and at all other choir duties; the other two are to be free to go about in the country *religiose et honeste*, but are bound to attend the mass and vespers unless for some reasonable cause the prior of the house grants a dispensation. This liberty next day is to be given to the other two. While all are to use the common dorter, the prior is to provide a room properly furnished with a fire and all things necessary for the visitors, and a special servant is to be appointed to wait on them.[1] But such excursions would be at present rare in the case of Dom John; for he had to be broken in to the willing monotony of monastic life. But the time was coming when he must leave his abbey for a while and go up to the university to take his degree,[2] and come back learned in the law, or perhaps a master in theology.

[1] *The Priory of Finchal* (Surtees Society, pp. 30, 31). See also the rules for the country house at Redburne belonging to St. Albans. *Gesta Abbatum* (Roll Series), vol. ii. pp. 202, 205.

[2] Sometimes the youths attached to a claustral school went up to Oxford to the benedictine houses and studied there and took their

In 1283 John Gifford, Lord of Brimsfield, during the abbacy of Reginald de Hamone, founded for thirteen monks of St. Peter's, Gloucester, a house at Oxford for students at the university. The church of Chipping Norton was appropriated for their support. The abbat, not able to carry on the house satisfactorily by his unaided efforts, got other houses to join with him. In 1290 the general chapter took up the matter of the higher education of their monks. They were pretty well forced to take some action, because the friars already at the universities[1] were carrying everything before them by the brilliancy of their studies and the hosts of students they attracted. The general chapter ordered that one monk in every twenty out of each house should be sent to the university, to the house known from its first owners as Gloucester Hall, and there go through his university course.[2] Each house had to support its own men, making them a fixed allowance for necessities besides contributing their share of the common tax. By degrees each of the principal

degrees in arts before becoming monks. Sometimes they returned to the university after they had been for some time in the monastery. We shall see later on (Ch. IX.) an example of this. See, also, an interesting account of the Canterbury claustral school, in Dom Gasquet's *The Old English Bible and other Essays*, p. 260.

[1] The dominicans made their first English house at Oxford 1221, and the franciscans settled there about the same time.

[2] The sister university of Cambridge also had its home of studies, the rebuilding of which was stopped through the attainder of the duke of Buckingham, its munificent benefactor, in the reign of Henry VIII. About three fourths of the benedictine students went to Oxford, and only one fourth to Cambridge.

houses who used this hall besides the original owners, St. Albans, Glaston, Tavistock, Burton, Chertsey, Coventry, Evesham, Eynsham, St. Edmundsbury, Winchcombe, Malmesbury, Norwich, Rochester, and others, built separate sets of chambers, existing to this day, for their own students, and marked with the heraldic device of their own monastery.[1]

To this house, then, was Dom John Weston sent from Lynminster. His mode of life was somewhat modified at the university, for he had to get in as much time for study as he could. But it was still a hard life, and contrasted greatly with the free and easy tone always found in university towns. He was kept strictly from intercourse with seculars, who might waste his time, and on no account was he allowed to study with them. He got up between 4 and 5 o'clock each morning; from 5 to 6 was spent in prayer; from 6 to 10 study and lectures, and then he broke his fast. Shortly after dinner he resumed his study until 5 P.M., when he supped much in the same way he had dined. Then study again until 9, when he went to bed.[2] Out of the

---

[1] The bishop of Durham founded a house in 1337 at Oxford, for thirteen students from his cathedral-monastery, as a memorial of the king's victory over the Scots at Halidon. From a letter of the prior, we learn that in this home the divine office had to be said daily in choir by all *vel ad minus duo*. On Sundays and all double feasts all were obliged to attend at the hours, which, although not sung, were to be said *tractim*. They sang both mass and vespers on these days, and on the principal feasts the whole office and the mass *si tempus hoc permiserit*.

[2] Fosbroke's *British Monasticism*, p. 186.

time allotted for study he had to find the time for
his office and the necessary recreation. After some
years of this severe life, Dom John returned to
Lynminster with the coveted degree of Doctor of
Theology, which meant much in those days, and
gave the holder a certain position in the community
as well as in the outer world.

He had now to look forward to the priesthood.
Already had he received the clerical tonsure and
the minor orders from his abbat; but for the
sacred orders he had to go to the bishop of the
diocese. Lynminster, not being exempt from episcopal control, could not call in any bishop at pleasure
for ordinations, blessings, and consecration. Most
likely Dom John had to go to the cathedral city
for the general ordination, and there receive his
priesthood together with the rest of the clergy.
But wherever it was, it was a great day for him;
and his first mass was the occasion of much rejoicing at Lynminster. He had to provide a feast
for his brethren, such was the custom, and wrote to
his friends and relatives to help him on the occasion.[1] Owing to his university training, or rather
to the good use he had made of his time there, he
was a man likely to rise in his house and to hold
high office—all of which came about in course of
time.

But meanwhile he had to take up the work of
teaching the novices; for his old teacher was past

---

[1] D. Gasquet's *The Old English Bible and other Essays*, p. 283.

his work, and his abbat was anxious to keep the intellectual tone of the monks up to the level of the best house in England. For the abbat who then presided over Lynminster knew well that a house, to be prosperous and vigorous, must have a high standard of intellectual life; otherwise its men become children, unable to think for themselves, or cope with any emergency, and, as a result of such a system, would by-and-by, like listless drones, live without any interests in life. This unhealthy tone the abbat was determined not to allow while he held rule. For in his younger days he had seen the ill effects of a contrary policy; and now that he was called to the abbat's chair, he was determined to do his best to remedy them. In the days of his predecessor (good but too easy-going man), studies had been neglected, a lax tone had crept in, and everything had gone down. Visitations, both diocesan and monastic, could keep things in check indeed, but could not get at the root of the evil. With the new abbat it took some time and the help of able obedientiaries to restore things to a proper efficiency.

In this abbey the chief office-holders were: the Precentor, whose duty it was to arrange all details of the services in the church: he also had the charge of the library, and had to provide parchment, colours, paper, ink, and other material for the monks. Then came the Sacrist, who had care of the church and its furniture: he was charged with the provision of vestments, lights, and wine, &c. Then there was the Almoner, who had to see to the distributions of alms to the poor; the Refectory Master and the Pitance Master,[1] important officials who were responsible for the meals and supplies of all kinds. Then there was the Chamberlain, who had charge of the dormitory and of the monks' clothes; the Infirmarian, Guestmaster, Treasurer, whose names denote their offices. The Cellarer, however, ruled supreme in the department of domestic concerns, and was looked upon as the second father in the monastery.[2] He held the most important place, for he was the business manager of the abbey; and upon him depended in a great measure whether life ran on as smoothly as it should.

The abbat was a wise man. Although he had the whole control over his abbey, yet he gave full scope to all his officers, and did not keep every detail in his own hands. He wanted his monks to be men, not children. As long as they kept within certain limits he left them free, and did not interfere or scold at every mistake. For it was by their very mistakes he wished them to learn how to rule and administer. If a monk turned out an irremedial failure in his office, he was removed and another substituted. The result of the abbat's wise policy

[1] An interesting manuscript [Harl. 1005] of about the latter half of the fourteenth century gives a full and detailed account of the nature and occasions of the pitances, or "scholastical and moderate congratulations," at St. Edmundsbury.

[2] *E.g.* at Peterborough.

was that Lynminster became a strong house in every way. Among its monks were to be found master-men and good solid religious, capable of fulfilling with credit any work set upon them. The good the abbat did, died not with him. There had been such a quiet, steady development of energy that the results were lasting; and Lynminster, when the day of trial came, was found one of "the solemn monasteries in which religion was, thank God! right well observed."

Under such an abbat, Dom John Weston was sure to get on; and in due course rose to the highest office. He went through various grades of administration, and then was set to rule his brethren as prior. He it was who carried out in detail the abbat's principles, and under him Lynminster was a happy and united brotherhood.

But alas! he was sent off to London on important business for the abbat and there caught the plague, which was making one of its periodical visits. When he was first seized, he was staying at a house belonging to his monastery which the abbat kept up for the use of his monks.[1] He did not die from the malady, but his health utterly broke down. He lingered on through the long summer days. His one desire was to get back home, to be with his brethren. Taking advantage of a fallacious rally, he was brought by slow degrees back to Lynminster

---

[1] The abbat of St. Albans kept up such a house. See *Gesta Abbatum* (Roll Series), vol. i. p. 289.

and put in the infirmary, a large building with its own chapel, on the north-east side of the church. There he was tended with loving hands. Three times was he solemnly visited by all the community, who came to pray by him. The abbat received his public profession of faith. Then was he houseled and annealed, and thus strengthened, could look with confidence to his coming passage into eternity.

And when in a few days the end came, the bells rang, and the monks came into the chamber of death with the crucifix, and sweet singing of the *Credo*, and psalms and litanies.[2] They found prior John Weston clad in his cowl and, in penitential spirit, laid on sackcloth and ashes. And as they watched and prayed his life gently ebbed away. At last the conversion of his life, promised at profession, was complete; he had been obedient until death, and his stability had been confirmed for ever. With sorrow his brethren paid the last offices. The body, wrapped in a shroud but uncoffined, was carried on a bier to the church. And *Placebo* and *Dirige* were chanted, and the abbat himself sang *Requiem*; and the monks said there were tears in his voice. Then was the body of prior John Weston borne forth, and was laid in the garth that was in the midst of the cloisters.

For thirty days his obsequies were celebrated with office and mass and daily visit to his grave. And

[1] *Officium Ecclesiasticum Abbatum sec. usum., Eveshamien. Monas.* (Henry Bradshaw Society), p. 117.

the prayers of the poor were also invoked for his soul. In the refectory during all that time a black cross was set in his place at table; and his portion of food and drink was bestowed on the poor. His name was written in the obit-book to be read out, year by year, as the date of his death came round. And word was sent round to all the monasteries in England to which Lynminster was united in spiritual relationship to beg for prayers for his soul. And each house did its share of prayers for the assoiling of his soul. His memory was kept green for a long time in his old home. For no love here below is so lasting and faithful as that between those who have given up all earthly loves and found them again in the Lord.

CHAPTER VI

WOMEN UNDER THE RULE

WHETHER St. Scholastica was a nun or not is uncertain, although St. Gregory tells us she was dedicated to God from her earliest childhood.[1] There are no historical traces remaining for us to decide the question; though venerable tradition records that St. Benedict founded also a community of virgins consecrated to God, and placed his sister at their head. While there is not a word in his Rule[2] about such a community, and St. Gregory in his dialogues is also silent, still, on the other hand, there is nothing in the teaching of the great lawgiver which cannot be applied to women. We know also that he seems to have undertaken the spiritual direction of his sister and had conferences with her, one of which was so beautifully illustrated by God granting a prayer the brother had refused.[3]

But whether St. Scholastica was a nun or not, one thing is certain, that before her brother's time there were cloisters of women dedicated to God.

---

[1] *Dialogues of St. Gregory*, book ii. chap. xxxiii.
[2] The word "woman" does not even occur in the Rule.
[3] *Ibid.*

They flourished in the East, whence St. Benedict drew much of his law. Cassian, at least, had introduced them into the West, and had founded a convent at Marseilles, whence Cesarius, bishop of Arles (542), persuaded his sister, Cesaria, to come and join him and preside over a convent he was then founding.

Tradition ascribes to St. Martin the foundation of various communities for women;[1] and in St. Gregory's time we know, from an account of the procession instituted on account of the plague then devastating Rome, that there were abbesses and nuns; for they were appointed to walk in the procession along with the priests of the first region.[2]

If St. Benedict founded a religious community for women it was nothing unheard of; but whether he did so or not, we may be sure it would only be a short time before he, too, was looked upon as guide and father to the many convents already existing. However this may be, here in England we have no doubt but that, as in the North, columban nuns existed at any rate very soon after the introduction of Christianity: so in the South, where the Roman benedictine influence was the stronger, it is almost as certain that the numerous convents, that sprang up as it were by magic, were benedictine. But, as we have elsewhere remarked, there was no antagonism between the two Rules; and the process of assimilation, or perhaps absorption, of the Celtic Rule by that

---

[1] Dupuy, A., *Histoire de S. Martin*, p. 176.
[2] Mabillon, *Annales Ordinis S. Benedicti* (ed. Paris, 1703), tom. i. p. 217.

of St. Benedict was so gradual as almost to be imperceptible. The Oriental tinge of severity so perceptible in the former would have to give way to the wider spirit of the West, which dealt with men as it found them. The two Rules were typical of their origins—that of the East unchanging and stereotyped; that of the West keeping in touch with the times, ever adapting itself to the unceasing flow and development of humanity.

Hilda in the north at Whitby, and Eanswith in the south at Folkestone, are the two prominent foundresses of the religious life for women in our land. Little is known of either of them; especially as to the beginning of their religious lives. Hilda was one of Edwin of Northumbria's household, and in her fourteenth year was baptized at York, on that Easter-day (627) that saw Paulinus, the benedictine monk, receiving the king and court into the Church of Christ.

"Nothing is known of the life of Hild (Hilda) between the ages of fourteen and thirty-four; but evidently she had not dwelt in obscure retirement, for the Scottish prelate Aidan in 647, knowing that she was living in the Midlands, begged her to return to the north. It is a noteworthy circumstance if, in an age when marriage was the rule, she remained single without taking the veil, but she may have been associated with some religious settlement." [1]

---

[1] Eckenstein, *Women under Monasticism*, p. 82. But Bede says "she withdrew to the province of the East Angles," with the intention of going to Chelles (lib. iv. cap. xxiii.).

She became foundress of Whitby, at first a columban monastery for men and women. It afterwards received the benedictine Rule as well, perhaps through the influence of Wilfrid. Of Eanswith we know still less. Her father, Edbald of Kent, after he had put away his heathen wife, married a princess of the Franks. About the year 630 he gave his daughter a piece of land at Folkestone, where she founded a convent. It would be a curious point for speculation to discover whether this beginning in Kent was due to the influence of the Northumbrian Edwin's widow, Ethelburga, who with her children and Paulinus had taken refuge at her brother's Kentish court, or whether the Frankish princess had taken the initiative. But there was Paulinus the benedictine at hand to give a direction to the new settlement. However, her convent was destroyed or deserted at the close of the century; for there is a charter of Athelstane (927) giving the land to Christ Church, Canterbury, "the house having been destroyed by the pagans."[1]

Queen Ethelburga was herself the foundress of a house at Liming. It would naturally be, coming from the north, that her foundation should be modelled on the great abbey of Whitby. But that is no proof that the house was governed by the columban Rule pure and simple. Sexburgh, queen of Erconbert, the successor of Edbald, founded another convent at Sheppy. At this time, says Bede, "there were

[1] Dugdale, vol. i. p. 451.

not yet many monasteries built in the regions of the Angles. Many were wont, for the sake of the monastic mode of life, to go from Britain to the monasteries of the Franks and of Gaul; they also sent their daughters to the same to be instructed and to be wedded to the Heavenly Spouse chiefly in the monasteries of Brie, Chelles, and Andelys."[1]

Mildred was the foundress of the famous abbey of Minster in Thanet. She had been brought up at Chelles, where, says the legend, the abbess Wilcoma wanted the girl to marry one of her kinsmen. Irritated by her refusals, she ordered her to be cast into a roaring fire whence she came forth untouched. She escaped back to England. Some time towards the latter half of the seventh century we find Egberht, king of Kent, giving her land in Thanet as a blood-fine for the murder of two of her brothers. "She asked for as much land as her tame deer could run over in one course, and received over ten thousand acres of the best land in Kent."[2] On this land she built a monastery; and her name as abbess appears signing a charter of privileges granted by King Witred to the churches and monasteries of Kent. Her name comes the first of the five abbesses who sign the document after the archbishop of Canterbury and the bishop of Rochester. A noticeable fact, the names of these five women

[1] *Hist. Eccles.*, book iii. chap. viii.
[2] Dugdale, vol. i. p. 447.

come before that of the priests who attested the charter.[1]

Of the other nunneries famous in Saxon days was Ely, founded (673) by Audrey or Etheldreda, the friend of Wilfrid. This seems to have been a double convent, or at least to have had a convent of monks hard by. One of her successors was Werburg, to whom was entrusted, by her uncle King Ethelred, the oversight of all the nunneries in his domains. She is known to have founded houses at Trentham, and at Hanbury, and at Weden.[2]

Coldingham was founded by Ebba, also a friend of Wilfrid's, and of Cuthbert too, that holy bishop of Lindisfarne who did so much by his gentleness and sweetness to introduce Roman usages among the columban monks in England. "Ebba wrote begging him to come and condescend to edify both herself and the inmates of her monastery by the grace of his exhortations. Cuthbert accordingly went thither, and tarrying for some days he expounded the ways of justice to all; these he not only preached, but to the same extent practised."[3]

Osith of Aylesbury, Frideswith of Oxford, Osburg of Coventry, Modwen of Burton, Everild of Everingham, are names which, as foundresses and abbesses

---

[1] Haddan and Stubbs, *Councils and Ecclesiastical Documents*, vol. iii. p. 240.

[2] During the Danish invasion her relics, which were at Hanbury, in 875 were carried off to Chester, whose patron she became.

[3] Bede, *Life of St. Cuthbert*, chap. x.

of holy houses, were sweet in the ears of our Saxon forefathers.

But among them all stands out pre-eminent Ethelburga, sister of Erkonwald (693), bishop of London, who made a home for his sister at Barking, which "he established excellently in the regular discipline."[1] This renowned house was also a famous place for the education of high-born children. The great scholar Aldhelm[2] wrote his treatise on Virginity for the nuns of this convent; and the whole tone of the book, besides several direct passages, shows that the intellectual life there must have been of a very high order. He quotes freely from the Fathers, and refers to the classics of antiquity. He praises especially the nuns for being devoted to study: like bees they gather, he says, everywhere material for study. Scripture, history, grammar, poetry, are among some of the subjects which he mentions. But evidently he looks upon Barking as an oasis in the worldliness which even then (the beginning of the eighth century) had entered into nunneries. He describes nuns elsewhere as wearing "a vest of fine linen of a violet colour. Above it a scarlet tunic with a hood, sleeves striped with silk and trimmed with red fur; the locks on the forehead

---

[1] Bede, lib. iv. cap. vi. Miss Eckenstein states that Barking was a double monastery. We can find no proof of this anywhere. Bede says: "In which (Barking) she could live as the mother and nourisher of devout women" (*ibid.*).

[2] Aldhelm was abbat of Malmsbury, and became bishop of Sherborne.

and the temples are curled with a crisping-iron; their dark head-veil is given up for white and coloured head-dresses, which, with bows of ribbon sewn on, reach to the ground; their nails, like those of a falcon or sparrow-hawk, are found to resemble talons."[1] This last reminds us that Aldhelm was a poet; and this may have been one of his licenses.

Wimborne, the last of the foundations of the early Saxon period, was founded from Barking by Cuthburg (725), a sister of Ina, king of Wessex, and wife of Ealdfrid of Northumbria. A famous inmate of this house was Lioba, one of the friends of Winfrid better known as St. Boniface. He wrote to the abbess Tetta begging her, "as a comfort in his wanderings and as a help in his mission, to send the virgin Lioba, the fame of whose holiness and teaching of godly life had penetrated across wide lands and filled the mouths of many with her praise."[1] She went, and became abbess of the famous house of Bischofsheim near Mainz.

In her life, written by Rudolf of Fulda (850), we get a glimpse of the life in these double monasteries. "There were two settlements at Wimborne, formerly erected by the kings of that people, surrounded by lofty and strong walls, and endowed with ample revenues. Of these, one was for clerics, the other for women. But neither, for such was the rule of their foundation, was ever entered by any members of

---

[1] *S. Aldhelmi: De Laudibus Virginitates* (ed. Migne), vol. 89, p. 157.
[2] *Vita S. Liobæ*, Pars II. *Acta Sanctorum* (Sept. 28), p. 713.

the other sex. No women had permission to come among the congregation of men, no men to enter into the dwellings of the virgins, the priests alone excepted, who entered their church to celebrate mass, and withdrew to their own part at once as soon as the service prayer was solemnly finished. . . . Moreover, the mother herself of the congregation, whenever it was necessary that she should give orders in the affairs of the monastery, spoke through a window, and decided whatever was considered to be best."[1]

Most of the nunneries perished during the invasion of the Danes, and but few were rebuilt. Only those which were in connection with the royal house of Wessex remained at the close of the tenth century. Those of the Northern and Midland districts had entirely disappeared. Some were deserted; others had been laid waste during the Danish invasion. It has been observed that with the return of tranquillity, not one of the houses for women was restored. Seculars "took possession of them, and when they were expelled, the Church claimed the land, or the settlement was restored to the use of monks. Some of the great houses formerly ruled by women were thus appropriated to men. Whitby and Ely rose in renewed splendour under the rule of abbats. Repton, Wimborne, and numerous other nunneries became the property of monks."[2]

The chief convents which survived to the Conquest

---
[1] *Ibid.*, Pars I. p. 711.
[2] Eckenstein, *Women under Monasticism*, pp. 201, 202.

were Shaftesbury (founded in 893 by Alfred the Great for his daughter Ethelgiva), Amesbury, Romsey, Winchester, Wilton, and Barking. Like all founded before the Conquest, these houses were abbeys,[1] and their abbesses were women of great political power in the kingdom. Those of Shaftesbury, Wilton, Winchester (Nunna-minster) and Barking held their lands of the king by an entire barony, and had the privilege, at a later date, of being summoned to Parliament, though this lapsed on account of their sex.[2]

The abbess had most of the privileges of the abbats, and in her possession were many lands, together with their churches, from which she drew her revenues, and to which she exercised the rights of presentation. She had to do service to the Crown and supply her quota of knights for the king's

---

[1] The houses founded after the Conquest were generally priories. Of the sixty-four benedictine convents founded for women after Saxon days, only three, viz. Godstow, Malling, and Elstow, were abbeys. "The explanation is to be sought in the system of feudal tenure. Women no longer held property, nunneries were founded and endowed by local barons or abbats. When power from the preceding period devolved on the woman in authority, she retained it; but when new appointments were made, the current tendency was in favour of curtailing her power." Cf. *Women under Monasticism*, p. 204. When the house was founded by an abbat it remained under his jurisdiction, and the house was visited both by abbat and by bishop, unless the abbey itself was exempt; then all houses depending upon it shared in the privilege, *e.g.* Sopwell nunnery in relation to St. Albans, and Kilburn to Westminster. Although the Lateran constitution gave general chapters the visitation of nunneries, yet we do not find any traces of capitular visitors going to any nunnery. Their oversight was left to the bishops.

[2] Dugdale, vol. ii. p. 472.

service.[1] She held her own courts for pleas of debts, and was altogether a most important personage. Of course she was elected for life, but could be deposed.

We will look a little more closely at the life of nuns, or "mynchyns," as they were called in the Southern parts of England, and make use of such information as we can glean from historical remains.

One feature of the life which strikes the reader at once is the fact that the benedictine nun in England, like her sister abroad, was not bound by the same law of enclosure as the nun of the last three hundred years. Her cloister was her home indeed; and there she loved to dwell in peace and retirement. But she did not hesitate to go out when the service of God required it. The pages of history are so full of examples, that one is surprised to find that any can doubt that the original benedictine nun had practically as much freedom as the monk. From the days of St. Scholastica herself, who came out to visit her brother, all during the Saxon times, and up to the Reformation, English benedictine nuns had a mitigated form of enclosure. And not the English "mynchyns" only, but in Germany, where the great names of Hildegarde,

---

[1] The abbess of Shaftesbury, Agnes Ferrar, in 1251 was summoned to Chester to take part in the military proceedings against Llewellin; and a successor of hers, Juliana Bauceyn, twenty years after, had a similar call made upon her. The abbesses of Shaftesbury, as baronesses, had to supply the king's service with a certain number of knights together with their full complement of soldiers. *Cf.* Dugdale, vol. ii. p. 473.

Gertrude, and the two Mechtildas were those of nuns as much unenclosed as their English sisters who went to help Winfrid and Willibald and Winibald in evangelising and civilising the German heathen.[1]

The majestic vision of Hilda taking part in synods, of Werburg inspecting the convents in her uncle's kingdom, of Withburga following the pilgrim-track to Rome, of Frideswide working a miracle on the public road at Oxford, of Edith at the court of her father Edgar; all come up at once to our memory as names of unenclosed nuns doing God's work in the world, and keeping themselves unspotted therefrom.

Later on we find many a reference to nuns being out of their convents. For instance, in the fourteenth century bishop Stapleton was on visitation in his diocese of Exeter, and among other decrees made for the benedictine nunnery of Polslo, was that they were not to be allowed to go out and visit their friends more than once in the year. They had to get the prioress' leave; and she was charged with providing a professed nun as a companion, who had to be changed each year.[2]

---

[1] It is a fact worth moralising upon, that no canonised saint has been found among the benedictine nuns since they kept strict enclosure. Other orders, in which enclosure is of the essence of their vocation, have had them in abundance.

[2] Hingeston-Randolph. *The Register of Walter de Stapledon* (1307-26), p. 317. We give here a license for a nun to go out for a while from her convent. P. C. Priorissæ E. Precibus charissimæ nobis in Christo filiæ Dominæ . . . consanguinis Domini . . . militis nostri diœcesis favorabilibus inclinatus, ut ad eam justis et honestis ex causis Domina . . . hujus dicti vestri prioratus commonialis, cum alia ejusdem prior-

Sometimes law business took the prioress away. "When I rode to London for the suit that was taken," says the prioress of Pree in her account for 1487–89, and notes down the money (20 shillings) paid for herself and "my priest and a woman and two men."[1] The abbess of Shaftesbury, Joan Formage, had leave from her bishop in 1368 to go to one of her manors to take the air and divert herself.[2] Nuns, however, did not always like this sort of thing; and when visitation time came round they would complain to the bishop that my lady abbess was always riding off somewhere or other; and they were quite sure it was not always on business.[3]

But they themselves could go out at times.[4] Their customs allowed them to go abroad, if they were ill, to take the waters, to console sick parents, to attend their funerals. They could be absent for three days only when out for relaxation or illness, but a special dispensation was needed for any further extension of absence.[5]

atus ipsam associente accedere valeant; valeant equestri, non obstantibus vestris consuetudinibus contrariis, dispensatione, ex causis licitis nobis sufficienter doctis, in quantum de jure possumus, quatenus obedientiam et honestatem disciplinæ regularis literarum tenore præsentium duximus indulgendam, &c. &c. (MSS. Harl. 2179, f. 78).

[1] Dugdale, vol. iii. p. 360.
[2] Hutchins, J., *The History and Antiquities of the County of Dorset*, vol. ii. p. 17.
[3] *Ibid.* p. 474.
[4] Blaauw, W. H., *Episcopal Visitations of the Benedictine Nunnery of Easebourne* (Sussex Archæological Collections), vol. iv. p. 7.
[5] Lyndewood, *Provinciale*, p. 212.

Chaucer was too true an artist to include, in the gay company meeting at Southwark that April morning all bound for Canterbury, two nuns, a prioress and her companion, if such characters would have been out of place in a band of pilgrims. His description of "Madame Eglentine" the prioress is full of charming touches, and shows us a lady, well-bred and friendly, in a dignified way, with all her company. She did not ride on demurely and silently. In the general entertainment she tells her tale of the little boy-martyr, a legend such as she would read at home in her convent. And her companion was not behindhand either, but contributes a prettily told story of St. Cecily.

How did the nuns occupy themselves in their convents? Study and intellectual pursuits have always been favourite employments with benedictine dames, and one may almost gauge the state of observance in a convent by the standard of intellectual activity which there obtained. When that was high, the convent flourished both in number and in exactness of rule. Where learning was neglected, almost everything else showed signs of decay. When Winfrid was in Germany he kept up an active correspondence with nuns in England, and from them received presents of books copied out with their own hands. "Often," says he in 725 to Eadburga, abbess of Minster, "gifts of books and vestments, the proofs of your love,

have been to me a consolation in misfortune. So
I pray you will continue as you have begun, and
write for me in golden letters¹ the epistle of the
holy apostle St. Paul, my master," &c.² Nor was
she an exception; for, as Montalembert says:—

"The Anglo-Saxon race above all was rich in
women of this kind: many are to be found among
the princesses established in the numerous abbeys
of England—such as Edith, natural daughter of
King Edgar; who, brought up by her mother in
the nunnery at Wilton, was famed there equally
for her knowledge and her virtue." He goes on
to speak of Lioba of Wimborne, who went to join
Winfrid. "She was so eager for knowledge that
she never left her books save for divine service.
She was well versed in all that were then called
the liberal arts; she was thoroughly acquainted
with the writings of the Fathers and canon-law;
cultivated Latin verse and showed her attempts
to St. Boniface (Winfrid) who admired them greatly.
. . . To her is due the honour of having trained
in Christian knowledge the young girls who filled
the new nunneries, founded under the teaching
of the Saxon missionaries. The Germans really
owe to her the introduction among them of that
monastic culture which, later, was to shine with

---

[1] Saxon nuns excelled in illuminating manuscripts. Wilfrid brought to England the art of writing in gold, and owned a copy of the Gospels written on purple-coloured parchments, in letters of pure gold.
[2] *S. Bonafacii Epistolæ* (ed. Migne), n. xix. p. 712.

such brilliance in the person of Hroswitha, the illustrious nun of Gandersheim, whose greatest glory was to have composed the plays which she caused to be acted in her abbey. These dramas astonish us by the extraordinary acquaintance they prove with the authors of classic antiquity—Plautus, Virgil, Terence, and Horace—and yet more by a knowledge of the human heart truly remarkable in a woman completely shut out from the world."[1]

The nuns knew Latin and could write it. For the superiors this was almost a necessity. It was not till after the rise of the universities, when learning ceased to be a monopoly of the religious houses, that documents for nuns began to be written in French, then as now the language of culture, or in English. This decline in learning coincided with the period when convents of women were at a lower ebb than they had ever been, both in point of numbers and of influence.

Besides intellectual studies of all kinds, needlework held an important place. The embroidering of our English nuns earned a reputation far and wide as the finest work to be had. Bishops and popes prided themselves on specimens of the famed *opus Anglicanum*, and were consumed with envy when they saw the richly embroidered vestments[2]

---

[1] *Monks of the West* (ed. Nimmo), vol. v. pp. 133, 134.

[2] Professor J. H. Middleton points out, in a note to his *Illuminated Manuscripts in Classical and Mediæval Times*, p. 112, that the popes of the period, when they sent the pall to a newly elected archbishop of England, suggested they would like in return some embroidered

of English bishops or abbats sitting in council with the rest of the clergy.

"The most famous embroidered vestments now preserved in various places in Italy are the handiwork of English embroiderers between 1250 and 1300, though their authorship is not as a rule recognised by their present possessors."[1]

The convents were almost the only houses of education for girls, and even for little boys. Dom Gasquet quotes old John Aubrey, as witness for what he knew of St. Mary's convent near Kington St. Michael in Wiltshire.

"There the young maids were brought up (not as at Hakney Sarum Schools, &c., to learn pride and wantonness) but at the nunneries, where they had examples of piety, and humility, and modesty, and obedience to imitate and to practise. Here they learned needle-work, the art of confectionery, surgery (for anciently there were no apothecaries or surgeons—the gentlewomen did cure their poor

---

vestments of English work. And Matthew Paris has an instructive passage on the point. When Innocent IV. saw the beautiful vestments worn (in 1246) by the English prelates who came to Rome, he asked where they were made; and on hearing in England, he exclaimed, "Truly England is our storehouse of delights, a very inexhaustible well: and where much abounds much can be extorted from many." He incontinently sent letters to the cistercian abbats here, ordering them to forward to him gold embroidery for the use of his chapel, "as though," says Matthew, "they could get it for nothing."—*Chronica Majora* (Roll Series), vol iv. pp. 546, 547.

[1] Middleton, p. 112. Such as the "Lateran Cope" in Rome, the "Piccolomini Cope" at Pienza, and those at Anagni, Florence, and Bologna.

neighbours: their hands are now too fine), physic, writing, drawing, &c. Old Jacques could see from his house the nuns of the priory come forth into the nymph-hay (*meadow*) with their rooks (*distaffs*) and wheels to spin, and with their sewing work. He would say that he had told three score and ten; but of nuns there were not so many, but in all, with lay sisters, as widows, old maids, and young girls, there might be such a number. This was a fine way of bringing up young women, who are led more by example than precept; and a good retirement for widows and grave single women to a civil, virtuous, and holy life."[1]

From this we may gather that convents afforded also a place of retreat and quiet life to women who, not having any vocation for the religious life, wished to share in some of its privileges without undertaking the obligations.

The religious life of the nuns was the same as that of their brethren. The ever-recurring sacrifice of prayer and praise formed their lives to a simplicity and singleness of eye.

The records of visitations[2] tell us there was a

[1] Dom Gasquet, *Henry VIII. and the English Monasteries*, vol. ii. p. 224.

[2] In the *Visitations of the Diocese of Norwich* (Dr. Jessop) we get a useful light on the inner life of convents in these parts; provided we bear in mind that these visitations record only the complaints made and the murmurings, without going into the question whether they were founded or unfounded; whereas, if all goes well, the whole business is despatched in a word or two: Omnia esse bene (Camden Soc. Publications, New Series, No. XCIII.).

great deal of human nature in convent life, then, as there must be always. One of the very charms of the monastic life is that it does not try to destroy nature but to elevate it. That this is a long process in some cases is clear, and one uncomfortable both to oneself and to others. But this is just the point in which the common life is of service in the work of moral education. Bearing and forbearing is the secret of happiness, when living with our fellow-men, and how much more in the family life of a monastery? This was one of the human sacramentals that St. Benedict relied upon so strongly in forming his disciples to the image of Christ. The various spiritual exercises of recent introduction are not of the essence of the benedictine vocation, though some find a use in them. But the large and deep minded Dom Baker (of whom anon), the most original and remarkable spiritual writer among English Catholics in the days of persecution, who was so fully possessed by the spirit of his state, lays the greatest stress on the careful fulfilling of the duties of the common life as a necessary requirement in those who, as the result of long probation, are called to the simple and direct union with God in contemplation.

Here we will leave the subject of the daughters of St. Benedict, closing with the words of a recent writer on their social influence:—

"It is unnecessary to speak of the many blessings which must have accrued to a neighbourhood by the presence of a convent of cultivated English ladies. Their gentle teaching was the first experience of the youthful poor; from them they derived their early knowledge of the elements of religion and of Catholic practice; to them they went in the troubles and cares of life as to a source of good advice; theirs was the most potent civilising influence in the rough days of the Middle Ages; and theirs was the task of tendering the sick and smoothing the passage of the Christian soul to eternity."[1] As has been well said, benedictine nuns "were indeed not of the world, but they were in it, actively and intelligently to do a good work to it—to elevate, to console, to purify, and to bless."[2]

[1] Dom Gasquet, *op. cit.* p. 221.   [2] *Ibid.* p. 220.

CHAPTER VII

CHRONICLES OF THE CONGREGATION. I

HITHERTO we have been occupied with the history of the black monks in England up to the period when the general chapter was appointed for the whole of England. We must now continue the history up to the eve of the fall of the monasteries.

The great abbeys at this period had reached their zenith, and by their wealth and numbers were some of the most important institutions in the country. Their influence was felt not only in the neighbourhood of each monastery—for great landlords, such as the monks were, will always have power—but also in Parliament. There the abbats of the black monks alone outnumbered even the bishops; for no less than twenty-eight of them sat as barons of the realm to some eighteen bishops.[1] And there are respects in which they were more in touch with the common feeling of the country than even were the bishops; for these last were rulers of large

---

[1] Together with the other abbats who had seats in Parliament, the number was fifty-two. The cathedral priors of Canterbury who were mitred also had a seat.

dioceses, were often statesmen, and immersed in affairs necessitating their absence from home; while the abbat was, with the exception of his attendance at Parliament, almost always living in the midst of the people. The mutual relations of benedictine abbat and secular bishop were on the whole good; for, with the exception of the five exempt monasteries, the bishop had all rights of visitation over the houses of black monks in his diocese.[1] With these exemptions friction was more likely to occur, especially when the exact limits of rights on either side were not defined. But for the last hundred or hundred and fifty years the mutual privileges were known and respected, and therefore a greater harmony existed.

Of the disputes between monastic chapters and their bishops (after the thirteenth century very rare), one very noteworthy example occurs in the case of the monks of Christ Church, Canterbury, who formed the chapter of the primatial church, and the archbishop of the see, Edmund Rich, known to history as St. Edmund. The dispute seems to have arisen (1237) in this manner. The archbishop was *ex-officio* abbat of the house: but this in reality meant less than appears. The affairs of the monastery and all internal discipline were governed by the cathedral prior, who however was appointed to

---

[1] It is to be understood that all the houses of the cluniacs, the white monks or cistercians, and the white canons or premonstratensians, were exempt.

his office by the archbishop after the convent had been consulted. He also had the power (a most important one) of admitting any one into the novitiate[1] and to profession, and also selected one out of the three names elected for the greater officers. These rights, together with a power of visitation, were about all the abbatial functions of the archbishop. But this did not satisfy archbishop Edmund. A saintly man, of great personal austerity, with a high ideal of his position, of inflexible purpose when he once saw what he considered to be his rights and duty, he was just the sort of man who naturally would not stay to consider any other view of things. He seems to have acted as though he had the faculty of intuitively arriving at a conclusion without being obliged to consider the steps by which it is reached. The result was inevitable. He found himself embroiled in perpetual disputes. The irony of fate was the more remarkable, for all his biographers state that personally he had the greatest horror of litigation. In these matters, unfortunately for himself and for all with whom he had to do, he trusted himself into the hands of others, notably Simon Langton, one of the archdeacons, a bitter and disappointed man. Whatever cause may be assigned to it, the fact remains

[1] At Worcester, and therefore more likely at the other cathedral monasteries, the prior, *sede vacante*, had also the right of admitting novices. See *Registrum Prioratus B. M. Wigorniensis* (Camden Soc.), p. 138. As to Christ Church, see *Literæ Cantuarienses* (Roll Series), vol. i. pp. 18, 117.

that the archiepiscopate of St. Edmund was by no means a peaceful one.¹

In the case of Christ Church, Canterbury, Edmund claimed as abbat the right of disposing of the monastic property, and had acted to the grave prejudice of the rights and liberties enjoyed by the monks in respect to certain churches appropriated to the monastery, to certain manors, possessions, perquisites, and services due from their tenants, &c. The monks in self-defence appealed to the pope (Gregory IX.). He, on December 22, 1235, appointed as judges in the dispute three abbats, who to avoid partiality were taken from the cistercian, premonstratensian, and augustinian orders.² The parties concerned were summoned in the pope's name to appear on May 10, 1236, at Rochester. The monks were represented there by their proctor, but no archbishop. Again was he summoned for June 20, but he took no notice. An attempt was made to settle the matter by compromise, but with no effect. At last, after several other citations, of all which the archbishop took no notice, when the final one was

---

¹ The state of the Church in England in St. Edmund's day was not happy. On one hand the kings, John and Henry III., were by no means nursing fathers; and on the other the popes, or those on whom they relied, were using it to enrich Italian clerics. Men who neither resided in England, nor knew a word of the language, were appointed to good livings in England, overriding the rights of patrons who either themselves or by their ancestors had founded these benefices. Deep and bitter was the resentment in the land; and it found expression in the laws excluding non-resident aliens from English livings.

² The abbats of Boxley, St. Radegund, and Lesnes.

issued for May 7, 1237 (a year after the first), then King Henry III. suddenly intervened and forbade the judges to proceed. At this sudden interference of the civil power in behalf of the archbishop, the judges dared take no further steps. Henry, who was anxious just then to keep on good terms with the pope (from whom he was daily expecting a legate to support his claims against the stand made by Edmund and others on behalf of English liberties), ordered (July 10) that nothing more should be done until he could talk over the matter with the legate. The pope meanwhile had also written ordering, in case of opposition, the whole case to be brought before his supreme tribunal. After the arrival of the legate, Otho, the judges saw him, and then held a meeting at Boxley, on August 31, whence they wrote a letter to the archbishop, who still kept away. After rehearsing all that had taken place in the matter, and stating they were hindered by the king from obeying the pope's commission, the abbats, in accordance with the apostolic mandate, fixed January 26, 1238, as the day upon which the litigants should appear before his holiness in Rome.

Edmund, perhaps, now had begun to see the matter in another light, and was anxious to make amends—the more so as it had reached his ears that he was being charged with ingratitude to the men who had elected him archbishop. This was a new aspect of things; and he began to realise that they were a body with rights of their own. To see this and promptly act was characteristic of the archbishop's impulsive and humble soul. He went to Canterbury and "entered the chapter-house in an attitude of deep humility, in the hope of allaying the commotion by calm reasoning and sweet moderation; for he did not wish to be thought unmindful of the confidence which the monks had bestowed upon him; indeed it cut him to the quick to think he should even appear ungrateful. Consequently he conceded all their requests so far as to remove any obstacle to an honourable and satisfactory arrangement being made. The monks, one and all, gladly consented to his terms, and they thanked God and the archbishop for this happy termination of the dispute. Edmund then announced to the chapter that he would go to Rome to get the approval of the Holy See to the arrangement that had been made."[1]

The archbishop had several other disputes on hand, with various houses of black monks who had appealed to Rome for protection against his claims. He wanted to make a visitation of Westminster abbey, a house exempt from all episcopal control, and, moreover, not even in his diocese. In this project he was opposed both by the monks, who claimed their privilege, and also by the bishop of London, who protested against his intrusion. St.

---

[1] Eustace's *Vita Sancti Edmundi*, f. 139, given in *Life of St. Edmund*, by Dom Wilfrid Wallace, O.S.B., and quoted at p. 235. The author was a monk of Christ Church, but attached to the person of the archbishop as chaplain.

Augustine's at Canterbury, too, was another stone of offence to the archbishop. Exempt itself, the abbey claimed for all its churches and manors freedom from episcopal visitation. A compromise, on the whole favourable to the monks, was entered into. They did not care, perhaps, to push matters too far, as it was said some of the bulls on which they relied would not bear too close inspection.[1] Then, again, in the neighbouring diocese of Rochester Edmund was involved in disputes with the monastic chapter; for he claimed the right of appointing the bishop, and would not allow of the monks' right of election. In all the cases that went to Rome, Edmund was worsted. He practically had no case except *sic jubeo sic volo*.

[1] Forgery, or the art of making history, was certainly not unknown in those happily uncritical ages; and one is constantly thwarted in research by documents which turn out not what they purport to be. We should doubt, however, if the intention of the writers of such documents always was to deceive. When the courts insisted, in cases of litigation, on the production of charters in regard to property held for four or five hundred years, the original deeds of which had been destroyed by foreign invasion or civil broils, the case was met by the production of documents, not original indeed but embodying the facts. "Forgery" applied to such a case needs a gloss, and it must not be at once assumed that the "forgers" were the rogues implied by our own modern use of the term. It is a commonplace in legal history, that when courts of law will press their conditions in a way which is felt to be undue, they will generally meet their match on their own ground; for instance, the whole question of conveying estates for uses or bequests for masses for the dead. In the twelfth and thirteenth centuries people went a much more simple way to work; but the principle was the same. The history of the methods employed to meet on their own grounds laws felt to be unduly pressed, is a subject worthy of the "Philosophic Historian."

When Edmund reached Rome (1238), he found, to his intense surprise, some of the Canterbury monks. A strong feeling had been gaining ground in that convent that they had gone beyond their legal rights in compromising many points with the archbishop. Their feelings had been touched, and, under that influence, had given a consent which after-thought did not warrant. The archbishop and his party were bitterly affected at finding an appeal pending on a matter they thought had been settled. Archdeacon Langton, Edmund's chief adviser, did not scruple to deny the validity of their grants; and, in the words of the continuator of Gervase, "vomited forth his venom before the pope, and said: 'Holy Father, there is no species of forgery which is not perpetrated in the Church of Canterbury. They forge in gold, in lead, in wax, in anything you please.'"[1] To settle this question, the pope sent orders to Otho to go to Canterbury and make a search into the monks' claims. All duplicate documents were to be shared between the archbishop and the chapter; but any found to be forged or of suspected authenticity were to be sent to Rome for the pope's inspection. When the charge of forgery was gone into, it turned out to be that a charter of St. Thomas à Becket, well known to exist, had been damaged beyond repair; and three of the monks, in all simplicity, had made a new copy to which they had attached the old seal.

---

[1] *Gervasii Opera* (Roll Series), vol. ii. p. 132.

But while at Rome, finding unavailing all hopes of a compromise with the agents of the monks, the archbishop was urged on to issue excommunication against all disturbers of the peace, or rather of his peace. He left Rome, as we have said, worsted upon all matters in dispute, and with the difficulty with his chapter still open. On reaching England, he went with the cardinal legate to investigate the charge of forgery, which resulted, as stated above, in a moral acquittal; although punishment was inflicted upon the monks who had appended the old seal to the new copy, and the prior was deposed by the archbishop.

The archbishop's pretensions were only increased by the firm opposition he met with; and now he went so far as to take steps to transfer the cathedral into the hands of secular canons. The dispute became a matter of life or death with the monks, and they fought the archbishop with grim pertinacity. Suspensions were issued and were treated with scant respect; for the archbishop had for the time being no longer jurisdiction over them on the disputed points, their cause being before the Holy See. He refused to appoint a new prior until the monks had returned to their obedience, a question which they persisted was still *sub judice*. Matters got graver, and each party more obstinate. At last, on January 9, 1239, he interdicted the whole convent, and later on excommunicated his primatial chapter, and on November 3, 1239, published the sentence throughout the whole province.

But meanwhile the cause at Rome was dragging on its weary length. At home it seems that the sentence of excommunication, certainly invalid, was not taken much notice of by the people of the diocese. This made the archbishop more determined to enforce his will; and he appealed to the secular power, in the shape of the sheriff of Kent, to enforce his decree. The idea got abroad that the archbishop intended to seize the temporalities of the monastery. The monks in alarm appealed to the king, who ordered his sheriffs not to interfere. Fresh excommunications are sent out against all who should support the monks; and then, all of a sudden, matters drop. The archbishop, sick at heart and hopeless, leaves his diocese and retires to the cistercian abbey of Pontigny, in the neighbourhood of which he died, November 16, 1240.

We have dwelt on this dispute in order to let the reader see the sort of trouble monastic chapters had to put up with until the situation was cleared; troubles in this case all the harder to bear, because the personal holiness of the archbishop was so great. It is no disrespect to the memory of a great saint to say he was not made of the stuff out of which a ruler is made, and was wanting in that tact so necessary for dealing with men.[1]

[1] A recent Life of St. Edmund, by Dom Wilfrid Wallace of Erdington, takes a view of the dispute diametrically opposite to the one given above. The conclusion we have arrived at is based primarily on the very evidence the writer brings forward to support his contention. The author, a former student of St. Edmund's College, Ware, seems to have

This dispute was the greatest and practically the last of the disputes between bishops and monastic chapters. It cleared the air and made the rights of either party known; and so the way of peace was henceforth smooth.

The Lateran Council had ordered certain reforms to take place among the benedictines of each country. As we have seen, steps were immediately taken in England (and England alone it was that obeyed unquestionably) to carry out the pope's desire. When the legate Otho came to England, he held a national council in London late in 1237; and among decrees affecting the English Church at large, he made some (No. XIX.) regarding the black monks.[1] But two years after, a conference of the benedictine abbats was held under his presidency in London, at which some of these regulations, notably about the perpetual abstinence, were modified. The decrees of this conference were carried out by the abbats. What these regulations were, it will be useful to mention; for unfortunately "reformation" has a bad sound in England, and, in

overlooked the fact that eminent personal sanctity does not necessarily imply those gifts which a governor, unless he is to fail, must possess. As a matter of fact, St. Edmund fell foul of every one from the highest to the lowest, priest and laymen, with whom his great office brought him in contact. Bishop Stubbs with his "best of archbishops" (Gervase of Canterbury, II. p. xx.) falls into the same mistake. Edmund's sudden retirement to the cistercian monastery of Pontigny seems evidence that the saint recognised himself, and had the courage to act on the knowledge.

[1] Wilkins, *Concilia*, vol. i. p. 653.

the popular mind, "reformation of monks" implies a state of immorality and vice as existent. While on one hand it would be idle to deny that, among so many, some few might be found who were unworthy, this is only to say that human nature exists, and is never destroyed. But when the aim of the monk's life is considered, the safeguards with which he is surrounded, and the public opinion, both in and out of the monastery, it is impossible for any unprejudiced mind, in face of the facts, for a moment to entertain the idea that monasteries could ever, unchecked, get to a depth of depravity such as the vulgar, for whom tradition has been falsified, love to imagine. The reforms, of which we give a summary, instituted by Otho, with the cordial consent of the abbats, show in what direction changes were considered desirable.

Monks were not to be professed before twenty years of age; novices, after their probation, were either to be professed at once or dismissed; no payment was to be exacted from those who wished to enter as monks; no monk to have anything of his own; they were not to farm landed property; no monk is to be set to a charge which will require him to live alone; all officers, three times a year, have to give in their accounts; the abbat once a year to all his community; possessors of private property were to be punished; silence duly observed; flesh meat forbidden (this was modified two years later); monks to be properly clothed, to sleep in one common dormitory, *all* to be present at divine office, at least for collation and compline; abbats and prelates to be moderate in their equipages and expenditure, &c.

No word, no hint of any deep-seated depravity, but only an endeavour to recall the monk to those observances which hedge in the higher paths to which he had bound himself by his vows.

We have now to consider the question of the alien priories, which were found to be a somewhat disturbing element in English monasticism as being under foreign influence (this holds good in particular of the cluniac houses), and ruled according to foreign modes of thought. The Normans, when they came to England, left friends behind them. They were also descendants of the founders of many noble monasteries. It was but natural that the conquerors should wish to share the sweets of victory with their friends. Consequently they gave English churches and tithes and manors to Norman and French abbeys. The monks of these houses abroad, in order to protect their rights, and gather in their rents and dues, built cells or small convents on their newly acquired property. This was the origin of the alien priories, which existed simply and solely for the benefit of foreign prelates. Having for the most part no interest in England except material profit, these alien priories formed the weak spot in monastic affairs; and it was not long before the civil power had to take cognisance of their existence.

The houses were of two kinds. Some, regular convents, only paying a yearly tribute (*apportus*) to the house abroad; and others, depending entirely upon the foreign prelates, who appointed at will superiors and subjects, with the main duty of reaping a harvest, and promoting the interest of those at home. As can be easily understood, the English found in these alien houses had to accommodate themselves to the law of those with whom they had incorporated themselves. The fact, too, that the monks were far away from their own superiors over the seas naturally opened the door to abuses. The general chapter began to take the matter in hand, and summoned the superiors to attend the meetings under pain of excommunication, unless they could show due cause of exemption. But before anything effectual could be done, the civil power took up the question.[1]

King John began the work and made the priories, then eighty-one in number, pay into his hands the money they used to send abroad.[2] But in 1294, on the occasion of his war for the recovery of Guienne, Edward, among other means of extorting

---

[1] From first to last there were between 100 and 150 of these alien priories. "The cluniac houses alone during the reign of Edward III. are said to have forwarded no less than £2000 a year (about £60,000 of our money) to the monastery at Cluni. When France and England were at peace, this transmission of wealth out of the country was tolerated by the English rulers; war however brought the subject prominently before them, and led to various acts of suppression and confiscation" (Dom Gasquet, vol. i. p. 42).

[2] Canon Dixon, *History of the Church of England*, vol. i. p. 321.

money, seized all the alien priories and used their revenues for the purposes of war; and, to prevent the foreign monks from acting as spies and helping his enemies, he removed them twenty miles from the sea-coast.[1]

So convenient a way of getting money, with the additional pleasure of knowing it was hampering the enemy, was sure to commend itself to other kings. Edward II., and then Edward III. (who at first had restored many of them) pursued the same policy.

Not only the king, but Parliament also saw the danger of these houses. Several acts had been passed declaring it unlawful for religious persons to send money to their houses beyond the seas. And a few years after the conclusion of the peace with France (1361), Parliament pointed out that, "in consequence of the priories and other religious houses subject to foreign monasteries being filled with Frenchmen who acted as spies," such houses were danger-spots in the whole body politic.

In the earlier years of Edward III., some of these monasteries became naturalised or made denizen on their own petition.[2]

[1] *Ibid.*
[2] In the cluniac houses, which in course of time numbered English subjects, there was for long a feeling of dissatisfaction, which at last found vent in a petition to Parliament (1330) stating their grievances, and asking for a remedy. The causes of such dissatisfactions may be sufficiently gathered from the record of the visitations published by Sir G. F. Duckett. "For example, the monks of Thetford abbey represented that the appointment of their superior was in the hands of

At last some of the foreign houses began to sell their English property for what they could get. Under Henry IV. their position became every day more precarious. The outcries of the Lollards against the wealth of the abbeys, and the clamours not only for their confiscation but for that of all church property, pointed out the approaching doom of at least the alien priories. Henry V. in 1414 took the final step, and suppressed them all. Their estates were vested in the Crown, and were mostly bestowed upon other monasteries or schools. In the instructions drawn up for his ambassador to the Council of Basle, where it was thought some of the foreign houses would attempt to regain their property, Henry V. declares he had applied to the pope (Martin V.) for leave to convert the revenues into endowment for religious houses and other sacred purposes. He also says that liberal compensation had been paid to the former owners for the loss of their possessions.[1]

Suppression or absorption was the inevitable end of the alien priories. Those houses which continued as denizen priories had not got rid of the foreign

the abbot of Cluni. This might have been tolerated when the religious were foreigners, but not when they and their prior were all of them English. They wished therefore to be free from their union with the French abbey, and from the subsidy required of them by their foreign brethren. In the same way the priory of Holy Trinity, York, asked to be declared an English foundation on the same footing as other religious houses" (Dom Gasquet, vol. i. p. 48).

[1] Beckington Correspondence. *Roll Series*, vol. ii. pp. 263-265.

influence when the dissolution came, and were some of the very first to succumb to the attack.

Another great feature in the Chronicles of the Congregation of English black monks was the terrible visitation called the "Black Death," in 1348-49. Its effects were lasting, and had a great deal to do, as Dom Gasquet[1] shows, in shaping the course of events leading to the Reformation. The monasteries felt the scourge to the utmost. For instance, at Westminster the abbat and twenty-six of his monks succumbed. The effect of this terrible disaster was felt for many succeeding generations. "According to Knighton's Chronicle there existed such distress and such a universal 'loosening of the bonds of society' as is 'only to be found,' says Mason, 'in the description of earthquakes in South America;' whole villages died out, cities shrunk within their walls, and the houses becoming unoccupied, fell into ruins. The agricultural population suffered as severely as that of the towns. The land fell out of cultivation on account of the difficulty of securing labourers, except at enormous wages. Flocks were attacked by diseases, and perished from want of herdsmen to watch them. The corn crops, which were unusually rich in the year 1348, rotted on the ground, as no honest men were to be found to reap them. The monastery of Christ Church, Canterbury, even with its rich endowments, felt the pinch of poverty. In asking from the bishop of

[1] *Cf.* "The Black Death," *passim.*

Rochester the impropriation of the Church of Westerham to help them to keep up their old hospitality, they pleaded excessive poverty, caused by 'the great pestilence affecting man and beast!' In furtherance of this suit they forward to the bishop a list of their losses in cattle, which amount to 257 oxen, 511 cows with their calves, and 4585 sheep, estimated to be worth in money £792, 12s. 6d., or more than £16,000 of our money. Nor is this all, for they declare that 1212 acres of land formerly profitable to them had been rendered useless by an inundation of the sea, from the impossibility of getting labourers to maintain the sea walls.[1]

The economic changes resulting from such a visitation were tantamount to a social revolution. The feudal system gave way. Retainers could no longer be kept on a land which failed to support even the owners. Only the largest landlords could possibly stand the strain. The peasant proprietor had to give up his holding and take to trade or handicraft in the town. In the course of the fifteenth century the old historic nobility of England became so impoverished, or reduced by the civil wars, that their power left them; and a new nobility arose, who looked to the king and depended upon him for their lives and possessions. The direct outcome was the despotism of the Tudors, who found none to question their wills.

[1] Gasquet, vol. i. pp. 4, 5.

One of the immediate effects on the monasteries was the diminution of the numbers of their inhabitants. The times were in a state of upheaval, and were thus unfavourable to the development of the peaceful benedictine life. Comparatively few new men came to fill the ranks thinned by death. Roughly speaking, the communities were reduced to one half, corresponding, as far as can be inferred, to the reduction of the population.

After the visitation of 1348-49, there had been a real difficulty in finding religious of mature age and of sufficient experience to take the place of the superiors who had succumbed. This, together with the other causes we mentioned, inevitably tended to a relaxation of the higher life. In 1422, Henry V. summoned the abbats and other prelates to meet him at Westminster to discuss the situation. It appears from Thomas of Walsingham, that certain false brethren had prejudiced the king against the order by asserting that many, both abbats and monks, had fallen away from the primitive institution and observance of the monastic state, and that a reform was urgently needed. It may have struck the reader, on the other hand, how all along the body was possessed of so much strength and vitality, that it was able from time to time to shake off, without outside pressure, any relaxations and abuses which had crept in unawares. So it was in this case. Sixty abbats and other superiors, together with over three hundred monks, assembled at Westminster.[1] The king, accompanied by only four persons, went to meet them in the chapter-house, and at his request Edmund Lacy, bishop of Exeter, one of his suite, addressed the monks. Then the king himself reminded them of the piety of his ancestors and others, in the foundation and support of so many religious houses; he expected them to remedy any abuses which they might find to exist, and to return to the former strictness which of old had made the orders so renowned. And here it may be mentioned in passing how the kings of England, comparing in this with the kings of France, had always fostered, protected, and defended the benedictines, until the days of the despoiler Henry VIII.; not only protecting them in their material interests, but by showing a regard for their best and highest welfare. The premier abbat, William Heyworth of St. Albans, presided at the following deliberations, and several articles were agreed upon and drawn up, to be presented to the next general chapter for approval.[2] From the decrees we see the nature of the reforms, which were entirely on the lines of former regulations. The abbats are to moderate their style of living, they are to live more among their brethren;[3] once

---

[1] It is useful to note how large these gatherings were, and how truly representative of all interests.

[2] Wilkins, *Concilia*, vol. iii. pp. 413-427.

[3] This was evidently a weak point, and the very greatness of their position was a real drawback in the case of men of a less high ideal.

a year they have to give in a full account to the monks of the state of the abbey; they are to take care of and not alienate the monastic property. The monks are to be clothed alike. The use of meat is regulated, and the monastic fasts enforced. The monks are not to handle money, but are to have their wants supplied in kind. They are only to go out once a year to visit their friends. The abbat is to supply them with the necessary funds, for which on return they must account. He also has to supply suitable companions for the journey. The old rule of sleeping in their habits to be enforced.[1] At the general chapter that followed, most of these reforms were accepted. One change was made as regards money supplied to the monks for any purposes of their own. They were, at least once a year, to give in an account of what they had spent, to the abbat, who could at will call for such account. Any balance that remained had to be returned to the house. As regards the fasts, it was decreed that as in all well-regulated monasteries they were no longer observed, so instead supper was not to be allowed on those days, unless to the weak or old.

Thomas de la Marc, Clement Lichfield, John Wheathamstead, and Richard Whiting, show how a great position might be united with a strict care for their primary duties as fathers of their convents.

[1] It must be remembered that St. Benedict legislated for the custom of his monks sleeping in an open dormitory. Some form of night-clothing was then required. But in the secular world, for centuries after, the use of night-clothes was unknown.

A new season of vigour came over the body. And when, a hundred years after, the dissolution came, it found the greater majority of the houses of the black monks living lives in edifying observances. All, both monks and abbats, seem to have risen to a sense of the requirement of the time. Piety and learning were flourishing in their houses at the moment when the hand of the destroyer was laid upon them, and the tendency was always in the upward direction.

But before taking up the story of the dissolution, we must just give a glance at the state of Benedictinism on the continent. For although the English houses were independent of all foreign control, as they were independent of one another, yet still, as brethren united by an intimate tie of far more efficiency than any outer bond, they were influenced by and felt the effects of a revival that was going on simultaneously in Italy and Spain and Germany. As these movements had a most important bearing upon the history of the benedictines of England after the Reformation, a word as to their nature and history is here necessary.

The great cause of the decline of the benedictine life on the continent, and especially in Italy and France, was the hateful system of *commendam*.[1] Laymen got possession of the revenues of monas-

---

[1] *Commendam* never obtained in England. The only case as regards the abbeys was that of Wolsey, who held the abbey of St. Albans in *commendam* (1521).

teries and bestowed them on their children, who received the tonsure only to avoid the law forbidding any but clerics to hold ecclesiastical benefices. To such a pitch did the evil get, that mere children held abbacies; who when they arrived at man's estate differed in their mode of life nothing from the laymen about them. Certain abbeys had come to be looked upon as the ordinary provision for the support of cadets of noble houses. The monks were themselves to blame in great part for a state which cut at the very root of monastic life. They had allowed the income to be divided into two portions; one for themselves and one for the abbat. This last became a "benefice"; and so an object of ambition on the part of crafty and unscrupulous persons. Then, moreover, the portion allotted to the support of the monks became cut up and subdivided among the various officers charged with the administration of the house. These also became looked upon as benefices, and were bought and sold and given away. No wonder was it, then, with this break-up of the common life, that the family idea, and with it monastic discipline, decayed. Once the system was introduced, those houses in which there was no division were, if anything, worse off, for their commendatory abbats possessed the whole income, and, almost without exception, concerned themselves with drawing the revenues and assigning a small pitance to the wretched and dwindling community, who had fallen into the position of mere rent-charges.

The natural remedy would seem to have been the reassertion of community life and of the rights of electing their own abbat and governing themselves; but such was the temper of the times, that all efforts at remedying the evil seemed in vain. Thirty synods had been held, and popes had issued decree after decree, but all had been ineffectual. At last the man appeared who should make the practice of *commendam* no longer possible among black monks. Barbo, abbat of the monastery of St. Justina at Padua, began the work and achieved it by what was no less than a complete revolution in the theory of benedictine government. He constructed a system, which, if it did not directly cut away the root of the evil, at least killed its offshoots, and stood ready to snip the bud of any attempt at future growth. In his reform no officer, not even the abbat, was to be appointed for a term of more than three years. Hence there could be no vested rights in an office, or anything approaching the nature of a benefice. By ordering a triennial chapter at which all officers had to give in an account of their administration, it was out of the power of any one to appropriate, or wish to retain, the property which belonged to all. A return was made to the common life both for abbats and monks, and the income was no longer divided. When this system was developed and other abbeys joined on to the reform of St. Justina, the election of abbats, &c., was vested in the general chapter alone; thus securing at least freedom of choice from outward interference. The reform of St. Justina, a drastic remedy for a terrible disease, was successful and rapidly spread through Italy; and when Monte Cassino itself adopted it, Julius II. gave the name of "Cassinese Congregation" to the whole body of these reformed benedictines of Italy.

The monasteries of Spain took up some of the features of this reform from Italy; and the famous congregation of Valladolid formed itself in many respects on similar lines to those of St. Justina's abbey.

In Germany, too, the movement spread; and the great congregation of Bursfeld took its beginning from John Dederoth, abbat of Rheinhausen, afterwards of Bursfeld, which house became the centre of the reform. The statutes of Bursfeld were gradually introduced elsewhere, until at last it began to be looked upon as the central house of the reformed monks of Germany. A general chapter was held in 1446; and by 1502 no less than ninety houses were on its roll. The Bursfeld Union made no such break with tradition as did the Cassinese. The abbats were elected for life.

In France a closer union of the black monks did not take place until the seventeenth century, when the congregations of St. Maur and St. Vannes renewed the benedictine glories of France. But the revolution in government, instituted by Barbo to remedy an evil, brought with it an inherent weakness which in time developed itself. This, the break-up of the *family*, a fundamental idea of St. Benedict, was the price that had to be paid.

CHAPTER VIII

THE DOWNFALL

In the previous chapter we have seen events in England, in the fifteenth century, shaping themselves in such a direction that, granted a man like Henry VIII., he might turn them to his own advantage with but little fear of consequences disastrous to his own position. And while the events we are now going to discuss resulted practically from the system he represented, they, by the lawless procedure characterising them, in their turn reacted upon it, and made the Tudor despotism a yet more potent weapon for evil in the hands of unscrupulous men.

The trend of political and social events had of recent years the effect of making monasteries in general unpopular with those parties in the state who looked to the king as the author of all their prosperity. Though they evidently were not unpopular with people at large, at any rate their great wealth was tempting to the Crown. And there were courtiers who said these were institutions which might easily become strongholds of the pope's authority.

Henry VIII. ascended the throne in 1509, and for many years won golden opinions from his subjects. If given, perhaps, rather too much to pleasure and prodigality, these were, it was hoped, but faults of a generous youth which, in time, would give way to the staider and graver virtues becoming a ruler. The minister upon whom he relied in everything was Wolsey, archbishop of York, chancellor of the realm, and cardinal of the Roman Church. This great man, who has never had justice done to him[1] (for great he was in spite of many failings arising mainly from his position and the corruption of the times), had arrived at the height of his power. In temporal matters he was practically supreme. "He is the person who rules both the king and the entire kingdom,"[2] says a foreign ambassador. The cardinal wanted powers as extensive in ecclesiastical matters. Perhaps, had he had them at first, and had reached to the papacy he was aspiring after, Wolsey might have come down to all times as the pope who had initiated the reform in head and members that for a century had been asked. His principles were excellent; when he had a free hand and no ulterior aim in view, we can see the lines he would have worked on. But this by the way.

[1] The way in which he spent the last months of his life in his own diocese of York, showed that he possessed qualities which had never had full play; and if he had not been a great statesman he might have been one of the greatest prelates of modern times.

[2] Quoted by Dom Gasquet, vol. i. p. 68.

In due course, and after much pressure, Wolsey did receive, as legate, powers perhaps more ample than had ever been given. But he had already committed himself to a policy which proved his ruin, and therefore his legateship was not advantageous to the Church. Unfortunately, he also thereby accustomed the people to see vested in the hands of one man, the supreme power both in Church and State. It was not so difficult, then, for them to acquiesce, later on, when Henry took into his own hands the powers his minister had wielded.

The cardinal wanted money. He had magnificent tastes, and was a founder of colleges and palaces. The pope had reluctantly given him extensive powers of visitation over certain smaller monasteries, even with power to suppress such of them as through fewness of numbers or poverty he might judge to be useless. Their funds were to be applied to the support of the colleges at Oxford and Ipswich he was then founding. Much pressure was used to force Clement VII. in 1524 to grant the powers, and even then the pope made limitations. Only such monasteries were to be suppressed as were absolutely necessary, and only to the total amount of 3000 ducats a year. The cardinal set to work, and in spite of all difficulties suppressed thirty monasteries in which the number had dwindled down to some five or six, or even fewer members. The visitors he employed to go round and inspect the houses were Allen and Thomas Cromwell, the latter of whom became so notorious. The visitors had many complaints (only too well founded) made about them; but this was beyond the intention of their master. Bribery and violence were the weapons they mostly used; and superiors of the threatened houses were led to believe they might buy off suppression by offering gifts to the cardinal's colleges. How much of these gifts stopped in the hands of the visitors it is impossible here to say. But Cromwell turned out later on such an adept in the receipt of bribes, that it is most likely he proved his powers on this occasion.

When Wolsey was impeached, the complaints made about the way in which the suppression of the monasteries was effected by the cardinal's agents were not forgotten. With his fall Henry lost the only check upon the downward course. In the place of the fallen cardinal was Thomas Cromwell, whose appetite for suppression had been whetted. He had seen practically how defenceless the monasteries were, and how easy it would be for the omnipotent Tudor monarch to make away with them on any convenient plea that could be raised; and also he had found out that in the process plenty of advantages would accrue to himself. The king had also cast his eyes on their wealth. And not cupidity alone influenced him; but he also saw in them institutions which might easily become, even after a final breach with Rome, means of keeping alive the pope's authority, which he was now attacking at its very foundation. Blood had already been shed in its defence. Fisher and More, and the carthusians had laid down their lives for the doctrine; and the people, restless and disheartened, were beginning to give trouble. Taxation was heavy: but the state of the country was such that it could not be paid. Cromwell was afraid of exasperating the people further by levying new taxes which Parliament had lately granted to meet the requirements of the king, who was, as is clear from state papers, at that moment reduced to great straits for want of money.

The monasteries offered themselves as an expedient to the fertile brain of Cromwell for supplying all these wants and remedying the complaints. " In determining to strike a blow at the monastic bodies, Cromwell had a twofold object, both of which appealed to the king's present state of mind: to overthrow the papal system in its principal strongholds, and to have the fingering of the riches with which the piety of ten centuries had endowed them. By the middle of the year 1334 [1534], commissioners were busily journeying through England tendering in the oath of supremacy to the religious. No special form of oath had been presented by Parliament, so Cromwell took advantage of the omission. He made his agents tender to the monks a renunciation of the papal supremacy and jurisdiction much more stringent and explicit than that rejected by More and Fisher, and already subscribed to by many of the secular clergy. The commissioners appear to have met with only partial success. The intolerable nature of the oath demanded seems to suggest that the intention of its framers was to drive the religious to refuse, and thus to create a pretext for falling upon and destroying their houses." [1]

An obsequious Parliament had transferred, along with other rights to the king from the pope, the power of visitation over monasteries. A royal commission was issued for the inspection of all religious houses, with an ulterior view to the speedy suppression of as many as possible. The chief men employed were Legh and Layton, Ap Rice, London and Bedyll, men whose names come down to posterity noted with infamy.

"They were furnished with a set of eighty-six articles of inquiry and with twenty-five injunctions, to which they had power to add much at their discretion. The articles of inquiry were, searching, the injunctions minute and exacting. Framed in the spirit of three centuries earlier, unworkable in practice, and enforced by such agents, it is easy to understand, even were there no written evidence of the fact, that they were galling and unbearable to the helpless inmates of the monasteries. . . . All religious under twenty-four years of age, or who had been professed under twenty, were to be dismissed from the religious life. Those who were

[1] Gasquet, vol. i. pp. 247, 248.

left became practically prisoners in their monasteries. No one was allowed to leave the precincts (which even in the larger monasteries were very confined as to limit) or to visit there. In many instances porters, who were in reality gaolers, were appointed to see this impossible regulation was kept. What was simply destruction of all discipline and order in the monasteries was an injunction that every religious, who wished to complain of anything done by his superior or any of his brethren, was to have the right of appeal to Cromwell. To facilitate this, the superior was ordered to find any subject the money and means for prosecuting any such appeals in person if he so desired."[1]

The object was clearly to drive the monks in desperation to surrender their houses, and thus save the king from the necessity of turning them out of house and home. Another plan, in order to give a colour to the project, was to see whether by any possibility scandals, or even any suspicions of scandal, might be found. The visitors, as is clear from their own letters, were determined that scandals should be found, and they scrupled not by threats to extort, or to invent so-called confessions: nay, even themselves to tempt to sin the helpless women in their power.

Dom Gasquet has once for all vindicated the memory of the monks and nuns of England at the time of the dissolution, and with masterly hand

[1] Gasquet, vol. i. pp. 255, 256.

analyses and shows the worthlessness of the royal testimony upon which Parliament acted in decreeing the suppression of the lesser monasteries. Six weeks only did these worthy styled commissioners spend in visiting the monasteries and finding out the state of religion. Short though the time was for any real inquiry, it was enough for the end they had in view. Their reports were sent in to Cromwell in time for the opening of Parliament in February 1536. These reports, the only evidence that ever existed against the monasteries, are preserved to-day in the State Paper Office, and after a careful examination Dom Gasquet says they are utterly valueless as proofs of anything more than "that these commissioners were ready to bring any accusation against the monks, and that the fair name of many, who possibly never heard anything of the matter, was blackened by mere reckless assertions."[1]

Parliament met on the 4th February. The only evidence laid before the nation, in the very words of the preamble to the Act passed by a packed House of Commons to legalise the suppression, was the king's own assertion that the reports of the commissioners were true, and his own testimony that he had received credible information that

[1] Layton, *e.g.*, writes from York to Cromwell, January 13, 1536: "This day we begin with St. Mary's, whereas we suppose to find much evil disposition, both in the abbat and the convent, whereof, God willing, I shall certify you in my next letter" (*Three Chapters of Letters relating to the Suppression of Monasteries* (Camden Society), p. 97).

vicious living was rampant in the smaller monasteries. On the king's word alone, and, as far as we know, without any further inquiry or even examination of witnesses, Parliament prayed the king to suppress and to take the property of such monasteries as had an income under £200 a year. On the strength, too, of the royal word, Parliament also publicly thanks God that in "divers and great Solemn Monasteries of the realm, religion is right well kept and observed."

It must also be noted that the Act does not give the property of these monasteries absolutely to the king, but only "in as ample a manner" as they were possessed by their former owners; that is, in trust for God and the poor. It was by no means the intention to grant them for the purpose to which Henry illegally afterwards applied them.

"It was ordered also that the king should provide occupation and pensions for the monks not transferred to other monasteries. It was further enacted that on the site of every dissolved religious house, the new possessor would be bound under heavy penalties to provide hospitality and service for the poor, such as had been given them previously by the religious foundations. By this provision not only is the patrimony of the poor recognised as being seized in the property of the monasteries, but a testimony is afforded as to the way the religious had hitherto discharged their obligations in this respect. The neglect of these rights of the needy by those who became possessed of the confiscated property is one of the greatest blots on our national history. It has caused the spoliation of monastery and convent to be regarded as the rising of the rich against the poor."[1]

To reconcile the people, Cromwell sent into the country preachers "who went about to preach and persuade the people that he could employ the ecclesiastical revenues in hospitals, colleges, and other foundations for the public good, which would be a better use than that they should support lazy and useless monks."[2]

These preachers spread abroad also that the money gained for these smaller monasteries would save the nation from any future taxation. Taxation already ground them down to an intolerable state; and this measure was held out to them as a promise of relief. The prospect of a share in the spoils, it was hoped, would quiet them, at least outwardly, for the time. Moreover, distinct affirmations were made that the king had no intention of touching the great houses. It was only the iniquity which existed in the smaller monasteries which forced so pious a prince to suppress them.

Having got legal colour for his work, the king appointed a court, "the court of Augmentations," to deal with the property of the monasteries. Surveyors

---

[1] Gasquet, vol i. p. 311.
[2] Marillac, the French ambassador. *Inventaire Analytique de Archives*, ed. Kanleck, No. 242.

were promptly selected to go round and, aided by the local gentry, decide which monasteries came under the limit of £200 a year.[1] The surveyors were instructed to make inventories of all plate, jewels, and other goods and property, to take possession of all deeds and muniments, and also of the convent seal. They were to lay a charge on the superior to take care of the king's property until he was released. The rest of the community were dismissed; to other monasteries if they could find admission; or, if not, they were, with "some reasonable reward," sent adrift in the world.[2]

"The system was the same in all cases, and the history of one dissolution is that of all. What the arrival of the six royal commissioners with their retinue of servants at monastery and convent must have been to the inmates can be well imagined. The Act of dissolution, it is true, had saved them from the necessity, to which many of their more powerful brethren were constrained, of surrender. Their houses, which pious benefactors had built genera-

[1] Whenever the local gentry, who would naturally know more of the reputation of any convent than the Government surveyor, pleaded for the preservation of a house and bore witness "that religion was right well observed," they made no impression upon Cromwell.

[2] What the effect of all these misdeeds was on a foreigner we see from a letter written July 8, 1536, by Chapuys, who says: "It is a lamentable thing to see a legion of monks and nuns, who have been chased from their monasteries, wandering miserably hither and thither seeking means to live; and several honest men have told me that what with monks, nuns, and persons dependent on the monasteries suppressed, there were over 20,000 who knew not how to live" (*Calendar S.P. Hen. VIII.*, vol. xi. No. 42).

tions before, and in which, for centuries, men and women of their order had served God and aided their neighbours, were passing away from them for ever; and the demand for and defacing of their convent seal was the ending of their corporate life. Henceforth they were to pass the remainder of their days as strangers in a larger house, or as wandering in a world which many had left years before, and to which they could never belong. The desecration of their churches, in which they and their forefathers in religion before them had gathered by night and by day for the service of God; the seizure for the king's use of their altar plate, in itself so often poor, to them always precious by the association of the past; the rude appraising of their bells and the lead which covered the roofs over their heads; the hurried sales of the mean furniture of their cells, and of the contents of church, cloister, and frater, were all so many heart-rending evidences of the passing away of all that for which most of the monks and nuns really cared."[1]

The work began in April 1536, and took some time to complete. According to Stowe, there were 376 houses dealt with, and the value of their lands alone was some £32,000 and more a year. Of their personal goods more than £100,000 was dealt with, and the same authority considers that "10,000 people, masters and servants, had lost their livings by the pulling down of their houses at that time."

Henry made some exceptions. Fifty-two houses

[1] Gasquet, vol. ii. pp. 13, 14.

gained a respite, bought of course at an enormous price, sometimes three times their annual income. Dom Gasquet points out that several of the houses there re-established were among the number of those gravely defamed by Layton and Legh, the prime managers of the visitation of 1535-36; and in more than one case a superior incriminated by them was reappointed on the new foundation.[1] In the course of the next year (1537) Henry actually founded one or two monasteries, one of nuns at Stixfold, to be called "the new monastery of King Henry VIII.," and an abbey of black monks at Bisham to pray for the king and Queen Jane. The king also granted to the abbat (but lately abbat of Chertsey, one of the suppressed houses) his royal licence to wear a mitre like any other abbat of that order, with large possessions in England. But this was not to last long.[2]

It is not our purpose to do more than refer to the popular risings on behalf of the monasteries in Lincolnshire in the autumn of 1536, nor of the Pilgrimage of Grace and other subsequent movements. They excited Henry's bitterest feelings against the helpless monks whom he falsely accused of fomenting them. They were the occasion of the wholesale destruction of the monastic orders. He wrote to the Duke of Norfolk, who was charged to put down the rebels :—

---

[1] Gasquet, vol. ii. p. 21.   [2] *Ibid.* p. 33.

"Our pleasure is that before you close up our banners again you shall cause such dreadful execution to be done upon a good number of the inhabitants of every town, village, and hamlet that have offended us, there may be a fearful spectacle to all others hereafter that would practise any like matter. . . . Finally, forasmuch as all these troubles have ensued by the solicitation and traitorous conspiracies of the monks and canons of these parts, we desire you, at such places as they have conspired and kept their houses with force save the appointment at Doncaster, you shall without pity or circumstance cause all the monks and canons that be in any way faulty, to be tied up without further delay or ceremony."[1]

Thus by force and blood all opposition was quelled; although the risings served as a temporary check upon the king's schemes for further suppressions. But a new expedient was found for getting hold of some of the larger monasteries which had hitherto escaped. This was by the attainder of such abbats as could be charged with high treason. Hitherto the penalties of attainder affected individuals, but not corporations. But Henry gave a new interpretation to the law, and took advantage of a clause slipped into the recent act, which put the whole abbey into the power of the king on the conviction of the abbat of high treason. Many of the cistercian, cluniac, and austin houses came into

[1] Blunt's *History of the Reformation*, p. 365.

THE DOWNFALL

the king's hands this way soon after the Northern risings. But there was the way of surrender also to be made use of, to give the king legal possession, "and every pressure was brought to bear upon the monks and nuns to induce them to resign their charges into Henry's hands;"[1] promises of pension to those who willingly consented, and threats of being turned out in utter destitution to those who refused.

Of forty convents of women that survived the first dissolution, thirty-three are on the rolls as having surrendered. But an inspection of the original papers, says Dom Gasquet, shows that in twenty-eight of the thirty-three cases the nuns never signed at all. Of the others, one (Shaftesbury) is signed by the abbess alone; another (Tarant) has twenty signatures, all in the same handwriting. The number of nuns turned adrift seems to have been 1560, more than one half of whom were benedictine dames.[2]

The commissioners were instructed, as we have seen, to try by every means to get a willing surrender. But at any rate they were to get possession of every house. This all the time, be it remembered, without any sanction from Parliament. Between 1538 and 1540, fifty-four monasteries of black monks,

---

[1] Gasquet, vol. ii. p. 225.
[2] *Ibid.* ii. pp. 228, 237. Before the dissolution there were eighty-four benedictine houses for women, and only twelve of them were worth more than the £200 limit settled by Parliament.

1300 in number, were cajoled or forced into surrendering their property. Besides, under various pretences Henry had deposed many superiors who proved too staunch to the oath taken when elected, and put in their stead creatures of his own to make the surrender when called upon. Three of the abbats, those of Glaston, Reading, and Colchester, condemned as it seems without trial even, were declared guilty of high treason and were hanged, drawn, and quartered on the spot in which they had ruled with honour for many years. Nothing stopped the king, neither pity nor reverence; and he rested not until not one house was left of all the monastic glories of England. It is not our purpose here to go into details of these surrenders; but a tale could be told as bitter and as heartrending as any known. It is just the bare facts of the dissolution and the way it was brought about that we have wished to set down here,[1] and we will end this chapter by words, written indeed of St. Peter's, Gloucester, but which may be applied to any case:—

"Having existed for more than eight hundred years under different forms, in poverty and in wealth, in meanness and in magnificence, in misfortune and in success, it finally succumbs to the royal will; the day came, and that a drear winter day, when its last mass was sung, its last censer waved, its last congregation bent in rapt and lovely adora-

[1] W. H. Hart's Introduction, vol. iii. pp. xlix., l., *Hist. et Cart. Mon. S. Petri Glouces.* (Roll Series).

tion before the altar there, and doubtless as the last tones of that day's evensong died away in the vaulted roof, there were not wanting those who lingered in the solemn stillness of the old massive pile, and who, as the lights disappeared one by one, felt that for them there was now a void which could never be filled, because their old abbey with its beautiful services, its frequent means of grace, its hospitality to strangers and its loving care for God's poor, had passed away like an early morning dream, and was gone for ever."

CHAPTER IX

JOHN FECKNAM, ABBAT

The monasteries were destroyed and the inhabitants dispersed. Many of those who received pensions[1] were as soon as possible promoted to livings; for then their pensions ceased. Others there were who sold their pensions for a few years' purchase, so sore was their need; and then, their money exhausted, went finally to swell the ever-growing crowd of beggars who after the suppression were daily becoming a most serious and dangerous element in society. Others, again, could not go to London to receive their money; for it was at first in the capital only that such pensions were paid. Some of these allowed their pensions to lapse; others had to employ agents who, at an enormous percentage, collected the money due.[2] The monastic colleges at the universities, particularly those of Gloucester, Durham, and Canterbury, were crowded with monks who retired there to continue their

---

[1] Only the superiors of houses under £200 income were granted pensions.

[2] The pensions were taxed sometimes to the extent of one fourth as "a loan" to the king. *Cf.* Gasquet, vol. ii. pp. 463-466.

studies and find a retreat from the world.[1] Among these was a young monk of Evesham, John (Baptist) Fecknam, whose name became illustrious as the last abbat of Westminster, and one of the confessors of the faith in the days of queen Elizabeth. As he was the restorer of the black monks, though but for a short while, and through him comes the link which binds the English benedictine of to-day to St. Augustine and his companions, we will sketch his life from the few details we have been able to gather. He will serve as an example both of what the dispossessed monks had to suffer and the manner of men they were.

John (Baptist) Fecknam was born in the district of Feckenham or Fecknam in Worcestershire, whence the name by which he is known to history. His family name was Howman, and his parents, Humphrey and Florence Howman, seem to have been of the yeoman class and fairly well off.[2] He was born about 1515, or perhaps earlier,[3] a few

[1] Wood's *Oxford*, p. xxiv., *note*.
[2] They left a bequest of xls. to the poor of Solihull during the rectorship of their son. See an old vellum book "containing the charitable alms given by way of love to the parishoners of Solihull, with the order of distribution thereof, begun by Master John Howman *alias* Fecknam, priest and doctor of divinity, late parson of Solihull aforesaid, in the year of our Lord MDXLVIII." This manuscript is preserved among the parish records of Solihull, and is quoted by Miss E. T. Bradley in her *Memorials of Westminster Abbey*, p. 163.
[3] It is said that Fecknam was about sixty at the time of his imprisonment with the bishop of Ely in 1579. If "about sixty" is to be taken literally, his age at the chief events of his life would be as follows: born about 1519, he would be twenty-one at the date of the suppres-

VOL. I. L

years after Henry VIII.'s accession, and received the first elements of his education from the parish priest. As Evesham was the nearest abbey, it is most likely that he was taken into the claustral school at an early age, and in due course became a monk. The first definite statement we find is, that in his eighteenth year he was sent to the benedictine establishment at Oxford, Gloucester Hall.[1] But whether this was before he became a monk is not certain. From the fact that a monk was not allowed to be professed till he was twenty,[2] it seems clearly evident, if he entered the university at eighteen, that he was not then in the habit; for one can hardly suppose that a mere novice would be sent to Oxford. It is much more probable that he really went as a benedictine student[3] to Gloucester Hall to take

sion of Evesham; thirty at his first imprisonment; dean of St. Paul's at thirty-five; abbat of Westminster, thirty-seven; second imprisonment, forty-one; at Ely, sixty; and died at Wisbeach, sixty-six. But these do not seem probable. He took his B.D. June 11, 1539. He would already have been at Oxford three years, and it is morally certain he could not have gone there for his divinity degree (which presupposes that of Arts) before his twentieth year *at least*. We are inclined to put his birth certainly not later than 1515, making him, at least, seventy when he died.

[1] A. Wood, *Athenæ Oxonienses*, ed. Bliss, vol. i. p. 507. "There is no doubt," says the Rev. Henry Anstey, "that the boys, as a rule, resorted to the university at a very early age, earlier, probably, than is usually supposed; and yet there appears to have been no statutable limit as to age, so that it may be assumed as certain that, while the majority would go from the age of ten to twelve years (*i.e.* supposing them to *commence their education* at Oxford, of which more will be said shortly), there would be found also a large number of more mature age" (Introduction to *Munimenta Academica* (Roll Series), Part I. p. lvii.).

[2] See page 89 *ante*.

[3] "Every religious house had, it would appear, its own schools, in

his degree in arts, and that after the course, generally three years, he returned to Evesham and took the habit and was professed.[1] That he probably returned to Oxford after profession seems certain; for, says Anthony à Wood, "I find him there in 1537, in which year he subscribed, by the name of John Feckenham, to a certain composition then made between Rob. Joseph, prior of the said college, and twenty-nine students thereof on one part (of which number Feckenham was one of the senior), and three of the senior beadles of the university on the other."[2]

It must have been shortly after June 1539 that he returned to Evesham, where he was set to teach the junior monks, and was perhaps engaged in this work when the suppression came. For this much we know, that in October 1538 he supplicated for

which its members performed all their academical exercises previous to inception. . . . Each such religious house had a school for every *purpose*, grammar as well as the higher faculties, to a great extent independent of the university, and yet a part of it, and subject to its *general* regulations and partaking of its privileges" (*Munimenta Academica*, p. lxii.).

[1] In the life of Richard of Wallingford, abbat of St. Albans, we get a similar picture, which throws light on the subject. "When hardly ten years old he lost his father, and soon after was, on account of his docility and promise, adopted as a son by William of Kirkby, prior of Wallingford, of good memory. Helped by his alms, he learnt grammar and philosophy at Oxford for about six years, and taking his degree in arts, according to the custom, in the twentieth year of his age he bade adieu to the world, and devoutly received the monastic habit in this monastery of St. Albans. After having been exercised for three years in the religious life, he was then sent to Oxford for the study of letters . . . where he spent nine whole years in philosophy and theology . . . so that he was promoted to read the sentences" (*Gesta Abbatum* (Roll Series), vol. ii. p. 182).

[2] *Athenæ Oxonienses*, ed. Bliss, vol. i. p. 507.

the degree of Bachelor of Divinity, and took it June 11, 1539.¹

Clement Lichfield, whose noble gateway is the only vestige left of the great monastery of Evesham, had been his first abbat. What sort of man he was appears from the report of the royal commissioners, who say he was " chaste in his living and to right well overlook the reparations of his house"; in other words, a good monk and a good administrator. The reformer, Latimer, who was bishop of the diocese, calls him a "bloody abbat," the evident animus and certain vagueness of which may be taken as praise. There was no chance of getting such a man to surrender his abbey, so the only thing was to force him to resign his charge and to place in his stead a more pliable man. From a letter of March 17, 1538, written to Cromwell by William Petre, the commissioner, we see how it was done.

"According to your commandment I have been at Evesham, and there received the resignation of the abbat, which he was contented to make immediately upon the sight of your lordship's letters, saving that he desired me very instantly that I would not open the same during the time of my being here, because, as he said, it would be noted that he was compelled to resign for fear of deprivation."²

The abbat bowed to *force majeure* and left his monastery. He was promptly succeeded by Philip

[1] Boase, *Register of the University of Oxford*, vol. i. p. 192.
[2] T. Wright, *Three Chapters of Letters* (Camden Soc.), p. 177.

Harford, "a true friend,"[1] who surrendered[2] the abbey to the king on January 27, 1540, and was rewarded with a pension of £240 a year,[3] which he lost when he was made dean of Worcester on the suppression of that monastic chapter. On the pension-list appears the name of John Fecknam, with a pension of 15 marks (£10) per annum. As the general pension for the younger monks was 10 marks, Fecknam was doubtlessly awarded the larger sum on account of his university degree. He went back to Gloucester Hall to continue his studies, but not for long, for the bishop of Worcester, John Bell, inviting him to become his chaplain, he entered his service until the bishop resigned in 1543.[4] He afterwards joined Edmund Bonner, the bishop of London; and stayed with him till 1549, when he was committed a prisoner to the Tower of London. It must have been while living in London that Fecknam received the living of Solihull, and

[1] Latimer to Cromwell. R. O. Crum. Corr. XLIX., 42, quoted by D. Gasquet, vol. ii. p. 310.

[2] Dom Gasquet points out that there is no deed of surrender and no enrolment on the Close Roll (vol. ii. p. 310).

[3] Clement Lichfield had paid £160 to the king for the restoration of his temporalities, and besides had to make heavy loans both to the king and to the cardinal. For a whole year he had to put up twenty-four of the royal household and provide for them and their horses. But in spite of these drains on his purse he did not forget the house of God. He added to the decoration of the choir and built chantries in the parish churches of All Saints and St. Lawrence, in one of which he lies buried. The memory of the "good abbat" remained for a long time cherished by Evesham and its inhabitants.

[4] The *Apostolatus*, i. p. 233, which on the whole is first-rate authority, is wrong here in giving the date of 1539 (Dugdale, vol. i. p. 578).

began to develop those oratorical powers for which he became famous. His keen intellect made him a formidable opponent in controversy with the reforming party; and it was most likely some public utterance of his that led to his first imprisonment. This was the time when the new Liturgy of the Book of Common Prayer was being forced upon the country under heavy penalties. Horne, later on the protestant bishop of Winchester, used to say that Fecknam was sent to the Tower because he first promised and then refused to receive the Sacrament after the new fashion. But Stapleton, in the *Counterblast to M. Hornes vayne blaste against M. Fekenham*,[1] says, "The cause of his imprisonment then, as I understand by such as well knoweth the whole matter, was not about the ministration of the Sacraments, but touching the matter of Justification by only faith and the fast of Lent; like as it doth appear in the archbishop of Canterbury's records, he being therefore, in a solemn session holden at Lambeth Hall, convented before M. Cranmer, then archbishop of Canter-

---

[1] This book was really written by Nicholas Harpsfield, sometime archdeacon of Canterbury, and a prisoner in the Tower from 1559 to 1575. Being himself a prisoner, it was not considered wise to bring out the book under his own name. But the fact that he was a fellow-prisoner with Fecknam at the very time he wrote, makes the biographical part of an unimpeachable authority. It was written about the year 1567–68, for the author says: "And God grant that Fecknam, after seven years' imprisonment, may find so much humanity and favour as he showed to others when he was in his prosperity." See Steven's *Addition to the Monasticon*, vol. i. p. 89.

bury, and other commissioners appointed for that matter. By the examination of the which records you shall be convinced of your untruth and error therein, as in all the rest, I doubt not, by God's help."[1]

While in prison, Sir Philip Hobbs, who had become the owner by purchase of the abbey lands at Evesham, remembered that the monk of Evesham, for whom his estate was charged a pension, and the famous disputant on the Catholic side were identical. So, to use Fecknam's own words, he was "borrowed out of prison" to hold disputations with the new men. "But the very intent of the borrowing of M. Fecknam for a time out of the Tower, like as he said himself, was that he should dispute reason, and have conference with certain learned men touching matters of religion then in controversie."[2] At seven of those exhibitions did he take part. Such disputations were in much favour in those days, and Fecknam was destined to have frequent experience of them. The first was in the house of the Earl of Bedford in the Savoy; the next at Westminster, in the house of Sir William Cecil, afterwards the famous secretary of state;[3] and the third at White Friars, in the house of Sir John Cheke, the Greek scholar, and the young king's tutor. Fecknam was then taken down to the diocese of Worcester, in which he was still a beneficed clergyman, and had to appear with Hooper as

[1] p. 36.   [2] *Ibid.* p. 4.   [3] *Ibid.* p. 36.

his opponent in four disputations. For though he had been imprisoned in the Tower he had not been deprived of the living of Solihull, to which he had been appointed in 1544. The first of these disputations was at Pershore, where Hooper was on visitation;[1] the last in the cathedral church, when he had as opponent, among others, John Jewel, afterwards the bishop of Salisbury.[2]

The disputations over, in which Fecknam, if he failed to change the mind of his opponents, certainly gave proof of his native charity and moderation, he was again relegated to the Tower. There he remained till Tuesday, September 5, 1553, when, with the rest of the prisoners for conscience' sake whom the new queen claimed as her own, he was released. By Sunday the 24th of that same month he was back in the pulpit again. According to Machyn, "the xxiiii day of September did preach master doctor Fecknam at Paul's Cross, the Sunday afore the queen's coronation."[3] He returned to Bonner as chaplain, and was made a prebendary of St. Paul's 1554. Preferment came to him rapidly. Nominated rector of Finchley on June 10, on September 23 he was transferred to the better living of Greenford Magna, and now resigned the

---

[1] Stapleton says: "The said M. Hooper was so answered by M. Fecknam that there was good cause why he should be satisfied, and M. Fecknam dismissed from his trouble" (p. 37).

[2] *Ibid.* Stapleton's account is the source of the account given in the *Apostolatus*, i. p. 234.

[3] Machyn's Diary, p. 44.

living of Solihull. Meanwhile the queen made him one of her chaplains and her confessor, and he had received the appointment of dean of St. Paul's on March 10 of that same year. The date of his installation does not appear; but he preached at the Cross as dean in the following November 25.[1] But his talents as a disputant were also called into requisition. In the April he was down at Oxford disputing with much charity and mildness against Cranmer, Latimer, and Ridley. John Fecknam had no sympathy with the ferocious measures that were being enforced against the innovators, nor in the application to them of the already existing laws. He did not believe in making men Catholics

[1] *Ibid.* Fecknam seems to have been the popular preacher of his day and a great favourite with Machyn, who mentions him as preaching twice on November 5, 1553—once at St. Stephen's, Walbrook, and once at St. Mary's, Overy; he was again at Walbrook on the 19th, where he "made the goodliest sermon that was ever heard of the blessed sacrament of the Body and Blood for to be after the consecration" (p. 48). One of his sermons, in November 1554, seems to have given offence to the Council, for in the *Acts of the Privy Council of England*, new series (vol. v. p. 35), we read: "At Westminster, the xxix of November 1554, Mr. Fekenham, dean of Paul's, being commanded by the Lords this day to make his appearance before them, did accordingly appear and exhibited the same day the sermon he made at Paul's on Sunday last in writing, which he was also commanded to bring with him." This sermon, Machyn says (p. 76), was "a godly sermon." It probably was one recommending mild measures with those opposed to the Catholic Church. Later on, as abbat, we find him on June 20, 1557, preaching at Paul's Cross, where he occupied the pulpit again on November 21, and on the following March 6; in his own abbey church on April 5 and on August 4, at the requiem mass held for one of the two widows Henry VIII. left behind him to lament his loss.

by force; and if he had to take part in the disputations then in fashion, it was from a sincere desire to prove the truth to the unhappy prisoners and reconcile them to the church they had deserted. Nor did he neglect to use his influence on their behalf; for, as Fuller says, "He was very gracious with the queen, and effectually laid out all his interest with her (sometimes even to offend her, but never to injure her) to procure pardon of the faults, or mitigation of the punishment for poor protestants.[1] The earls of Bedford and Leicester received great kindness from him; and his old friend, Sir John Cheke, owed his life to Fecknam's personal interest with the queen. He took up the cause of the unfortunate Lady Jane Dudley, and remonstrated with the queen and Gardiner upon the policy of putting her to death. He visited the poor young girl in prison; and though unsuccessful in removing the prejudices of her early education, he was able to help her to accept with resignation the fate that awaited her. Neither did he forsake the hapless lady until she paid by death the penalty of her father-in-law's treason and her own share therein (1554). When the princess Elizabeth was sent to the Tower (March 18, 1554) for her supposed part in Sir Thomas Wyatt's rebellion (on account of the proposed Spanish match), Fecknam, just then elected dean, interceded so earnestly for her release that Mary, who was convinced of her sister's guilt or at any

---

[1] *Worthies of England*, ed. 1811, vol. ii. p. 477.

rate of her insincerity, showed for some time her displeasure with him. But Elizabeth's life was spared; and she was released mainly by his importunity, after two months' imprisonment.[1]

In her proposed restoration of the Catholic Church to its former state, Mary found zealous helpers, not only in Fecknam, but in other benedictines. Bishop Thornton, once a monk of Christ Church, Canterbury, suffragan to the archbishop, was the first to restore the mass in that cathedral. Six benedictine bishops altogether took part in the revival.[2] But the queen's

[1] Fuller, *The Church History of Britain*, vol. v. p. 95 (ed. Oxford). Later on, when abbat, Machyn tells us that in 1557, on "the xii day of November, there was a post set up in Smithfield for three that should have been burnt, butt (?) both wood and coal; and my lord abbat of Westminster came to Newgate and talked with them and so they were stayed for that day of burning" (p. 157).

[2] Of these benedictine bishops, Wharton, abbat of Bermondsey, was made bishop of Hereford March 17, 1554; John Holyman, a monk of Reading, was made bishop of Bristol November 18 in the same year. Four others, Salcot of Salisbury, Chambers of Peterborough, the abovementioned Thornton of Dover, and Kitchin of Landaff, had fallen into schism but were reconciled by Pole and reinstated in their sees. Chambers died in 1556, Thornton and Salcot in 1557, Wharton and Holyman in 1558. Anthony Kitchin, whose name in religion was Dunstan, had been a monk of Westminster and became prior of Gloucester Hall, and abbat of Eynsham in 1536. He acknowledged the king's supremacy August 10, 1534, and surrendered his abbey to the king December 4, 1538. He received a pension of £133, 6s. 8d., and became one of the king's chaplains; was elected bishop of Llandaff March 26, 1545, and consecrated the following May. He was unfortunately the only one of the Catholic prelates who fell away under Elizabeth, and so kept possession of his see, of which in after years he was called "the Calamity." But there were certain lengths he would not go to; he absolutely refused to have anything to do with the foundation of the Anglican Succession. He died, aged ninety, on October 31, 1565.

wish was to restore to the monks some at least of their houses.

And here we are able, from the Venetian State Papers of the period, to trace the steps of the restoration of Westminster abbey. On March 19, 1555, the Venetian ambassador, Giovanni Michiel, writes to the doge and senate:—

"The queen is intent on its augmentation (*the Church*) and diffusion here, having sent for many English friars of the orders of St. Dominic and St. Francis, who, to escape the past persecutions, withdrew beyond the seas and lived in poverty in Flanders, in order to give them monasteries and the means of subsistence; and they, showing themselves in public everywhere, are tolerably well received and kindly treated. Sixteen benedictine monks have also resumed the habit and returned to the order spontaneously, although they were able to live and had lived out of it much at ease and liberty, there being included among them the dean of St. Paul's (*Fecknam*), who has a wealthy revenue of well-nigh 2000 (?); notwithstanding which they have renounced all their temporal possessions and conveniences, and press for readmission into one of their monasteries. The entire sixteen last week appeared in their habits before the queen, who from joy, immediately on seeing them, could not refrain from shedding tears; and for [the adjustment of] this matter she has appointed six of the leading members of the council, including the chancellor, the treasurer, the comptroller, and secretary Petre, so that, together with the legate, they may according to their judgment decide what is most fitting and beneficial for the realm, both about these monasteries and all the Church property in possession of the Crown. Her Majesty wishes it to be entirely restored to those who were deprived of it, should any of the original possessors be alive."[1]

Already we see that as early, then, as March 1555 some benedictines, with Fecknam, had resumed their habit, although as yet they had no house. The queen had some difficulty in getting her husband to consent to her project of a bill passed to allow her to give back such abbey lands as were vested in the Crown ; for by this she was giving up an income of some £60,000 a year. Parliament, after considerable opposition, did pass in the following October a bill legalising the renunciation. But there was the secular chapter at Westminster to be removed, and they were not willing to go. Promotion was given to the dean, and the interests of the others were duly looked after.[2] Pole also had to make his arrangements. Himself the protector of the Cassinese benedictine congregation, he was determined that the home at Westminster should be refounded on the Italian model. Fearing *commendam*, he de-

[1] *Calendar of Venetian State Papers*, vol. vi. No. 32.
[2] There is a bond for £30 between the abbat and a Spanish canon, by which the abbat, "as well as any other person to whom the said monastery should come," is bound to pay. See Bradley's *Illustrations of Westminster Abbey*, p. 163.

cided that the abbat was to be appointed only for three years, no *congé d'élire* was to be required for his election, neither was the royal confirmation to be sought for. Pole sent for monks from Italy, whom he intended to introduce the more rigid discipline of the continental houses, and took advantage of two "father visitors" the Cassinese had sent into Spain, for purposes of their own, to ask that they might come on to England. Pole writes to the president of the Cassinese congregation under date of February (1556?) that he was anxiously expecting the arrival from Spain of the "father visitors," as he hoped they would render good service for the restoration of the monastery which is about to be effected.[1]

The royal consent to the restoration was given in a deed signed by Philip and Mary at Croydon on September 7, 1656, and Fecknam was appointed abbat. Not only was he the most prominent man of his order then in England, but his praise was in every one's mouth. In another letter, written by the Venetian ambassador on September 28, 1556, he says:—

"The queen, thank God, continues in her good plight, rejoicing to see the monks of St. Benet return to their old abbey of Westminster, into which the canons having been removed, they in God's name will make their entry to-morrow—and this will be the third monastery and order of regulars, besides

[1] *Cal. V.S.P.*, vol. vi. No. 403.

one of nuns, which has hitherto been re-established, to whom will soon be added the fourth of the carthusians [at Sheen], who have already made their appearance."[1]

Once more, then, in possession by the end of September 1556, the house had to be got into order and some restorations made before the monks could enter. Dean Stanley says "the great refectory was pulled down," and "the smaller dormitory was cleared away," and other conventual buildings either destroyed or adapted to other uses.[2] To make all straight would necessarily take time; and it was not till 21st November that they began their regular life. Machyn in his quaint style relates the event.

"The same day (21st of November) was the new abbat of Westminster put in, Doctor Fecknam, late dean of Paul's, and xiv more monks sworn in. And the morrow after, the lord abbat with his convent went a procession after the old fashion, in their monks' weeds, in cowls of black saye, with his vergers carrying his silver-rod in their hands; at evensong time the vergers went through the cloisters to the abbat, and so went into the church afore the high altar, and there my lord kneeled down and his convent; and after his prayer was made was brought into the choir with the vergers, and so into his

[1] *Cal. V.S.P.*, vol. vi. No. 634. The dominicans were refounded at Smithfield, the franciscans at Greenwich, the bridgettines at Syon House, the carthusians at Sheen, the hospitallers at Clerkenwell, and a hospital at the Savoy.

[2] *Historical Memorials of Westminster Abbey*, fifth edition, p. 398.

place, and presently he began evensong xxii day of the same month that was St. Clement's Even last."[1] Michel in his account mentions "as many as sixteen[2] having taken the habit on that day, it was a very beautiful sight most agreeable to those who witnessed it."[3]

A few days after, the abbat was installed amidst a large assemblage of the English Church.

"On the 29th day, at Westminster abbey, was the lord abbat stalled and did wear a mitre. The lord cardinal was there and many bishops, and the lord treasurer and a great company. The lord chancellor sang mass, and the abbat made the sermon."[4]

Fecknam had lost no time in setting his house in order, in receiving others to the habit,[5] and in vindicating the privileges belonging to his venerable church. On the feast of St. Nicholas (December 6) our gossiping diarist tells us :—

"The abbat went on procession with his convent;

---

[1] Machyn's Diary (Camden Society), pp. 118, 119. A date always celebrated by English benedictines as the *Dies memorabilis*, on account of the many important events which have taken place on this date.

[2] There seems to be some mistake about the number. Writing a few days after (December 1), he says : "Yesterday . . . the twenty-six monks and their abbat made a fine show and procession." The community seem to have numbered in reality some twenty-eight.

[3] *Cal. V.S.P.*, vol. vi. No. 723.

[4] Machyn, pp. 119, 120.

[5] Owing to the present difficulty of obtaining access to the Westminster abbey records, it is not possible to identify all the monks of Westminster. But the principal interest centres round D. Sigebert Buckley, who passed on the benedictine succession nearly fifty years afterwards.

before him went all the sanctuary men with cross keys on their garments; and after went three for murder; one was the Lord Dacre, son of the North, who was whipt with a sheet about [him for] killing of one Master West, squire, dwelling beside . . ." Another finding shelter was one of the abbey boys —"a boy [that] killed a big boy that sold papers and printed books, [with] hurling of a stone, and hit him under the ear in Westminster Hall; the boy was one of the children that was [at the] school there in the abbey; the boy is a hosier's son above London stone."[1]

The queen was not long in paying the monks a visit. Giovanni Michiel writes, December 21, 1556:—

"Yesterday, St. Thomas' eve, the queen, before her departure for Greenwich, which will take place to-morrow, chose to see the benedictine monks in their habits in the abbey of Westminster, whither she went to vespers, being received in state by them and their abbat, twenty-eight in number, all men of mature age, the youngest being upwards of forty, and all endowed with learning and piety, as proved by their renunciation of the many conveniences of life; the poorest having a fixed annual rental of 500 crowns, besides ready money, and some 1500, besides the abbat, who had upwards of [2000?], and was dean of St. Paul's, which after that of the bishops is the chief dignity of the English

[1] *Ibid.* p. 121.

clergy. Words cannot express how much this rejoiced the legate, who is already preparing another monastery for the regular canons who are coming shortly."[1]

Besides his duties as abbat and constantly preaching, we find him giving time and money to beautifying his church. On January 5, 1557, he began to set up St. Edward's shrine again and the altar with divers jewels that the queen sent hither.[2] While on the following 20th of March, says Machyn:—

"The xx of March was taken up at Westminster again with a hundred lights, King Edward the Confessor in the same place where his shrine was, and it shall be set up again as fast as my lord abbat can have it done, for it was a godly sight to have seen it how reverently he was carried from the place that he was taken up, where he was laid when that abbey was spoiled and robbed, and so he was carried and goodly singing and censing as has been seen, and mass sung."[3]

Machyn dearly loved a function.

Fecknam was a lover of the old customs, and did not forget the benedictine spirit of hospitality. One more extract from Machyn must be allowed, for the sake of the glimpse it gives of the geniality of his

---

[1] *Cal. V.S.P.*, vol. vi. p. 2, No. 771. Priuli writes to Beccatello, December 15, 1556, in the same strain, and gives the same number. According to him they were "tutte persone benissimo qualificate di dottrina e di gran pietà." See the letter in Tierney, vol. ii. p. ccxxiii.

[2] Bradley, p. 166.   [3] P. 130.

rule. On March 21, 1558, the feast of St. Benedict, was held the traditional festivity connected with the making of the gigantic paschal candle for the approaching Easter. "xxi day of March was paschal for the abbey of Westminster, made there the weight of 300 lbs. of wax: and there was the master and the wardens of the wax-chandlers with twenty more at the making, and after, a great dinner."[1] Evidently the head of the trade-gild of chandlers took a representative part in the day's doings, and shared, too, in the great dinner. There is a touch of fellowship between the abbey and the gild which tells of the good feeling of earlier days, and which the "great dinner" would, no doubt, *more anglico*, help to knit up again, if not increase.

Fecknam, while thus fulfilling the duties of his high charge, had also to attend Parliament as a mitred abbat of the realm. The rights of sanctuary at his abbey were being questioned, and the Speaker of the House of Commons called on the abbat to produce the proofs of the privilege. "Accordingly on Saturday the 11th of February [1557] came the abbat, accompanied with no council learned, but only with one monk attending on him, bearing two old muniments—the one whereof was the charter of sanctuary granted to the house of Westminster by King Edward, the saint; the other the confirmation of the same charter . . . by Pope John." "He begged the house, if he had no other instruments to

[1] *Ibid.* p. 169.

show,[1] they would not thereby take advantage, but impute it to the iniquity of the times wherein they were perished, declaring how, as by a miracle, these were preserved, being found by a servant of my lord cardinal's in a child's hand playing with them in the street."[2]

Westminster being thus restored, the hope of the monks ran high that other houses, too, would be reopened. There seems to have been a project for restoring one of the Canterbury houses. Cardinal Pole writes from Croydon on the 28th May 1557, to the abbat of St. Paul's, Rome, saying: "Your paternity will perhaps have heard that the affairs of St. Peter's monastery go on well, and thus by God's grace they still continue proceeding from good to better; and I am not indeed without hope that one of the two monasteries at my church of Canterbury may soon be restored.[3]

Abbat Fecknam was zealous for the restoration of other houses of his order, and used his influence on their behalf both with the cardinal and the queen, as is clear from the following petition of four Glastonbury monks, then at Westminster:—[4]

---

[1] Bradley, p. 170. Miss Bradley gives no references to all these statements, and it has been a cause of ceaseless trouble to identify them, a task not always successful.

[2] *Ibid.* p. 171.

[3] *Cal. V.S.P.*, vol. vi. p. 904, *note.*

[4] This letter was probably written after Pole's letter to the abbat of St. Paul's and before the end of the year which found Philip soon back to the continent.

"*To the Rt. Honble.* LORD CHAMBERLAIN *to the Queen's Majesty.*

"Right Honourable, in our most humble wise your lordship's daily beadsmen, some time of the house of Glastonbury, now here, monks in Westminster, with all due submission we desire your honour to extend your accustomed virtue, as it hath been always heretofore propense to the honour of Almighty God, to the honourable service of the king and queen's majesties, so it may please your good lordship again, for the honour of them, both of God and of their majesties, to put the queen's highness in remembrance of her gracious promise concerning the erection of the late monastery of Glastonbury, which promise of her grace hath been so by her majesty declared that upon the same, we your lordship's daily beadsmen, understanding my lord cardinal's grace's pleasure to the same by the procurement here of our reverend father abbat, have gotten out the particulars; and through a warrant from my lord treasurer, our friends that have builded and bestowed much upon reparation: notwithstanding all now stands at a stay. We think the case to be want of remembrance, which cannot be so well brought unto her majesty's understanding as by your honourable lordship's favour and help. And considering your lordship's most godly disposition, we have a confidence thereof to solicit the same, assuring your lordship of our daily prayer while we live, and of our successors' during the world, if it may so please your lordship to take it in hand.

"We ask nothing in gift to the foundation, but only the house and site, the residue for the accustomed rent, so that with our labour and husbandry we may live there a few of us in our religious habits, till the charity of good people may suffice a greater number; and the country there being so affected to our religion, we believe we should find much help among them towards the reparations and furniture of the same, whereby we would haply prevent the ruin of much, and repair no little part of the whole to God's honour and for the better prosperity of the king's and queen's majesties, with the whole realm. For doubtless, if it shall please your good lordship if there hath ever been any flagitious deed since the creation of the world punished with the plague of God, in our opinion the overthrow of Glastonbury may be compared with the same, not surrendered as other [abbeys] but extorted; the abbat preposterously put to death with two innocent virtuous monks with him; that if the thing were to be scanned by any university or some learned council in divinity, they would find it more dangerous than is commonly taken; which might move the queen's majesty to the more speedy erection; namely, it being a home of such antiquity and fame through all Christendom, first begun by St. Joseph of Arimathea, who took down the dead body of our saviour

Christ from the cross and lieth buried in Glastonbury. And him most heartily we beseech to pray unto Christ for good success unto your honourable lordship in all your lordship's affairs, and now specially in this our most humble request that we may shortly do the same in Glaston[1] for the king and the queen's majesties as our founders and for your lordship as a regular benefactor.

"Your lordship's daily beadsmen of Westminster.

"JOHN PHAGAN.
JOHN NEOTT.
WILLIAM ADELWOLD.
WILLIAM KENTWYN."[2]

[1] The restoration of Glastonbury to English monks is, we hope, only deferred. The prayers of the martyred abbat Whiting, now beatified, must plead strongly for the restoration of his house to his own brethren. After the dissolution, several of the old monks remained in the neighbourhood. One, D. Austin Ringwode (died in the odour of sanctity in 1587), had not the heart to tear himself away from the home round which so many gracious memories clung. He dwelt in a little cottage hard by, where in poverty and solitude he kept his rule as strictly as if he had been in his cell. His days were passed in prayer, in fastings and vigils for his unhappy country. The country folk said the old man saw visions and had the gift of prophecy, and they tell that he said: "The abbey will one day be repaired and rebuilt for the like worship which has ceased, and then peace and plenty will for a long time abound" (Lee's *Church under Queen Elizabeth*, vol. i. p. 216). D. Austin Ringwode's name does not appear on the pension list. Some of the relics which had been venerated for centuries at Glastonbury were secured by the monks at the time of the dissolution, and have been handed down from generation to generation. One most valuable one, "The Holy Thorn"—a thorn from the crown of thorns—is now venerated at St. Mary's abbey, Stanbrook, in a chapel built for the purpose.

[2] Dugdale, vol. i. p. 9. These names do not appear on the pension list of Glastonbury, which bears their surnames. The signatures here give their names in religion.

St. Albans was also to be restored. The former abbat, Richard Boreman or Stevenage, had remained in the neighbourhood and hoped one day to see his house reopened. To his great joy, consent was given to his prayer. This must have been late in 1558; for Mary died before anything could be done. And for very grief the abbat took to his bed and died two weeks after of a broken heart.[1]

Mary died on the morning of Nov. 17, 1558, and on the same day cardinal Pole breathed his last at Lambeth.[2] The prospects of the Church were gloomy and uncertain; for although Elizabeth had not begun to disclose her hand, yet what was known of her did not warrant any hopeful future. Mary's funeral rites were duly solemnised, and Fecknam preached one of the funeral sermons,[3] and White, bishop of Winchester, the other.

The new queen took umbrage at the bishop's sermon, and ordered him to be confined to his own house. She soon began to show the direction of her policy. Perhaps it is wrong to say she was herself personally in favour of the reformation as a religious movement; but policy forced her into a position which could only be preserved, as things

[1] Dugdale, vol. ii. p. 207.
[2] There have been all sorts of statements about the date of Pole's death, some placing it on the 19th. But all doubt is now set aside by a letter from Priuli to his brother in Venice: "On the 17th instant, seven hours after midnight, the queen passed from this life, and my most reverend lord followed her at seven o'clock on the evening of the same day" (*Cal. V.S.P.*, vi. n. 1287-1292).
[3] MS. Cott. Vesp. D. xviii. fol. 92.

then seemed to stand, by cutting England off once more from the centre of Unity, and by rejecting the cardinal point of Catholic worship, the mass.[1] But still she had a liking rather than otherwise for such of the outward forms of Catholicism, and even of its discipline, as were compatible with her own supremacy. She had no sympathy with the iconoclastic rage of the Puritan party, who were now struggling for the upper hand.[2] Besides

[1] Paul IV. it seems refused to recognise her, which of course he could have done without any reference to the matter of her father's divorce; for there was no question of legitimate birth, but of the fact, that by law and the will of her father, as well as by the acceptance of the nation, she succeeded. Then again Henry II. of France had lately ordered the arms of England to be quartered with those of Scotland upon the marriage of his son with Mary Stuart; and Elizabeth's advisers convinced the queen that this was a direct questioning of her title, as Mary Stuart was by legitimate birth the heiress to the English throne. All this made the queen determined at any cost to secure her position.

[2] In her own private chapel Elizabeth kept many of the ornaments of Catholic usages. "The altar was furnished with rich plate, two fair gilt candlesticks with tapers in them and a massy crucifix of silver in the midst thereof" (Heylin, p. 296). "She had honourable sentiments of the use of the cross, of the blessed virgin and other saints, and never mentioned them without regard and reverence" (Collier, vol. ii. p. 412). In fine, she was so fixed in this practice that all Parker's "learning and zeal could not persuade her to part with the crucifix and lighted tapers in her own closet. She thought, 'tis likely, that the arguing against the use, from the abuse, was short of an exact reasoning" (*ibid.* p. 435). Her Catholic instinct also revolted against the idea of a married clergy, which she only tolerated as the surest method of alienating them from the pope. Parker writes to Cecil, and reports some speeches uttered to him by the queen against the marriage of the clergy: "I was in a horror," says he, "to hear such words to come from her mild nature and Christianly learned conscience, as she spake concerning God's holy ordinance and institution of *matrimony*. . . . Insomuch that the queen's highness expressed to me a

intending to preserve such a hierarchy as she could (Providence arranging that matter), she also wanted, as we shall see, to keep at least Westminster as a monastery, if such an institution could find place in her scheme of religion. This, in view of her strong and ineradicable notions as to the marriage of the clergy, seems to be the most likely explanation of her sending for the abbat of Westminster at a very early period of her reign. But Fecknam, whatever the nature of the private interview may have been, could not enter into her measures, for the proposal meant treason to his conscience. It is said she even tried to bribe him to come over to her side by the promise of the vacant archbishopric of Canterbury. But all was in vain.[1]

The new Parliament opened ominously for the monks. The queen assisted at the usual mass of the Holy Ghost in the abbey on the 25th of January. "On arriving at Westminster abbey, the abbat,

---

repentance that we were thus appointed in office, wishing it had been otherwise, which inclination being known at large to queen Marie's clergy they laugh prettily, to see how the clergy of our time is handled, and what equity of law is ministered to our sort. But by patience and silence we pass over, &c., and leave all to God ; in the meantime we have cause all to be utterly discomforted and discouraged" (Strype, *Life of Parker*, Appendix, vol. iii. pp. 50, 51).

[1] Fuller, *Worthies of England*, vol. ii. p. 477. This interview was most likely before her coronation, January 14th, or before the opening of Parliament, January 25th; for on that latter date the queen began her course of reformation. According to the old custom, the abbat of Westminster had some days previous to the coronation to wait on the sovereign and give instructions upon the forthcoming ceremony. See *Missale Westmon.* (H.B.S.), p. 676.

vested pontifically, with all his monks in procession, each of them having a lighted torch in his hand, received her as usual, giving her first of all incense and holy water; and when her majesty saw the monks who accompanied her with the torches she said: "Away with those torches, for we see very well!"[1]

The various bills introduced for the recognition of the queen's title (without any reference, however, to the validity of the marriage of her mother, Anne Boleyn) and the restoration of the first-fruits, the all-important bills relating to the royal supremacy and to the new liturgy, came before a house of commons packed for the occasion, and a house of lords which included only a few bishops, who, together with Fecknam, were left to defend the cause of the Church.[2] The abbat in a vigorous speech opposed any changes in religion. He said—

"My good Lords, when in Queen Mary's days, your honours do know right well how the people of this realm did live in an order; and would not run before laws nor openly disobey the queen's

[1] *Calendar of Venetian S.P.*, vol. vii. No. 15.
[2] The state of the English hierarchy on Elizabeth's accession was as follows: Six sees were vacant by death, viz. Canterbury, Oxford, Salisbury, Bangor, Gloucester, and Hereford; although nominations had been made to the five last, they were all set aside by the new queen. Before the end of the year four more bishops died, Rochester, Norwich, Chichester, and Bristol. When Parliament met on January 25, 1559, the bishops of Durham, Peterborough, Bath and Wells, and St. Davids were absent, but had appointed Heath of York their proxy. Lincoln was ill; Ely away on an embassy (but returned and took his seat in April); St Asaphs was not summoned. So out of twenty-six sees, only nine were present.

highness's proceeding and proclamation. There was no spoiling of churches, pulling down of altars, and most blasphemous treading down of sacraments under their feet and hanging up the knave of clubs in the place thereof. There was no skurching nor cutting of the faces and legs of the crucifix and image of Christ. There was no open flesh-eating, nor shambles keeping in the Lent and days prohibited. The subjects of this realm, and in especially the nobility and such as were of the honourable council, did in queen Mary's days know the way unto churches and chapels, there to begin their daily work with calling for help and grace by humble prayer and serving of God. And now since the coming and reign of our most sovereign and dear lady queen Elizabeth, by the only preachers and scaffold-players of this new religion all things are turned upside down."[1]

Fecknam opposed in all their stages the bills[2] for the supremacy and for the restoration to the crown of the first-fruits, though he does not seem to have been present in the house of lords during the debates of April 26, 27, and 28, on the act of Uniformity of Common Prayer and Service.[3]

---

[1] MS. Cott. Vesp. D. xviii. fol. 86. See also Strype's *Annals*, vol. i. Part II. p. 436.

[2] D'Ewes, *Journals of all the Parliaments during the Reign of Queen Elizabeth*, p. 30.

[3] Heath, archbishop of York, refers in his speech to the pope, Paul IV., in terms which show that considerable irritation existed against him personally, and only makes the pronouncement in regard to the

But before it was passed and the new liturgy authorised, a public dispensation was appointed to be held at the end of March, under the presidency of Sir Francis Bacon. As the queen and her ministers had arranged the meeting only as a pretext for breaking down the opposition of the bishops, and to secure their subsequent punishment, Fecknam, although an acknowledged champion of the Catholic Cause, when at the end he was called upon by Bacon to take part, refused to do so. On April 3rd the disputation broke up, and two of the bishops, Lincoln and Winchester, were sent to the Tower. Those of Lichfield, Chester, and Carlisle, with three doctors who had taken part in it, were otherwise punished.

In spite of the unanimous opposition of the bishops, the act of the Royal Supremacy was passed and became law May 5, 1559. Il Schifanoya writes the next day to the castellan of Mantua: "Parlia-

pope as the centre of unity all the more remarkable. On this point Heath is explicit. "If by this our relinquishing of the see of Rome, there were none other matter therein than a withdrawing of our obedience from the pope's person, Paul the fourth of that name, which hath declared himself to be a very austere stern father unto us ever since his first entrance into Peter's chair, then the cause were not of such importance as it is; as will immediately appear. For by relinquishing and forsaking the church or see of Rome, we must forsake and fly, first, from all general councils; secondly, from all canonical and ecclesiastical laws of the church of Christ; thirdly, from the judgment of all other christian princes; fourthly and lastly, we must forsake and fly from the holy unity of Christ's church, and so, by leaping out of Peter's ship, we hazard ourselves to be overwhelmed in the waves of schism, of sects and divisions" (Strype's *Annals*, I. Appendix 8).

ment will rise this week, the two houses having enacted that all the convents and monasteries of friars, monks, nuns, and hospitallers of St. John of Jerusalem, are to be suppressed as heretofore, and all their religious to be expelled. Such of them who will take the oath against the pontifical authority, and approve of the new laws abjuring their own professions, are to receive pensions for their maintenance; but the greater part of them have left the kingdom in order not to take such oaths."[1] A week afterward he writes: "Westminster abbey with the monks and the rest of the monasteries and friaries will be appropriated to the Crown, pensions being given to those who will swear to and approve of the laws."[2]

Commissioners were appointed to administer the oath; refusal involved forfeiture of all benefice and office, and disablement for any further promotion. It is to be noted that the mere refusal of the oath only incurred deprivation, not imprisonment, which was illegal. It was an expedient for getting out of office all opposers of the royal policy. But, after thirty days of the passing of the act, script, or word, or deed in defence of the newly abolished papal supremacy, entailed for the first offence loss of all property, for the second the penalties of *premunire*, and for the third death. Any active opposition was thus punishable: but a simple

---

[1] *Cal. V.S P.*, vol. vii. No. 68.
[2] *Ibid.* No. 71.

passive refusal to accept the queen as supreme in matters ecclesiastical was tolerated even after the deprivation of the refuser.

The letters to the commissioners were signed May 23, 1559. But they proceeded slowly, in the hopes of winning over some.[1] By the end of the year the oath had been offered to all the bishops, who, with the exception of Kitchin, refused, and were therefore deprived but were not as yet imprisoned.

During the time of the debates in Parliament on the changes in religion, abbat Fecknam was quietly going on at Westminster unmoved by the approaching storm. He kept his soul in peace through it all. He knew the consequences of his refusal of the queen's offer, but let the evil of the day take heed to itself. So he went on. The story goes that he was engaged in planting elm trees in his garden at Westminster when a message came to tell him that a majority in the house of commons had declared for the dissolution of all religious houses,[2] and remarked that he planted in vain, for that he and his monks would soon have to go. "Not in vain," replied the abbat. "Those that

---

[1] How slowly they set to work is clear from the date of the depositions. Bonner they disposed of that very month; Lichfield, Chester, Carlisle, Lincoln, Winchester, and Worcester in June; York, St. Asaph, Ely, in July; Durham in September; Bath and Peterborough in October; Exeter in November. When St. David's was voided is not known.

[2] This was on April 29. The bill passed the Lords, May 5. See Strype's *Annals*, I. (ed. Oxford), vol. i. Part I. p. 99.

come after me may perhaps be scholars and lovers of retirement, and whilst walking under the shades of these trees they may sometimes think of the olden religion of England, and the last abbat of this place." And so he went on with his planting.[1]

Il Schifanoya, who was a Mantuan correspondent, seemingly official, tells us hitherto unknown details about the second dissolution of Westminster. Writing on June 6, he says :—

"The poor bishop [Bonner] has taken sanctuary at Westminster abbey to avoid molestation from many persons who demand considerable sums of money from him; but the abbey cannot last long, as the abbat made a similar reply [of refusal] when it was offered him to remain securely in his abbey with his habit and the monks, to live together as they had done till now, provided that he would celebrate in his church the divine offices and mass, administering the sacraments in the same manner as in the other churches of London, and that he would take the oath like the other servants, officials, pensioners, and dependents of the crown, and acknowledge this establishment as from the hands of her majesty. To these things the abbat would by no means consent; so after St. John's day, the term fixed by Parliament for all persons to consent and

---

[1] Fuller, *Church History of Britain* (ed. Oxford), vol. v. p. 96, says this took place soon after the accession. But Heylin, *Examen Historicum*, p. 167, with much more probability, puts the story at the time when the dissolution of the monastery was decreed.

swear to all the statutes and laws or to lose what they have, all of them will go about their business, though no one can leave the kingdom." [1]

On the 27th of June he writes again: "Six or eight bishops have been deprived not only of their bishoprics but of all their other revenues, being bound also not to depart from England, and not to preach or exhort whatever in public or in private, and still less to write anything against the orders and statutes of this parliament; nor [to give occasion to] insurrection or any other scandalous act, under pain of perpetual imprisonment; [the queen's ministers] demanding security and promise to be given by one bishop for the other. . . . *Yesterday these good reverend fathers* [2] *underwent their deprivation, and received orders where they are to dwell, before the council which assembled here in London in the house of a sheriff for this purpose, they being humble, abject, and habited like simple and poor priests—a sight which would have grieved you.* . . .

"The abbat of Westminster with all his monks did the like, and are therefore deprived of the revenues of the monastery and of all the rest of their property." [3]

Little time was now lost in putting into effect the result of Fecknam's refusal. The end came on July 12, 1559. The abbat and his monks were

[1] *Cal. V.S.P.*, vol. vii. No. 78.
[2] The six bishops were those of London, Worcester, Chester, Carlisle, Lichfield, and Llandaff. Winchester and Lincoln were already in the Tower.
[3] *Cal. V.S.P.*, vol. viii. No. 82.

turned out, and Westminster knew the benedictines no more. As they had refused to take the oath of supremacy, they received no pensions, which were only promised on that condition.[1]

The day after, Fecknam and one John Moulton, most likely one of the monks, raised the sum of £40, on what was evidently private plate, from Sir Thomas Curtis, the same to be considered as a loan if paid back before the feast of All Saints next.[2]

A few days after the suppression, the commissioners appointed to survey, examine, and order concerning the state of the late monastery, directed the receivers to pay over to the abbat the sum of £374, 14s. 6d. for various considerations.[3]

What became immediately of the abbat and his monks we do not at present know; but it is most likely that, like the bishops, he received orders where to dwell.

[1] It is generally said by writers that the monks had pensions. There is, we believe, no pension list extant, and the testimony of Il Schifanoya, quoted above, seems entirely to do away with any such idea. Perhaps those who, like Fecknam, had been in receipt of pensions under Henry VIII. now resumed those. This perhaps is likely the meaning of dean Stanley's assertion, based on the chapter-book of 1569 (see *Memorials*, p. 406, *note*), which book unfortunately, like the rest of the Westminster documents, is not accessible.

[2] *Historical MSS. Commission, Fourth Report*, p. 178.

[3] *Ibid.* This is the sum Miss Bradley (*Dictionary of National Biography*, sub *Fecknham*) has evidently mistaken for a pension, and of which she says Fecknam generously gave up a part to dean Bill. A few years later he made over to the dean and chapter (with the hope doubtlessly of a future return of England to the Church) certain ecclesiastical vestments and altar hangings specified in an inventory attached to the deed of gift (April 4, fifth of Elizabeth).

But very soon it was considered to be injurious to the new order of things that the bishops and abbat should be at liberty. There had been, as yet, no complaint of any overt act on their part against the new statutes. But at the following Easter (1560) their continued absence from the state worship was made a cause for excommunicating and then imprisoning them. This was the resolution taken by the queen and her council: "The xx of May was sent to the Tower master Fecknam, doctor Watson, late bishop of Lincoln, and doctor Cole, late dean of Paul's, and doctor Chadsay; and at night about viii of the clock was sent to the Fleet doctor Score, and master Fecknam, the last abbat of Westminster, to Tower."[1] Parker,[2] the new archbishop of Canterbury, it was who sent the abbat to prison.

Of his life in the Tower we have gathered a few particulars. He had to pay heavily for his food and accommodation. The charges, for instance, in the Fleet prison were then £1 a week for board and the privilege of a single bed; this sum, be it re-

[1] Machyn, p. 235. Jewel writes to Peter Martyr (May 22, 1560): "Bonner, the monk Feckenham, [Dr.] Pate, [Dr.] Story the civilian, and Watson [bishop of Lincoln] sent to prison for having obstinately refused attendance on public worship, and everywhere declaiming and railing against that religion which we now profess." And two years (February 7, 1562) after he again writes: "The Marian bishops are still confined to the Tower, and are going on in their old way. If the laws were but as rigorous now as in the time of Henry, they would submit themselves without difficulty. They are an obstinate and untamed set of men, but are nevertheless subdued by terror and the sword." *Zurich Letters* (Parker Society), First Series, pp. 79, 101.

[2] Stowe, *Annals of the Reformation*, vol. i. Part I. p. 211.

membered, is equal to £10 a week; the charges were most likely the same at the Tower. Even at this high cost, his cell was damp and unhealthy, the food was bad, and he was subjected to close confinement. The prisoners were kept separate, and of this they so complained, that Sir Edward Warner, lieutenant of the Tower, in writing to the council (June 14, 1560), says:—

"First he put your lordships in remembrance that the late bishops, with Mr. Fecknam and Mr. Boxall, being all eight in number, be close and severally kept, for which they continually call upon him to make on their names humble suit to have more liberty; informing your lordships therewith how troublesome it is to serve so many persons severally so long together."[1]

The council wrote on 4th September to the archbishop giving leave that the prisoners, unless he had any objection, might dine at two tables, together with the order in which they had to sit. The archbishop of York, the bishop of Worcester, abbat Fecknam, and Boxall, dean of Peterborough and secretary of state under queen Mary, were to dine at one table; and the bishops of Ely, Bath and Wells, Exeter, and Lincoln at the other. Parker consented, and (September 6th) authorised the lieutenant to make the change.[2]

[1] *P.R.O. Dom. Eliz.*, vol. xxiii. No. 40, quoted by Bridgett and Knox in *Queen Elizabeth and the Catholic Hierarchy*, p. 165.
[2] *Parker Correspondence* (Parker Society), pp. 121, 122.

This new arrangement would be better at least, for they would have the help of each other's society to resist the insidious attacks made to bring them to conformity. As each Easter came round, threats of death were reported for those who would refuse to partake of the new sacrament.[1] In March 1563 Parliament had given authority to administer the oath, with the penalty now of death for those who refused it.[2] But so far the oath had not been again tendered to the prisoners. They were first to be tried in another way. Occasion was taken of the plague, then raging in the City, to remove them from the Tower and commit them to the custody of the new bishops. They had themselves petitioned the council "to be removed to some other convenient place for their better safeguard from the present infection of the plague."[3] But this slight grace shown to them did not please the preachers of the new religion. Stowe in his *Memoranda* says: "Anno 1563 in September the old bishops and divers doctors were removed out of the tower into the new bishops' houses, there to remain prisoners under their custody (the plague being then in the city was thought to be the cause); but their deliverance (or rather change of prison) did so much offend the people that the preachers at Paul's Cross and on other places, both of the city and the

---

[1] Bridgett and Knox, p. 42.
[2] Lingard (ed. Dolman, 1849), vol. vi. p. 83.
[3] *Parker Correspondence*, p. 192.

country, preached (as it was thought of many wise men) very seditiously, as Baldwin at Paul's Cross wishing a gallows set up in Smithfield, and the old bishops and other papists to be hanged thereon. He himself died of the plague the next week after."[1]

Abbat Fecknam was sent, first of all, back to his old home at Westminster, to the care of Goodman, the new dean. There is a letter from Grindal, bishop of London, to Cecil, of the date October 15, 1563, suggesting that Fecknam should be sent to some bishop.

"The bishop of Winton, when he was with me, said if he should have any, he could best deal with Fecknam, for in king Edward's days he travailed with Fecknam in the Tower and brought him to subscribe to all things, saving the Presence and one or two more articles. Ye might do very well (in my opinion) to ease the poor dean of Westminster, and send the other also to some other bishop, as Sarum or Chichester."[2]

The suggestion was taken, and the dean was relieved of the unwelcome presence of the abbat; and that same winter Fecknam was sent to Horne, bishop of Winchester, who was boasting he could prevail over the abbat's constancy. With what results will appear. In the bishop's house he was treated very uncivilly and roughly. "We must not think of these

---

[1] *Three Fifteenth-Century Chronicles, with Historical Memoranda*, by *John Stowe* (Cam. Soc.), p. 126.

[2] Grindal's *Remains*, p. 282 (Parker Society).

first intruders into the Catholic sees of England as if they were modern Anglican bishops, gentlemen of refinement and of enlarged and liberal minds, who, if we could imagine them in the position of unwilling jailors to Catholic bishops, would seek by every means to alleviate their lot."[1]

We shall see later on what the treatment was the prisoners had to endure at the hands of their episcopal jailors.

Horne began to ply the abbat with questions on the dangerous subject of the oath. Fecknam wrote a clever paper in answer, giving the reasons which would hinder him from taking the oath. We see the old dialectical skill which made him so feared as an opponent. Among other difficulties, he says: "The fourth and last point is that I must swear to the observation of this oath, not only to the queen's highness, and our sovereign lady that now is, but also unto her heirs and successors, kings and queens of this realm; and because every Christian man ought to be careful to avoid perjury therein, I would right gladly know that if any her highness successors should by the refusal of the said title of supremacy bind her subjects by the like statute law unto the clean contrary [experience whereof was of late made in this realm, that it is yet fresh in the memories of all men]; in this case I would right gladly know what authority is able to dispense again with the oath? And if there be none at all, then

[1] Bridgett and Knox, p. 94.

the subjects of this realm in this case are bound, and that by book-oath, to live in a continual disobedience to the laws of their sovereign lord or lady, king or queen, the case whereof is very lamentable"[1]

The abbat was always ready to listen;[2] and was able at least to prove to his opponents that his refusal to submit to the royal supremacy in ecclesiastical affairs was solely a matter of conscience. Horne complains that Fecknam used to point to his heart and say: "The matter itself is founded here, that shall never go out."[3] In spite of frequent reports spread abroad of an approaching recantation, day and hour being even fixed by the gossips, Horne, finding that all his endeavours were unavailing to bring over the abbat to his own way of thinking, kept him for six weeks a close prisoner in the house, and after allowing him to be grossly insulted at his table, made complaint to the council and procured his return to the Tower.[4]

In April 1564 archbishop Parker had a conversation with Cecil, and urged the enforcement of the oath according to the recent act. But Cecil gave him to know that the queen was unwilling to have the oath tendered for the second time, for that meant death. The archbishop acted under the instructions

---

[1] Horne's *An Answer to M. Fekenham*, p. 101.

[2] "I hear said Mr. Fecknam is not so precise (*as Watson, who refused all conference*) but could be contented to confer" (Grindal to Cecil, p. 282).

[3] Horne's *An Answer to M. Fekenham*, p. 3.

[4] *Ibid.* p. 129.

he received, and sent round a circular, the draft of which Cecil corrected, to the rest of his bishops ordering them not to tender the oath to any one a second time without previously referring the matter to him. But this instruction had to be kept secret.[1] An exception, however, was made in the case of Bonner, a fellow-prisoner with the abbat, who had incurred the special hatred of all the reformers by his severity under the last reign. How that wily old lawyer Bonner checkmated Horne and all Elizabeth's government on the plea that the intruded bishop of Winchester was no bishop in the eyes of the law, is a well known story.

We have seen how Horne, having failed to convince the abbat, was glad to get rid of him; and Fecknam on his side preferred, it is said, to go back to the Tower rather than stay with the bishop. We find him there in custody in January 1565, and he probably returned on the occasion of Horne's fiasco with Bonner. In the Tower he lingered on; and we know but little of his imprisonment.[2] As Horne had complained to the council of the abbat's intractability, Fecknam in a letter to Sir W. Cecil

---

[1] *Parker Correspondence*, pp. 173–175.
[2] A poem *In Laudem Joannis Fecknam*, by an unknown author, printed in the *Downside Review* (vol. i. p. 430), tells us some particulars of his life at this time. It was his own choice to return to the Tower; for he said, "A prison is better than a bishop's palace." And on one occasion when Cecil expressed his wonder that the abbat lived so long, "The reason is," said he, "because I live shut up in the prison and not the prison in me. I willingly bear my chains."

(March 14, 1565) puts the matter into its real light.

"According to your honour's pleasure, signified to me by the lieutenant, I have sent to your honour such writings as have passed between my lord bishop of Winchester and me, touching the oath of the queen's highness' supremacy, in perusing whereof I do most humbly beseech your honour to observe how slenderly his lordship hath satisfied my expectations therein: who in requesting of his lordship to be resolved by the authority of the scriptures, doctors, general councils, and by the example of the like government in some one part and church of all Christendom: his lordship in no one part of his resolutions hath alledged any testimony out of any one of them: but only hath used the authority of his own bare words, naked talk and sentences; which in so great and weighty a matter of conscience I esteem and weigh as nothing. And if his lordship shall at any time hereafter (and especially at your honour's request) be able to bring forth any better matter, I shall be, at the sight thereof, at all times in readiness to receive the said oath, and to perform my promise before made in the writings. But if his lordship shall be found (notwithstanding your honour's request) to have no better matter in store, I shall for my duty's sake towards the queen's majesty, considering the degree and estate her highness hath placed him in, abstain from the plain speech which

I might justly use (his lordship first beginning the complaint), yet that notwithstanding your honour must give me leave to think that his lordship hath not all the Divine Scriptures, doctors, general councils, and all other kinds of learning so much at his commandment as I have oftentimes heard him boast and speak of. And this much to write of my own secret thought, either against him or yet any other, it is very much contrary to the inclination of my nature: for I being a poor man in trouble am now, likewise at all other times, very loath to touch him or any man else. But whensoever it shall please your honour by your wisdom to weigh the matter indifferently between us, your honour shall be sure to have this short end and conclusion thereof: that either upon his lordship's more pytthyer (? pithier) and learned resolutions, your honour shall be well assured that I will receive the oath, or else, for lack of learned resolutions, your honour shall have certain and sure knowledge that the stay so long a time on my part, made in not receiving of the same oath, is of conscience and not of will stubbornly set; but only of dread and fear to commit perjury, thereby to procure and purchase to myself God his wrath and indignation: finally to inherit perpetual death and torment of hell fire, and that remedyless, by a separation making of myself from God and the unity of his Catholic Church, being always after unsure, how or by what means I may be united and knit thereunto again. The upright and due consideration of this my lamentable state is all that I do seek at your honour's hands, as knoweth our Lord God, who long preserve your good honour with much increase thereof.

"From the Tower, this xiiii of this present March, by your poor orator,   JOHN FECKNAM, *priste*."[1]

Whilst in the Tower (1570), Fecknam wrote a pamphlet which casts a light on the "gentle persuasiveness," used in his regard. It was written in answer to Sir Francis Jobson, the lieutenant of the Tower, on Mr. Pellam's request, "upon Sunday last [January 15, 1570], as I came from the church, to know my liking of M. Gough's sermon. Whereunto I answered: that I was very loath to find any fault with the sayings or doings of any man, being already in trouble as you know. You replied and said: that I was not able to find fault where no fault was. I had not then no leisure to make any further answer, you departing homewards and I to my prison." He then discusses the various opinions broached in the course of the sermon, and ends up with these words: "I desire, I say, to make my humble suit unto your worships for myself and my prison-fellows both, that hereafter we may not be haled by the arms to the church in such violent manner against our wills, against all former examples, against the doctrine of your own side (Luther, Bucer, Zwinglius, Oecolampadius, Melancthon, and the rest,

[1] Dom Eliz., xxxvi. 23.

every one writing and earnestly persuading that all violence be taken away in matters of religion), there to hear such preachers as care not what they say so they somewhat say against the professed faith of Christ's Catholic Church; and there to hear a sermon, not of persuading us, but of railing upon us. This, if your worships will incline unto for charity sake, we shall have to render you most humble thanks, and whatsoever else we may do in this our heavy time of imprisonment."[1]

Some time after the abbat was removed to the Marshalsea, but the exact date has not been yet discovered.[2] He was still in the Tower 1571, for in the March of that year he was allowed to have his meals at the table of the lieutenant of the Tower,[3] and is known in the June to have attended his fellow-prisoner, Dr. John Story, at the scaffold

Stevens says: "Many protestants, being ashamed to see a man who had deserved so well so inhumanly treated, prevailed that he should be put out of the Tower and removed to the Marshalsea, where he had a little more liberty."[4] But on July 17, 1574, the council ordered the keeper of the Marshalsea to take him before the archbishop of Canterbury at his grace's leisure, and "upon bonds taken of him by the said lord bishop, to set him at

---

[1] L. T., *An Answer to Certain Assertions of M. Fecknam*, &c., p. 17.
[2] Bradley's *Westminster*, p. 179.
[3] *Acts of the Privy Council* (New Series), vol. viii. p. 21.
[4] *Additions to the Monasticon*, vol. i. p. 289.

liberty." And they also wrote the same day to the archbishop empowering him to accept bail for Mr. Dr. Feckenham on the same conditions as those lately made (July 5th) in the case of bishop Watson. These were that he "shall not by speech, writing, or any other means induce or intice any person to any opinion or act to be done contrary to the laws established in the realm for causes of religion," and that he should dwell in a specified place, "and not to depart from thence at any time without the license of the lords of the council," and that he was not to be allowed to receive visitors.[1]

After fourteen years' confinement, Fecknam was now released on parole and went to live in Holborn, where, no sooner had he partly regained his liberty, than he was engaged in works of charity and usefulness. Benevolence was so marked a feature in his character that, as Fuller says, "he relieved the poor wheresoever he came, so that flies flock not thicker about spilt honey than the beggars constantly crowded about him."[2] Large sums of money seem to have been at his disposal, for the charitable were assured, from their knowledge of his character, that their alms entrusted to his care would reach the most needy and the most deserving of the poor. In Holborn he built an aqueduct for the use of the inhabitants.[3] He distributed every day the

[1] *Acts of the Privy Council* (New Series), 1574, vol. viii. pp. 269, 264.
[2] *Worthies of England*, vol. ii. p. 477.
[3] Stevens, vol. i. p. 28a.

milk of twelve cows among the sick and poor of the district, and took under his special charge the orphans. He encouraged the youth of the place in manly sports by giving prizes, and thought it better they should on Sundays have games, such as all English lads love, rather than attend the new fashion of worship.[1] Thus spending himself for others, and already broken down by the rigours of his long imprisonment, he fell ill. On July 18, 1575, the council ordered "the Master of the Rolls, or in his absence the Recorder of London, to take bondes of Doctor Feckenham for his good behaviour, and that at Michaelmas next he shall return to the place where he presently is, and in the meantime he may repair to the Baths."[2] Whilst in this town he built, in 1576, a hospice for the poor "by the White Bath," that they too might come and get the benefit of the waters.[3]

Whilst thus a prisoner on parole, reports had reached the ears of the Council (June 24, 1577) that Fecknam and the others "have very much abused themselves by suffering certain of her majesty's evil-disposed subjects to resort unto them, whom they have perverted in religion."[4] For Aylmer, the bishop of London, had lately written to Burghley signifying "that he liked not that Fecknam, late

[1] *Hymnus in Laudem J. Fecknamis*, Harl. MS. 3258, fol. 45.
[2] *Acts P.C.*, vol. ix. p. 8. On June 19, 1576, he got a similar license.
[3] See *Downside Review*, vol. xiv. p. 323.
[4] *Acts*, vol. ix. p. 371.

abbat of Westminster, Watson, late bishop of Lincoln, and Young, another active popish dignitary under queen Mary, should continue where they were, in London, in the Fleet or Marshalsea, where by their converse and advice they might instigate and do mischief; advising that they might be placed again, as they had been before, with some three bishops, at Winchester, Lincoln, Chichester, or Ely, and that for his part, he, if he were out of his first-fruits, could be content to have one of them."[1]

So in the following month Walsingham wrote to the bishops who had formerly been charged with these prisoners, saying that as inconvenience and mischief is daily found to increase, not only to the danger of her majesty's person but to the disturbance of the common quiet of the realm on account of the lenity shown to such as obstinately refused to come to church for sermons and common prayer, he appoints a consultation to be held which should be attended by the bishops and their chancellors and others they think fit. The secretary then goes on to say :—

"And fore-as-much as the special point of the said consultation will stand upon the order that may be taken generally with all them that refuse to come to the church, and in particular what is meetest to be done with Watson, Fecknam, Harpsfield, and others of that ring that are thought to be the leaders and pillars of the consciences of great

[1] Strype, *Life of Bishop Aylmer*, p. 25.

numbers of such as he carried with the errors, whether it be not fit they be disputed with, all in some private sort and after disputation had with them, and they thereby not reduced to conformity; then whether it shall be better to banish them the realm or to keep them here together in some straight sort as that they may be kept from all conference."[1]

The result of these consultations was soon made known, for by the end of July (1577) the council ordered Cox, the bishop of Ely, to receive abbat Fecknam, and divided the rest of the prisoners among other anglican bishops. The real cause of this second incarceration was that Elizabeth, at last driven to desperation, began to apply the penalty of death attached to the act of 1571, which was her answer to the deposing bull of Pius V. The act had not hitherto been enforced, although its provisions were such as made illegal any communication, under any shape or form, with Rome. But just then the seminary at Douai, about which more in the next chapters, was beginning to pour priests into England in defiance of her laws, and the first blood for conscience' sake was shed in this year by the heroic Cuthbert Mayne. The queen, rightly or

---

[1] *P.R.O. Dom Eliz.*, cxiv. 69. Walsingham also suggests that, if Fecknam and the others are to be kept in durance, the cost of their keep was to be found in taxing such of the bishops and clergy as are non-residents and have pluralities some yearly contribution for the finding of them, and a convenient stipend to be given to their keeper. See Bridgett and Knox, p. 178.

wrongly, was in terror of plots against her life; and the government had determined upon taking stringent measures, and keeping in custody the most prominent of those who were known to be disaffected to her religious policy. Together with the order of the council, the notorious Cox, bishop of Ely, received a stringent code of regulations for the treatment of the aged abbat—they were to this effect:—

"1. That his lodgings be in some convenient part of your house, that he may be both there in safe custody and also have no easy access of your household people unto him, other than such as you shall appoint and know to be settled in religion and honesty, as that they may not be perverted in religion or any otherwise corrupted by him.

"2. That he be not admitted unto your table except upon some good occasion, to have ministered to him there in the presence of some that shall happen to resort unto you, such talk whereby the hearers may be confirmed in the truth; but to have his diet by himself alone in his chamber; and that in no superfluity, but after the spare manner of scholars' commoners.

"3. That you suffer none (unless some one to attend upon him) to have access unto him, but such as you shall know to be persons well conformed in true religion, and not likely to be weakened in the profession of the said religion by any conference they shall have with him.

"4. That you permit him not at any time and place whilst he is with you to enter into any disputations of matters of religion, or to reason thereof, otherwise than upon such occasion as shall be by you or in your presence with your good liking by some others ministered unto him.

"5. That he have ministered unto him such books of learned men and sound writers in divinity as you are able to lend him, and none other.

"6. That he have no liberty to walk abroad to take the air, but when yourself is best at leisure to go with him, or accompanied with such as you shall appoint.

"7. That you do your endeavour by all good persuasion to bring him to the hearing of sermons and other exercises of religion in your house, and the chapel or church which you most commonly frequent."[1]

This disposes of the pleasing fiction some writers maintain, that the abbat and others of the deposed clergy were kept as guests under gentle restraint in the houses of protestant bishops. To be deprived of liberty, company, the solaces of their religion and all they held dear, was bad enough treatment; but to be harassed on religious topics on every conceivable occasion, to have to take the air, on the rare occasion permitted, tied to the strings of a protestant bishop's apron, and to have only such books of sound divinity as

[1] Lansdowne MS., No. 155, fol. 201.

the reformers delighted in, were unnecessary aggravations.

The bishop did his best to convert the abbat, for Elizabeth, it is said, ordered him to bring the abbat, "being a man of learning and temper, to acknowledge her supremacy and come to church." But Cox wrote to Burghley, August 1578, and gives this report of the abbat: "That he was a gentle person; but in popish religion too, too obdurate." And that he had often conference with him: and other learned men at his request had conferred with him also touching going to church, and touching the oath to the queen's majesty. The bishop added that he had examined him whether the pope was not a heretic . . . that when there was some hope of his conformity he (the abbat) said unto him, "All those things that he said against me with leisure I could answer them." And further said, "That he was fully persuaded in his religion, which he will stand to." "When I heard this," said the bishop, "I gave him over and received him no more to my table;" and in some zeal subjoining, "Whether it be meet that the enemies of God and the queen should be fostered in our homes and not used according to the laws of the realm, I leave to the judgement of others. What my poor judgement is I will express, being commanded. I think my house the worse being pestered with such a guest." . . . This letter the bishop dates from Ely, styling it "that unsavoury isle with turves and dried-up loads," the 29th of August 1578.[1]

The council on October 23, 1579, understanding that Fecknam had "lately broken out into an open discommending of her majesty's godly proceedings in matters of religion," required Cox "to cause him to be kept close prisoner in some fit room within his house, not suffering him to have any man of his own choice to attend upon him, and that such person as his lordship shall appoint of his own servants to resort unto him, to deliver him his necessary food (which their lordships wish to be no larger than may serve for his convenient sustenance)."[2]

A so-called "confession"[3] exists in the Lans-

[1] Strype's *Annals* (ed. 1824), vol. ii. Perne, the dean of Ely, had been set on to Fecknam some months before Cox wrote to Burghley, and in his turn writes on May 11, 1578, to the effect that the abbat had said of the Book of Common Prayer: "That as he liked well of prayers therein that were made to Almighty God in the name of His Son, Jesus Christ; so he would also have added the invocation of our blessed Lady and other saints and prayers for the dead" (*ibid.* pp. 176, 177, 186).

[2] *Acts of the Privy Council*, vol. xi. p. 291.

[3] Endorsed in Burghley's writing, "Feckehamis Confessio before the bishop of Ely and his Chaplaines. Papists 1580." Two years earlier Perne had written to Burghley that it was impossible to get Fecknam to sign this or a similar document. Burghley evidently wrote to Fecknam about this confession, for Strype reports the abbat as writing in answer words to the effect: "That he was persuaded of a singular good will (he said) both that her majesty and his honour bore unto him, if he should show himself anything conformable. That he thought verily that were it not for her majesty and his honour, it would have been worse for him and others of his sect than it was at that day; for the which he said, that he did daily pray for the long preservation of her majesty, and also for his lordship's honourable state. But yet to subscribe he did refuse; saying that if he should subscribe and fail in one thing, he had as good failed in all" (*ibid.* p. 180).

downe MSS.,[1] which shows the pertinacity of his jailors and his own constancy :—

> "A True Note of Certain Articles confessed and allowed by Mr. Dr. Fecknam, as well in Christmas holidays last past as also at divers other times before, by conference in learning before the reverend father in God the L. Bishop of Ely, and before Dr. Perne, Dean of Ely, Master Nickolas, Master Stanton, Master Crowe, Mr. Bowler, Chaplains to my L. of Ely; and divers others whose names be here subscribed.
>
> "*First*, he doth believe in his conscience and before God that the xiiii chapter of the first to the Corinthians is as truly to be understanded of the common service to be had in the mother tongue, to be understanded of the vulgar people as of the preaching and prophesying in the mother tongue.
>
> "*Secondly*, that he doth find no fault with anything that is set forth in the Book of Common Service now used in the Church of England, but his desire is to have all the rest of the old service that was taken out to be restored again, as the prayer to the saints and for the dead, and the seven sacraments and external sacrifice, and then he would most willingly come thereto. He liketh well to have the sacrament ministered under both kinds unto the lay people, so it were done by the authority of the Church.

[1] No. 30, fol. 199.

"*Thirdly*, he doth very well allow of the interpretation of the oath for the queen's majestie her supremacy as it is interpreted in her highness injunctions, that is that the queen's majestie under God have soveranty and rule over all manner of persons born within her realms, dominions, and countries, of what estate either ecclesiastical or temporal soever they be; the which oath he offereth himself to be at all times ready most willingly to receive whensoever it shall be demanded of him by authority.

"*Fourthly*, he being demanded why he will not come to the service in the Church of England as it is set forth this day, seeing he doth find no fault with it, and doth think it in his conscience that it may be lawful to have the common prayer in the mother tongue. He answereth, because he is not of our Church for lack of unity; some being therein protestants, some puritans, and some of the family of Love, and for that it is not set forth by the authority of general council to avoid *schisme*.

"*Lastly*, Mr. D. Fecknam will not conform himself to our religion, for that he can see nothing to be sought but the spoil of the Church and of bishops' houses and of college lands, which he saith maketh many to pretend to be puritans, seeking for the fruits of the church, and always requesting Almighty God to put in her majesty's mind and her honourable council to make some good stay therein, otherwise he saith it will bring in ignorance in her highness' clergy, with a subversion of Christian religion, and finally all wickedness and paganism.

(Signed) "JOHN FECKNAM, *Priest*.[1]

"Richard Ely.
Andreas Perne.
Gulihelmus Stanton."

How well the abbat knew the temper of the times. He would be willing to accept the Prayer-Book if it ceased to be protestant. As regards disciplinary laws he was free to hold his own opinion as to their utility, but he denied the Church of England was an authority with power to make such changes as had been made. He saw plainly the state of schism the established church was in, and that alone was proof to him that it was outside the unity of *his* church. He would not object to an oath expressed in the terms explained in the queen's injunction; but the oath that had actually to be tendered to him under the act of Parliament, he would not take at all on any understanding whatsoever as to its implied meaning. There is in this confession always a saving "but" to every approach to an agreement with the reformers, and it was just these exceptions that made the "Confession" useless to them.

In June 1580 Cox writes a piteous letter to Burghley.[2] He is ill and has paralysis, and cannot

[1] It is signed in a very feeble and shaky handwriting.
[2] "To take one view more of the ancient, pious, learned confessor and bishop Cox, which take from his own pen to his old friend, the lord Burley; complaining of two evils that now oppress him in his very

put up with the abbat any longer, and begs that he may be taken away. The truth is that the anglican bishops were worn out with the quiet but unconquerable constancy of men who entrenched themselves absolutely behind the invisible but all-powerful barriers of conscience. It was an open rebuke to them in the face of the whole kingdom; for not one of these had they succeeded in bringing over to the new religion. Parker, as we have seen, was only following the current when he was anxious to cut the difficulty by enforcing the oath, the refusal of which meant death. Jewel, too, had been hinting at the use of the sword in confidential intercourse with his friends, regretting that this means was not used upon these irreconcilables. And Aylmer had written in 1577 to the lord treasurer: "I speak to your lordship as one chiefly careful for the state, and to use more severity than hitherto hath been used; or else we shall smart for it."[1] The unholy blood-thirst, we cannot call it anything else, displayed by the new bishops excited the anger of Elizabeth. Bernadino

old age: one might have a redress by favour of that lord; the other only from God. Thus writing *Duo mala me premunt*, the one, *hospes malus et inutilis*; i.e. a bad guest and good for nothing. He meant Fecknam, sometime abbat of Westminster, that had been committed to his house and had remained there so long till he was weary of him. . . . The other inconvenience . . . *corpus nimirum dimidia parte languidum*, his poor paralytic body" (Strype, *Annals of the Reformation*, ed. 1824, vol. ii. Part II, p. 381).

[1] Strype, *Life of Bishop Aylmer*, p. 24. Cox, writing in 1578, says: "I trust hereafter her highness and her magistrates will prosecute severely the same trade" (*Annals*, p. 196).

de Mendoza, the Spanish ambassador, writing to his king, March 23, 1580, says: "This (the armament) has caused her recently to revoke the commission given to her bishops to ascertain who were catholics. She told them with her own mouth that they were a set of scamps, for they were oppressing the catholics more than she desired."[1]

As a consequence of Cox's appeal, at the end of the month (June 24) the council gave leave that Fecknam should be transferred from the bishop's immediate neighbourhood. So sometime in July the abbat was once more moved; this time to Wisbeach Castle, a disused and partly ruinous house belonging to the bishop of Ely. Here he met several of his old fellow-prisoners, bishop Watson among the others.

Wisbeach Castle was a dreary place. "During the winter the sea mists drifting landwards almost always hung over and hid the castle walls. Broad pools and patches of stagnant waters, green with rank weeds, and wide marshes and sterile flats lay outspread all round for miles. The muddy river was constantly overflowing its broken-down banks, so that the moat of the castle constantly flooded the adjacent garden and orchard. Of foliage, save a few stunted willow-trees, there was little or none in sight; for when summer came round, the sun's heat soon parched up the rank grass in the courtyard, and without, the dandelion and snapdragon

[1] *Calendar Spanish State Papers* (Simancas), vol. i. p. 22.

which grew upon its massive but dilapidated walls."[1]

Such was Wisbeach, a place which in a few years more was to gain so sad a notoriety as the theatre of dissensions which, it is no exaggeration to say, inflicted a blow upon Catholicity in England the effects of which are felt even to-day. But while the benedictine abbat was there, his gentle spirit sorted well with the fraternal charity which possessed the hearts of his fellow-confessors. There was no emulation, no prelature. Even Watson would not accept of any superiority on account of his episcopal dignity. They were all fellow-prisoners, he said, all equal.[2]

The life passed a few years later in this prison is described by Fr. Weston, the jesuit, in his account of his imprisonment.[3] The prisoners were kept in separate rooms under bolts and locks. Dinner and supper they had in common; and for half-an-hour before and after the meals they could take exercise in the open air. Wisbeach was then a public prison, common to all thieves and criminals. After the time of Fecknam the prisoners seem to have had more liberty, as we shall see in the next chapter. But when the abbat first came there the system was in all its rigour. There is a letter from the keepers of

[1] F. G. Lee, *The Church under Queen Elizabeth*, ed. 1892, p. 198. Among the state papers is a document of July 1579, as to the evil state of the river at the time. *P.R.O. Dom Eliz.*, vol. cxxxi., No. 48.

[2] Bridgett and Knox, p. 204.

[3] Morris' *The Troubles of our Catholic Forefathers*, second series, pp. 239, 240.

Wisbeach, George Carleton and Humphrey Michell, to the Privy Council (Oct 16, 1580),[1] in which they report the recusants as being eight in number. "The bishop of Ely has appointed a preacher, Dr. William Fulke, a puritan; but the prisoners refuse to attend his sermons or prayers, saying that they are not of our church, and they will neither hear, pray, nor yet confer with us of any matter concerning religion." The keepers mention that, according to instructions they had received, all books " saving the canonical scriptures and the allowed writers " have been taken away from the prisoners, to the great grief of their hearts. They end up by asking whether the permission of taking meals in common may be withdrawn.

This durance did not extinguish Fecknam's benevolence nor his desire of doing good all round. Here, at Wisbeach, he paid for the repairing of the road, and also erected a public market-cross in the town.[2] But the life of this venerable confessor was drawing to a close. Worn out with the rigours of an imprisonment of twenty-three years,[3] he died a

---

[1] Bridgett and Knox, p. 197.

[2] Stevens, p. 289. "And there was also a cross, probably dedicated to St. Peter, which was afterwards converted into an obelisk . . . [but was] taken down in the year 1810" (*History of Wisbeach* [1883], p. 258).

[3] In the poem before mentioned, the unknown author says:—

"Fama refert igitur quod dira venena dabantur;
Fecknamo; neque res suspicione caret."

He also mentions that the abbat was consoled before death with the

martyr for his faith in 1584, and on October 16 was buried in an unknown grave in the parish church of Wisbeach.

Abbat Fecknam, says Stevens, was of "a mean stature, somewhat fat, round-faced, beautiful and of a pleasant aspect, affable and lively in conversation."[1] Camden calls him a man learned and good, who lived a long time and gained the affection of his adversaries by publicly deserving well of the poor.[2] Bishop Kennet mentions as a trait in the abbat's character that he "left what he had to the church at Westminster, and gave the dean good directions about such lands leased out, which could not otherwise have been easily discovered, in letters which are still preserved among the records."[3]

To the last he never forgot Westminster, and, as was characteristic with him, the poor of Westminster. From the overseer's accounts of the parish of St. Margaret's is recorded, 1590: "Over and besides the sum of forty pounds given by John Fecknam, sometime abbat of Westminster, for a stock to buy wood for the poor of Westminster, and to sell two faggots for a penny, and seven billets for a penny, which sum of forty pounds doth remain

Holy Viaticum, and said when the Blessed Sacrament was brought to him:—
"Tu bona cuncta mihi tecum sapienter portas
Tu letitia es, tu mihi vita, salus."

[1] Ibid.
[2] Annales Rerum Anglicarum, ed. Hearne, vol. i. p. 48.
[3] Lansdowne MS., No. 982, fol. 62.

in the hands of the church-wardens."[1] He also left a bequest to the poor of his first monastic home of Evesham.[2]

According to Anthony à Wood, Fecknam, with the benedictine instinctive love for the Office, wrote a commentary on the Psalms of David, and also one on the Canticles. Among the Sloane MSS. is an autograph work of about 400 pages bearing the following heading:—

"This booke of sovereigne medicines against the most common and knowne diseases both of men and women was by good proofe and long experiences collected by Mr. Dr. Fecknam, late abbat of Westminster, and that chiefly for the poor, which hath not att all tymes the learned phisitions att hande."[3]

Thus in the odour of sanctity lived and died John Fecknam, the last abbat of the monastery of St. Peter's at Westminster. A true monk and a staunch witness for the faith of Christ.[4]

---

[1] These accounts have been privately printed. Westminster, 1877. See also Malcolm's *Londinium Redivivum*, vol. iv. pp. 139, 140.
[2] May's *History of Evesham*, p. 398.
[3] Add. MSS., No. 3919.
[4] Among bishop Kennet's collection in the Lansdowne MSS. (No. 982) are some notes in addition to Anthony à Wood's notice of Fecknam. From them we gather that in 1556 Fecknam resigned the deanery of St. Paul's in the January; the living of Kentish Town was voided November 22, and that of Greenford Magna December 7, "*per religionis ingressum magistri Johis Fecknham cleric. in mon. S. Petri Westmon. noviter erecti*" (from Bonner's Register). Among the pensions recorded in the year 1555 *Com. Wigorn. Evesham. Pensio Johi Fecknham, Decani D. Pauli,* × *libr.*

CHAPTER X

THE STATE OF ENGLISH CATHOLICS, 1559–1601

THE immediate effect of tendering the oath of supremacy was the deprivation of all the bishops, 15 in number, with the exception of Kitchin of Llandaff. They were followed by 7 deans, 10 archdeacons, 7 chancellors, 25 heads of colleges, 37 fellows, 35 prebendaries, 44 doctors and professors, 17 heads of schools or religious houses, 197 dignitaries and men of weight.[1] This by no means completes the list of deprivations. The number of parochial clergy that were either gradually deprived or gave up of their own accord is numbered by competent judges as something like 2000.[2] It is only by some great exodus like this that the great dearth of clergy, of which the new Elizabethan

---

[1] See a list (avowedly incomplete) printed in Tierney, vol. ii., Appendix.

[2] "In the visitation of the province of York in August and September 1559, out of 90 clergymen summoned, 21 came and took the oath, 36 came and refused to swear, 17 were absent without proctors, 16 were absent with proctors. . . . In the province of Canterbury . . . out of the 8911 parishes and 9400 beneficed clergymen, we find only 806 subscribers, while all the bishops and 85 others expressly refused to subscribe, and the rest were absentees.' See R. Simpson's *Campion*, ed. 1896, p. 197.

bishops were constantly complaining, can be accounted for. Of those who remained in outward union with the Anglican Church there were great numbers we know who kept to their livings in the hopes of another change, looking forward "to a time," as it was said. They had already seen so many variations within the last twenty years, why not keep quiet and wait for better days? So many argued, and would, at least in country parts, say mass privately for those of their parishioners who were of their mind, and then would perform the new rite publicly in the parish church to fulfil the law. Most of these, by thus tampering with their consciences, at last fell away entirely. But of that large body of clergy known as the "Old Priests," or the "Marian Priests," some few retired for a while to the universities and thence went abroad to Rome, Louvain, Douai, Paris, &c. Others were received into private families, where they acted as chaplains and attended in secret the catholics who would not admit the ministrations of the new clergy. They were not molested as a rule, for many of those who kept to their livings were friends and secretly admired their constancy.

This, then, was the state of the Church in England in a few years after Elizabeth's accession. The bishops were in prison, and a large body of clergy was scattered here and there and left without head or organisation. The sacrament of confirmation ceased; and it became difficult even to get the

THE STATE OF ENGLISH CATHOLICS

holy oils for extreme unction. These had to be smuggled over from Ireland or the continent. Sometimes, at rare intervals, an Irish bishop would come over in secret and try to supply the more pressing wants of the district he visited. But practically Elizabeth had achieved her end. She wanted to crush all opposition and deprive of place, power, and influence those who would not allow of her religious policy.

The desperate state of the church was brought under the notice of the Roman authorities, and steps were proposed (which, alas! came to nought) to apply a remedy. Among the letters of cardinal Morone *de rebus angliæ* (written between July 1560 and September 1563) is a proposal for a new arrangement of the English sees.[1] Heath was to be translated from York to Canterbury, Watson from Lincoln to York, and Scott from Chester to Durham. The others were to retain their sees; and names were proposed for filling up the vacant ones. There was no idea of submitting quietly to the intruders, and thus tacitly admitting their claim. Had this policy prevailed in England as it did in Ireland, we to-day should have been in possession of our old historical hierarchy.

What hindered the project has not yet fully appeared. But it can be sufficiently accounted for. Twice did the pope (Pius IV.) send ambassadors to

---

[1] *Episcopal Successions* (M. Brady), vol. ii. p. 322. This must have been written before it was known that Heath and the others were imprisoned.

the queen assuring her he would give every satisfaction. But the envoys were refused admittance into the kingdom.[1] When this conciliatory pontiff died, he was succeeded (1566) by a pope of very different policy. Pius V., a dominican friar, of stern and inflexible ideas, was determined to crush the queen by the censure of the church, and to impose by force of arms the recognition of a temporal headship, which an united Christendom had, of free will, given to his predecessors. Had the *Curia* recognised that the political world was indeed moving, the history of the church in England would have been very different. But easy enough as it is for us to see the errors of a past time, it was not so easy for those then at the helm to divine the trend of affairs. A pope is necessarily influenced by his *entourage;* and the temporal policy of one pope will not necessarily be that of his predecessors. The government of the church is vested in human hands, which are moved by human hearts swayed by every manner of human motives.[2]

[1] May 5, 1560, the pope wrote to Elizabeth asking her to receive Vincent Parpaglia, abbat of St. Saviour's, as *persona grata* to the queen. But he was stopped at Calais. The pope renewed his attempt the next year, and sent abbat Martinengo, who got as far as Brussels, and there received notice that he too was refused admittance into the kingdom. As neither was allowed to fulfil his embassy, it is not possible to say, with the means at present at our disposal, what were the terms of the papal message. Any reports as to the pope's willingness to accept the changes introduced by the queen, are mere valueless conjectures.

[2] In a letter of Bernardo Navagero, Venetian ambassador at Rome, to the doge and senate (March 14, 1556), he says: " Yesterday I had audience of the pope, who said to me . . . 'It is a miracle, lord ambassador, how this holy see has maintained itself, preceding pontiffs having,

But Providence, while leaving men to work out their own measures and to take the consequences of their own acts, overrules all for its own predestined end.

We shall be better able to understand the action of Pius V. in regard to Elizabeth, if we remember that he was brought up and was surrounded by men imbued with a tradition of universal sovereignty even in temporal matters. It was one of long standing. What was more natural, when Christendom was united by the bonds of one faith, than to look up to the pope as to the common father and head of all kingdoms; as the arbitrator in all disputes, between king and king and also between king and subjects? But that which was the free concession of a loving flock, in course of time became to be regarded by some as a divine right. It was held and publicly taught by many that the pope had, by a right inherent in his pastoral office, the power of deposing monarchs and of releasing subjects from their allegiance — even more, of transferring their allegiance to whomsoever he pleased to give the forfeited crown. The church of course was not committed to this doctrine; but it formed in those days a very important element in practical teaching and in the run of men's thoughts; just as in the thoughts of other people who abhorred the pope it was held that there was a divine or a natural right

---

one may say, done everything to destroy it; but it is founded on such stones that there is nothing to fear" (*Calendar of State Papers* (Venetian), vol. vi. No. 425).

in temporal princes to dictate the religion of their subjects according to the formula *cujus regio ejus religio*. The Curia saw England slipping away; that England which, if of late the cause of much trouble, was yet "a very garden of delights." Fears were entertained that other nations, too, would follow in her wake. So an example must be made of the English queen. A judicial inquiry into her case was begun in Rome and resulted in a declaration that she had incurred all the canonical penalties of heresy. A bull *Regnans in Excelsis* was issued on February 25, 1570, which denounced her as excommunicated. But when it goes on to declare her deprived of her "pretended" right to the crown, and to absolve all her subjects from their allegiance, and moreover to proclaim excommunicated all who henceforth presumed to obey her laws or acknowledge her as queen, there was an assertion here of a temporal right which could only result in deadly resistance.

The effects were disastrous. The queen was driven to desperation. Against the determination of the man was pitted the obstinacy of an infuriated and unscrupulous woman. Though she affected to treat the sentence of deprivation with contempt, yet she knew not what complications might ensue. The excommunication, of which she knew the spiritual force, wounded her also to the quick, and she endeavoured to get the stigma removed. The pope was inflexible. The bull was received with dismay by the English catholics, who could only fear from it a fresh excuse for ill treatment. While they were proving their loyalty as no other nation has ever done to the pope's divine right, the verities of the catholic religion, they felt it hard indeed to be called upon to be implicated in temporal matters, based as they were upon grounds which, even in catholic kingdoms, were held at least to be questionable. The English catholics were thus ground down between the upper and the nether millstones.

The queen's answer to the bull was an act of Parliament cutting off all communication between her subjects and Rome, and declaring traitors all who denied her title. Another made it treason to use or procure any bull from Rome, or to reconcile or be reconciled, to have in possession any objects blessed by the pope, or even to maintain or harbour any offenders against the act. The pope, on his side, was determined to enforce his bull, and called upon Christian kings to invade England. To this period belong the many plots, real or feigned, with which the queen was threatened.[1] In after years the

[1] That there were real plots on the part of some catholics against the queen cannot to-day be denied; nor that churchmen were unfortunately mixed up in them. On May 2, 1583, the papal nuncio writes from Paris to the cardinal of Como: "The duke of Guise and duke of Mayenne have told me that they have a plan for killing the queen of England by the hand of a catholic, though not one outwardly, who is near her person, and is ill affected towards her for having put to death some of his catholic relations. This man, it seems, sent word to the queen of Scotland, but she refused to attend to it. . . . The duke asks for no assistance from our lord [the pope] in the affair. . . . As to putting to death that wicked woman, I said to him, that I will not

Armada appeared (doubtlessly rather than was) the result of the pope's appeal. The immediate effect of the bull was to widen the breach between England and the holy see. It was the devoted English catholics who felt all the weight of the papal bull, and saw with dismay a still trembling scale sent down with a violent impetus in a direction contrary to catholicity. During this time of open rupture the one thought that was uppermost at Rome seems to have been to crush the queen.

There was now no more talk of sending over bishops, and the flock was left to itself. Meanwhile "the old priests" were either leaving the country or were dying out. It was an Englishman who first came to the rescue of the unhappy catholics in England by starting the seminary at Douai in Flanders to provide priests for the English mission. William Allen, an exile himself, in 1568 invited some of the Oxford and Cambridge men scattered over France and Flanders to unite with him in forming a small establishment at Douai. Several came at his call, and a house was bought. The benedictine abbats of the neighbouring monasteries of Arras (St. Vedast), Marchienne, and Anchin, contributed generously to the undertaking, and

write about it to our lord pope (nor do I), nor tell your most illustrious lordship to inform him of it; because, though I believe our lord the pope would be glad that God should punish in any way whatsoever that enemy of His, still it would be unfitting that His vicar should procure it by these means" (Knox's *Historical Introduction to Letters and Memorials of William, Cardinal Allen*, pp. 46, 47).

helped to support the great number who flocked in as soon as the doors were opened. Soon there were 150 persons gathered at Douai under the presidency of Allen. But he had no fixed means of support for his new college. Pius V. had indeed applauded his work and encouraged him to go on: but it was not until 1575, in the third year of Gregory XIII., that any substantial help came from the holy see. In that year Allen determined to go to Rome to beg for assistance; and the good abbats gave him strong letters of recommendation, in which the university of Douai joined. His journey was successful: and the pope, it is said at the special entreaty of Mercurianus, the general of the jesuits, gave the college a moderate yearly allowance. The king of Spain, to whose dominion Douai then belonged, also gave them an annual pension.

A few years after, at the instigation of Owen Lewis, afterwards bishop of Cassano, the pope about 1578 opened, near St. Peter's, a similar college in Rome, and placed it under the charge of Dr. Maurice Clenock, then warden of the old English hospital. In 1579 the two institutions were united. Two Italian jesuit fathers were employed; one as procurator, the other as prefect, to help on the new establishment. But after a year a rebellion broke out among the students. A strong party began to clamour for the expulsion of the president, and the introduction of jesuits as superiors. Without going into the reasons which led up to this *émeute*, it will be sufficient to state that Dr. Maurice Clenock was removed; and the direction of the college successfully passed into the hands of the society under the headship of Fr. Alphonso Agazzari.

We now come to consider a painful page in our history, a page which is however fraught with deep lessons. It was a bitter experience. We should have been tempted to pass it by; but, as Fr. John Morris, S.J., says—

"At this distance of time, and after this happy lull in the controversy, we can afford to look at the whole dispute with greater impartiality, and not feel it necessary to say that all that was done on one side was right, and all that was done on the other was wrong."[1]

Moreover, we think more harm than good is done by catholic writers who entirely pass over the matter, for the story is known outside the church. Surely it is wisdom to see that mistakes, and grave mistakes, too, have been made by good, zealous people. We profit by their failings. We also get a wider and truer view of life and history by looking these questions full in the face; and by ever remembering that men are men, and that human nature has to be taken into account in all things and at all times. Moreover, unless the real case in point be stated, history becomes unintelligible. And the lessons, which Providence has allowed, must be for our benefit, if we know how to use them: for Truth is

[1] See *Dublin Review*, April 1890, p. 255.

THE STATE OF ENGLISH CATHOLICS 233

always edifying in the true sense of the word. It is therefore necessary to sketch the events which lead up to the troubles and their subsequent history. We have no case to plead, but only a plain story to tell. And in the telling we shall follow the method Lingard professes in the preamble to his history—

"To admit no statement on trust; to weigh with care the value of the authorities on which I rely; and to watch with jealousy the secret workings of my own personal feelings and prepossessions."[1]

At the very time Henry VIII. was engaged in his nefarious work of suppressing the monasteries, St. Ignatius Loyola, a Spaniard, was engaged in laying the foundation of his society. In 1537 he went, with five companions, before Paul III. for his blessing. The pope, three years after, gave his solemn approval of the new institute. Its members were at first restricted to sixty in number; but such was their startling success, that, by 1608 the new men were already possessed of 293 colleges, 123 houses, and formed an army of 10,581 devoted men.[2] Started at a desperate emergency, they flung themselves into the breach, and changed a threatened disaster into victory. They took possession, so to say, of the catholic world. Universities, colleges, pulpits, and confessionals were peopled with the new religious.

[1] Preliminary notice to the *History of England*, ed. 1849, p. xxi.
[2] See also Ribadeneira's *The Life of B. Father Ignatius*, ed. 1616, pp. 327, 328.

The fame of the great St. Francis Xavier, one of Ignatius' first companions, cast a glory upon them as missioners. In every department of learning, their men were acknowledged masters; and the number of their admirers was enormous. They were, of set purpose, the apostles of the rich and influential. And this, besides giving them the disposal of boundless wealth, also initiated them into the secrets of courts, and made of them, whether they sought for it or not, a power to be reckoned with in the state. Their device, "*All to the greater glory of God,*" if it was the secret of their brilliant success, was also undoubtedly the cause of many difficulties. Some, who had not gained by their religious training that width of mind which makes the perfect religious, came to accept their own society as the one hope for the regeneration of a fallen world; and their sole and solitary aim, the object of their lives, the end of each day's occupation, being the promotion of what they conceived to be the greater glory of God, this, they concluded, could not but be promoted by the advancement of their society. Taking a broad view of their action, this really seems to have been with them a practical, though perhaps not a reasoned conviction. Unfortunately it was so in some of the more prominent of those who had secured the direction of English affairs. This, it seems, is a position warranted by facts, and is the only key to the situation.

But looking at the matter calmly, is it any wonder if it were so? Success so complete, so sudden, so well-deserved and so brilliant, as that which befell the jesuits, is rarely given to any body of men. Was it, then, we say, any wonder that some might have become intoxicated therewith, and carried away to the point of making a means an end? They certainly had no warrant in their rule for their conduct; and one cannot help feeling that their superiors, in not checking the dabblers in politics, secular and spiritual, brought on in later years a heavy retribution.

It was at this time, when the fame of the society was at its height, that, in reply to Allen's repeated request, the general of the jesuits promised to send some of his English subjects to help in the mission field which had already become one of death.[1] In the spring of 1580 the first two jesuit missioners set out for England, and arrived in the June following. The two were Robert Parsons[2] and Edmund Campion. As these two were typical of the currents

[1] When Pole was restoring the church in England, the jesuits suggested to him "that whereas the queen was restoring the goods of the church that were in her hands, there was but little purpose to raise up the old foundations; for the benedictine order was become rather a clog than a help to the church: they therefore desired that those houses should be assigned to them for maintaining schools and seminaries which they should set on quickly," &c. (Burnett, *History of the Reformation*, ed. Oxford, 1865, vol. ii. p. 526. Taken from a Venetian manuscript.) St. Ignatius wrote a beautiful letter to Pole, January 24, 1555, speaking of the desire he had of saving souls in this realm. See *Epist. Card. Poli.*, vol. v. p. 117; and More's *Historia Provinciæ Anglicanæ S.J.*, p. 11.

[2] Robert Persons or Parsons was born at Nether Stowey, near Bridgewater, in Somerset, in the year 1546. He received his education from the vicar of the parish, who sent him to Oxford in 1564. Two years

which then began to flow from the society we must sketch their characters, and do not believe we can do better than by quoting the masterly analysis given by the late Mr. R. Simpson in his *Life of Campion*. He says the protestants describe Parsons as the "lurking wolf," and Campion as "the wandering vagrant." And goes on—

"There was more truth in this colouring than in the subsequent notion which Camden promulgated, that Parsons was a violent and fierce-natured man, while Campion was of a sweet disposition and good breeding; the first seditious, turbulent, and confident; the other modest in all things except his challenge.[1]

"Campion, it seems to me, was the quick-tempered man, open, free, generous, hot, enthusiastic yet withal modest, gentle, and fair. Parsons more slow, subtle, cool, calculating, and capable of ex-

---

later he entered Balliol College. He took his degree of M.A. in 1572, and became fellow of his college and then bursar and dean. He was also a noted tutor. He went abroad intending to become a physician; but falling in with a jesuit he became a catholic, and joined their order July 4, 1575. He was made rector of the English college in Rome 1587, and again after his return from Spain. He died April 15, 1610. He was of middle size, swarthy complexion, strong featured, and of somewhat forbidding appearance. But he was agreeable in manners and had powers of conversation. His friends claim that his mind was penetrating, his judgment solid and well regulated, and that he was calm in consultation and patient under disappointments. He was a great reader, and a master of an emphatic style of controversy.

[1] This refers to a challenge Campion wrote offering to dispute with any one a certain number of priests. The paper was committed to the care of a friend, to be produced only under certain circumstances. But it was prematurely published.

hibiting either violence or modesty as the occasion seemed to demand. If Campion had the wisdom, Parsons had the prudence. The first knew how to move, the other to guide; one, if I may use offensive terms without offence, had the gifts which make an agitator; and the other those that make a conspirator. The rules of the jesuits, as I have shown above, linked together characters thus dissimilar in order that united they might act with more force and more completeness. And this would have been the case if their function had been all in common; but though the men were linked together they had separate work to perform. As their instructions directed them to use the lay members of the confraternity to prepare the preliminaries of conversion and then themselves to finish the work, so in this work of finishing there were different grades; for it is one thing to be a thorough catholic, and it is something beyond to take part in the pope's intentions and desires, and to devote oneself to their furtherance and fulfilment.[1] The instructions sufficient to make a man a catholic are not sufficient to make him an ultramontane. Campion thought that all was done when he had reconciled his convert to the catholic church, and taught him the faith and made him partaker of the sacraments. Parsons looked further; he desired and laboured for the conversion of England, and he thought nothing

[1] Mr. Simpson is to be understood, of course, as referring to the papal secular policy.

could effect this but the overthrow of Elizabeth; therefore his aim was the organisation of a party on which he could rely when the pope gave the signal for the attack. But there was no reason for him to blab of this design. The seed sown would, he thought, grow all the stronger for not being prematurely forced. It thus happened that there was not always perfect community between the jesuit missionaries; a polarity began to declare itself, as it afterwards did in the society at large, sending off those like Campion to fight under the banner of St. Francis Xavier against heathenism, whilst it retained those like Parsons in Europe to direct the consciences of princes, and to influence the councils of state."[1]

When they arrived in England,[2] there were already here some four-score seminary priests who had been trained either in Rome or Douai, besides a number of the old Marian clergy. These latter knew but too well the position of the country; they had acquired that knowledge in a bitter school. The enthusiasm of youth was passed; and they were contented for the most part, perhaps, at this time of day, too well contented, to regard things as they were, not as they would have wished them to be. Hence they looked rather askance at the new ways

---

[1] R. Simpson, *Edmund Campion* (1896), pp. 275, 276.
[2] Parsons landed at Dover on June 11, 1580, disguised "in a captain's uniform of buff trimmed with gold lace, with hat and feathers to match." Campion followed on the 25th, and passed himself off as a merchant of jewels. The disguises were characteristic of the men.

THE STATE OF ENGLISH CATHOLICS 239

and new ideas of these men who were flocking into England from the seminaries; and above all upon the jesuits, who from their very founder were devoted to the Spanish policy. It was feared, moreover, that these two men would introduce a political influence under the guise of religion. How well in this the "old priests" forecasted the event, history tells.

When Parsons and Campion arrived in London, July 1580, they were met by certain representatives of the secular clergy who told them plainly their fears. Parsons assured them they had no political object in view; that they came only "to treat of religion in truth and simplicity, and to attend to the gaining of souls without any pretence or knowledge of matters of state."[1] The general had given them special instructions, and directly forbidden them even to discuss such matters. Parsons told them this, and said—

"Not that we would have meddled in these matters if it had not been forbidden us; but we wish that by making public the general's charge we may prevent all who are informed of it from starting such discourses in future."[2]

[1] *Edmund Campion*, p. 183.
[2] "Those instructions, says Fr. Morris, S.J., were intended to be strictly secret, and they were not kept secret. They were meant to be obeyed, and Father Parsons at first, and blessed Edmund Campion to the end of his short career, obeyed them. It would have been good for religion if Fr. Parsons had continued to obey them, and his superiors to enforce them. But for a time he was busily engaged in Spain acting in the very teeth of them" (*Dublin Review*, April 1890, p. 251).

The fears of the secular clergy were allayed and the jesuits made very welcome as helpers in the mission field. But soon Parsons threw obedience to the winds and began political intrigues. He could not resist it. His mind was filled with the vision of the regaining of England by force of arms, and he felt he must prepare the way for that. The Armada was talked about abroad as a certainty;[1] the ground must be prepared here. With all the energy of his impetuous nature he adopted, solely, we think, from the conviction that he was thereby advancing God's greater glory, the dangerous rôle of a conspirator in the hope of helping on the restoration of England to the holy see or of dying a martyr in the cause. But he had misjudged his means. Within a year Campion, the brave and chivalrous missioner, was the martyr. And Parsons fled away, in prudence

[1] It is instructive to find Parsons, while engaged in the tangles of politics, being himself duped by those he served. Philip II. wrote thus on February 11, 1587, to Count Olivares: "You will maintain Allen and Robert (Parsons) in faith and hopefulness that the recovery of their country will really be attempted in order that they may the more zealously and earnestly employ the good offices which may be expedient with the pope; but let it be in such a way that they do not think the affair is so near at hand as that it will make them expansive in communicating it to others of their nation for their comfort and consolation, and so cause it to become public, for this is the way in which during these past years many things which were well begun for the benefit of that kingdom have come to nought. Go on, then, counterbalancing and drawing profit from them; and in everything do as you are accustomed with just prudence and dexterity according to what the affair requires; and I confide it to you, and you will inform me of what is done." See Knox's Introduction to *Letters and Memorials of William, Cardinal Allen*, p. lxxxvi.

it has been called, to the continent, never again to put his neck in jeopardy on English soil.

Father Parsons could never more resist the attraction of politics. His life henceforth was devoted to intrigue. Restless and untiring, he wandered up and down the continent exerting directly or indirectly, for the one end in view, all his vast powers of organisation and leadership. He obtained the foundation of seminaries for secular priests, which he placed under the direction of the fathers of the society, at Valladolid (1589), Lisbon, and Seville (1592); and also founded a college for lay youths at St. Omers (1594). With his influence at the Spanish court, whose interests he was always labouring to advance, he got pensions for these houses. He collected alms from the nobility for the same purpose, and also for helping the English exiles. This command over money gave him great power and influence with his countrymen abroad; and his words came to be looked upon as so many oracles. He wrote treatises, political and spiritual; he was the adviser upon English affairs at Rome, especially after the death of cardinal Allen (1594); and in fact his opinion seemed to be at one time all powerful. Everything was done through him and according to his views. It is extraordinary to think of the wonderful influence one man could exert over superiors, and that he, a religious, not a statesman, should as irresponsible be allowed to hold the threads of a hundred affairs in his own hands.

What were the results as we see them? His intrigues were failures; the monopoly he laboured at such cost to create was destroyed; and he did more than any other man to create an ill feeling among Englishmen towards his order. Blackwell, who afterwards became the first arch-priest, lamented his coming into England, saying:—

"The President of Rheims[1] played a very indiscreet part to send him hither, as being an unfit man to be employed in the cause of religions."[2] His political ventures, and the way in which he proposed first one and then another as successor to the English throne, could not but excite the amusement of the Romans. Pasquino tells Marforio, "If there will be any man that will buy the kingdom of England let him repair to a merchant in a black square cap in the city, and he shall have a very good pennyworth thereof." It was well enough for the Romans to laugh at Parsons' schemes and projections. But in England our forefathers had to suffer for them.

His plan, which seems to have developed into a fixed and orderly purpose, was that his society should have the glory of regaining England to the faith. He, without doubt, honestly believed that

---

[1] Allen had been obliged to remove his college from Douai in 1578 to Rheims, on account of reports adverse to his loyalty to Spain, which were found afterwards to have been spread by the emissaries of queen Elizabeth. The college remained at Rheims till 1599, when it returned to Douai.

[2] *A Sparing Discoverie*, by W. W., 1601, p. 45. Dr. Ely, in his *Certaine Briefe Notes*, mentions the same opinion of Blackwell.

the jesuits could do so, and also that they alone could do so. For that end, accordingly, he was convinced that they must have full control over all ecclesiastical affairs in this country. He impressed this upon his men, and there were some who openly avowed it. More does not hesitate to write :—

"Perhaps even these missions might with greater propriety and greater convenience (let not the expression offend) be entrusted to members of our society than to other men."[1]

Parsons, in the plan he drew up for the reorganisation of the English Church which was hoped for upon the success of the Armada, takes measures to exclude from England all who would interfere with the monopoly he was so carefully planning for the greater glory of God as he understood it. The benedictines, it was true, were the old apostles of England; the jesuits, under his guidance, should now have the glory of recovering the land to the Faith.[2] When in 1596-7 the students of the English secular college at Rome were petitioning the pope to remove the jesuits from the control over the house, he hurried to the Eternal City and "undertook to oppose the prayer and to assign the reasons for its rejection. The society, he assured the pontiff, was essential to the existence of religion

[1] *Historia Provinciæ Anglicanæ Societatis Jesu collectore Henrico Moro* (1660), p. 152.
[2] See *Memorial for the Reformation of England*, by R. P., 1596, Part I. chaps. vi., viii.

in the country. To the laity its members were necessary, to counsel, to strengthen, and to protect them; to the clergy to support, to correct, and to restrain them. Already the latter, by their vices and their apostacy, had become objects of aversion[1] or of distrust to the catholics. Were the fathers to be removed, the people would be left without advisers, the clergy without guides; the salt would be taken from the earth, and the sun would be blotted from the hearers of the English Church."[2]

With such assumptions it was not likely that peace could long be kept in England, where we must now return to the coming of the jesuit missionaries in 1580. The great question which was agitating the consciences of catholics, was how far the excommunication of Pius V. bound them. Left to themselves, a certain sense of most told them not at all; but some were scrupulous about it. Parsons and Campion brought with them some instructions from the pope (Gregory XIII.) on the subject. Catholics were to be told "that

[1] Father J. Morris, S.J., thus writes about Parsons' abusive language: "It is to be profoundly regretted that Father Parsons should have allowed himself to make such terrible accusations against the personal character of his opponents. . . . Still, considering all that can be alleged in excuse, the language used by him is, if I may be allowed to judge so great a man, absolutely indefensible. It seems to have been impolitic likewise. . . . But on this point of hard, uncharitable language I for one cannot be the defender of Father Parsons, and indeed I look upon it with the deepest regret and concern" (*Dublin Review*, April 1890, p. 253).

[2] Tierney's edition of Dodds' *History of the Church in England*, vol. iii. p. 45, *note*.

the bull of Pius Quintus should always oblige the queen and heretics, and should by no means bind catholics as matters stood; but thereafter bind them when some public execution might be had on the matter." In other words, according to this theory, catholics were to be loyal as long as they could not help it. The knowledge of this instruction goes far to discount the professions of loyalty so many of them made then and afterwards.[1]

When Campion was taken and Parsons fled, there were in England but two more jesuits, Frs. Holt and Haywood, who came over in the summer of 1581. Fr. Haywood was taken prisoner, and Fr. Holt went to Scotland on a political mission. Soon two others came; but a long time the jesuits were only a handful. Fr. Gerard says:—

"On my arrival in London (1588), by the help of certain catholics I discovered Fr. Henry Garnet, who was then superior. Besides him, the only ones of our society then in England were Fr. Edmund Weston, confined in Wisbeach, Fr. Robert Southwell, and we two new comers"[2] (Frs. Oldcorne and

---

[1] Father Gerard in his autobiography speaks of his examination at the Guildhall, and says: "They asked me then whether I acknowledged the queen as the true governor and queen of England. I answered: 'I do acknowledge her as such.' 'What,' said Topcliffe, 'in spite of Pius V.'s excommunication?' I answered: 'I acknowledge her as our queen notwithstanding I know there is such excommunication.' The fact was, I knew that the operation of that excommunication had been suspended for all England by a declaration of the Pontiff till such time as its execution became possible" (*Quarterly Series*, p. 118). [2] *Ibid.* p. 21.

Gerard). Three years after the jesuits only numbered nine or ten. But they were a united, determined body with a superior of their own, and thus were able to work in unison. The secular clergy, on the other hand, were still left without bishops or superior.

Before the arrival of Fr. Gerard, however, the troubles had begun. And they came about in this way. At Wisbeach Castle in the year 1587 were confined thirty-three prisoners for conscience' sake, many of whom were old priests of tried virtue and learning, and among whom was an old monk of Westminster, D. Sigebert Buckley. The others were seminarists either from Rome or Douai, many of whom, be it remembered, were educated, directly or indirectly, under the influence of the society.[1] Fr. Weston, the Jesuit, was one of the prisoners. He was not content with letting things be as he found them. It seemed to him that it would be highly advantageous if the prisoners were reduced to the regularity of the life to which he had been accustomed.

[1] To understand the situation we will quote from Tierney's remarks: "Originally introduced as the assistants, the jesuits, with the advantage of a resident superior, had gradually become the most influential members of the English mission. They possessed more extensive faculties than the clergy. They were attached to the principal families, were consulted by the catholics in their principal difficulties, and were the medium through which the funds for the maintenance of the clergy and the poor were chiefly administered. The younger missioners, educated in the colleges of the fathers, and still looking to them for support, naturally placed themselves under their guidance. The elder clergy, on the other hand, superseded in their authority and deprived in great measure of their influence, regarded the members of the society in the light of rivals. . . . Human nature on both sides yielded to the impulse (vol. iii. p. 43, *note*).

His first step was to get his confessor, a secular priest, elected as superior of the prisoners. This plan was negatived. Other proposals of a like nature were made; but were invariably rejected. This went on for seven years; until at last Weston, having arranged the plan with his adherents, suddenly withdrew from the common table. His absence being remarked, he was questioned as to the reason, and promptly declared that unless his companions submitted to a regular mode of life, his conscience would not allow him any more to join their society. He had a following of nineteen, one of whom was a jesuit lay-brother. It is not necessary here to follow the details of a story on which at present we can only look back with shame and humiliation. The scandal went on for months, and its effects were felt far beyond the prison walls. Remote as was the stage on which this unhappy drama was enacted, and petty as were the actors, the stir such schisms created in fact, was natural. For it was inevitably felt that here first came into evidence the forces which had been long, though secretly, in conflict; and, nay, in this quarrel, obscure and sordid in some aspects, principles were, in the last resort, involved which were of the widest range and of the deepest import to both church and state. The suffering English catholics were now divided into two factions: those who through thick and thin favoured the jesuits, or in other words Parsons' schemes; and those who opposed them just as vehemently. Many attempts were made during nine months by some of the most reverend of the "old clergy" to heal the breach at Wisbeach. After many efforts difficulties were overcome, a new code of rules was drawn up, and on November 6, 1597, the two parties met again at the common table.

It was a fallacious peace, however; for already steps were being taken by Fr. Parsons in Rome to complete the subjugation of the secular clergy. These latter, feeling the want of some head, were beginning to take steps towards forming themselves into an association for mutual help.[1] This alarmed the jesuits. The necessity of some form of government was apparent, but Parsons now knew that the revival of government by bishops would be fatal to his schemes in regard to the clergy, and would interfere with his political views. And, upon Allen's death (1594), Parsons, having got into his place, was practically the sole director of English ecclesiastical affairs.

Attempts after the Armada had been made to get the succession of bishops kept up; but hitherto without avail. Several petitions went up for at least an episcopal superior to rule and confirm the stricken flock. Parsons at one time (1580), when

---

[1] See Colleton's *Just Defence*, pp. 123-5. In the preface to the rules, they declared, "for our parts, we wish and intend no other thing hereby, but God's honour, the furtherance of His church's cause, with perfect unity and concord amongst ourselves by the mutual offices of love, comfort, and succour, one towards another" (Quoted by Tierney, vol. iii. p. 45, *note*).

he first came to England, and before politics wholly carried him away, was an advocate for sending over a bishop. In 1591 he still held to the idea, and had fashioned a kind of hierarchy of his own.[1] He had secured the promises of a competent support for two or three bishops. But when the news of the proposed association reached him, at once he saw the danger, and determined on a bold stroke. To give the clergy a superior, yes; and one not merely friendly to the society, but in dependence on it. The scheme took some little time to mature, and at last burst upon the astonished clergy, filling them with dismay. Cardinal Cajetan, who only saw as Parsons wished him to see, was then protector of the English mission. After some kind of approval (so it turned out afterwards) on the part of the pope, Clement VIII., who had been kept by Parsons in ignorance of the real state of affairs, the cardinal, in his own name and by his own authority, issued letters appointing one George Blackwell to be arch-priest, with full jurisdiction over all the secular clergy. He assigns him six persons as assistants, and tells him to select six more. This document, constituting an office unheard of before in England, ends by exhorting him to cherish a feeling of brotherly love towards the jesuits, "who neither have nor pretend to have any portion of jurisdic-

[1] His idea was an archbishop to live in the Spanish domains and one bishop to live in England. The latter was to have certain assistants, half of whom Parsons practically was to nominate.

tion or authority over the secular clergy." And effectually to contradict this last official statement, a secret instruction was sent with the letter ordering the arch-priest in all matters of importance to follow the advice of the superior of the jesuits.[1]

To make a painful story short. The heads of the secular clergy demurred to the legality of the document; and, while giving obedience to Blackwell, appealed to the holy see. They had not been consulted, although the cardinal hinted the appointment[2] had been made at the prayer of the secular clergy. Two priests, Mr. Bishop (who afterwards became a bishop) and Mr. Charnock, were deputed to go to Rome, and set out. But care had been taken to traduce their characters and to represent them as turbulent and seditious men. Soon after their arrival, at Parsons' advice, they were both seized (December 28, 1598), by the cardinal's orders, and put into prison apart at the English college. Their gaoler was none other than Parsons himself.[3] Here

[1] The arch-priest and his assistants were bound to write to the cardinal every six months, *but every week to Parsons.*

[2] The persons consulted were Parsons and Baldwin, jesuits, with Haddock, Array, and Standish, who soon after joined the society, and some other secular priests at Rome, avowed partisans of the society, whose opinions were supported by letters from their friends not only in England but also Spain and Flanders.

[3] How this arbitrary act was viewed in England Dr. Ely, author of the *Certaine Briefs Notes*, shall tell us, and his words are of weight, for he may justly lay claim to the title he gives himself, "an unpassionate secular priest, friend to both parties but more friend to the truth": "Cloak and disguise it so well as you can now, the posterity hereafter will wonder to hear or read that two catholic priests, coming

they were kept in prison for four months, and then, after a so-called trial, under Parsons' management, they were expelled from Rome without having even seen the pope, and were forbidden to return to England.

"It is evident," says Tierney, "that these proceedings were adopted principally, first entirely, as a matter of precaution. A great political object was in view. Had Bishop and his companion been permitted to approach the pontiff or to converse freely with his officers, a new impression might have been created as to the wants and wishes of the English catholics; and, in that case, the institutions of the arch-priest, which in the minds of its projectors was to determine the future destinies of the throne, might have been overturned. By first sequestering and afterwards dismissing the deputes this danger was avoided. The pontiff heard nothing but what might be prudent to lay before him, his impressions were left undisturbed; and he willingly subscribed the breve by which Blackwell's authority was confirmed."[1]

as appellants to Rome out of an heretical country in which they maintained constantly with danger of their lives the honour and preservation of that see, and one of them had suffered some years' imprisonment with banishment afterwards for the articles of St. Peter his successor's supremacy over all other princes and prelates, that these priests (I say) should before they were heard what they had to say be cast into prison, yea, and imprisoned in the house and under the custody of their adversaries, never was there heard of such injustice since good St. Peter sat in the Chair" (p. 107).

[1] Vol. iii. p. 53.

The arch-priest denounced all opposers to his authority as rebels and abettors of schism, and branded the supporters of the two priests with opprobrious epithets. When two of the clergy, Mush and Colleton, complained of his injurious language, they were answered only by suspension. His jesuit friends were not behind-hand; Fr. Lister wrote a *Treatise of Schism* in which he declared the appellants to be "fallen from the church and spouse of Christ," &c. How bitter the feelings excited on both sides it would be hard to tell.

When the breve arrived, the appellants promptly bowed to the decision. But this was not enough for the arch-priest, who now made his great mistake. He insisted upon a declaration that they had been guilty of schism in disputing his right. The result of this was another appeal to the holy see. But this time the secular clergy were determined to bear the winning side. The Government knew everything about these dissensions. The face of affairs had changed from that of twenty years before; and at that time of day nothing could better suit Elizabeth than the ruinous tactics pursued by Parsons. Elizabeth had watched the progress of the quarrel; "she was aware of its political origin, and while on one hand, perhaps, she sought to weaken the body by division, on the other, she not unnaturally inclined towards that party whose loyalty was less open to suspicion."[1] Some of the appellants were allowed to be prisoners

[1] *Ibid.*

THE STATE OF ENGLISH CATHOLICS 253

at large, in order to correspond with one another. Facilities were given them to print the numberless tracts and pamphlets to which the controversy gave rise. About the end of June 1601 Bluet, one of the Wisbeach prisoners, had an interview with the queen herself. She consented to allow four of them to be released and go about the country getting money for their journey to Rome. They were then *pro forma* expelled the country, with passports however; and went off to Rome with nearly £1000 for their expenses. Just as they were starting a breve came from Rome, which Blackwell suppressed as unfavourable to himself.

The deputies reached Rome February 16, 1601, and were kindly received by the pope. They were, however, shy of Parsons' offer of hospitality at the English college, and of his desire to be on friendly terms. They wisely kept their distance. The petition for bishops was indeed foiled by their adversaries, but all the rest was granted. On the 5th of October another breve was issued, condemning the conduct of the arch-priest, and doing justice to the appellants. Blackwell was declared to have exceeded his powers, and the appellants not to have lost their faculties. The arch-priest was to have jurisdiction only over the seminarists, and in future he was forbidden to communicate either with the superior of the jesuits or their general in Rome. He was finally ordered to take three of the appellants to fill the first vacancies in the number of his assistants.

Tierney so well sums up the history that we willingly make his words our own:—

"Thus terminated this unhappy contest, leaving behind it, however, a rankling feeling of jealousy and dislike which cannot be too deeply or too lastingly deplored. Yet in closing this imperfect sketch, let me not forget to remind the reader of the real nature of the dispute; let me point once more to its political origin; and, above all, let me remark that however reprehensible may have been the conduct of any of the parties immediately engaged in it, that conduct of itself will neither detract from their real merit upon other occasions, nor diminish our legitimate respect for the bodies to which they belonged. To the services of Parsons, to his comprehensive mind and indefatigable energy in the foundation and management of many of the foreign seminaries, the world will continue to bear witness in spite of all his failings. Yet his existence was not necessary to the greatness of his order. Its glory needs him not, and without detracting either from his merits or his powers, the disciples of Ignatius may still assure themselves that their body 'hath many a worthier son than he.'"[1]

We have in this chapter led our readers up to the point when the benedictines come upon the mission field. It was necessary to touch upon unpleasant details, otherwise much of what follows

[1] *Ibid.* p. 55.

THE STATE OF ENGLISH CATHOLICS 255

would be unintelligible. The position in English affairs at the moment we have now arrived at, the beginning of the seventeenth century, was this. The jesuits had full control over the education of the clergy in all the seminaries, even in Douai; for the new president of that college, Dr. Worthington, had made a vow of obedience to Fr. Parsons and was wholly devoted to him. No student from the seminaries could enter England without their leave; for he got his faculties for the mission from them or from Dr. Worthington. And in England itself the arch-priest, though checked, was still working in their interest.[1]

In all this there was no other motive but the honest and fixed conviction that they, and they alone, were the best persons to undertake the conversion of England, a work so much to the glory of God. Granting this premise, the conclusion—therefore no one else was to be permitted to interfere—was legitimate.

So matters stood at the moment we once more take up the thread of the history of English benedictines.

[1] Before the appointment of the arch-priest, Garnet, who had very extensive faculties, a source of considerable influence, had also the power of subdelegating them to secular priests. But now all faculties for secular priests were ordered to be given only by the arch-priest. In a letter to Parsons Garnet laments this, for says he: "By this also have I lost the chiefest means I had to win the favour of good honest priests."

APPENDIX

APPENDIX

THE CONSUETUDINARY OF ST. AUGUSTINE'S, CANTERBURY

[THE following *résumé* of the old consuetudinary of the great exempt house of St. Augustine's, contained in the Cotton MS. *Faustina* C. xii., is of peculiar interest as being *mutatis mutandis* identical with that of Westminster, the largest part of which was lost in the fire of 1731. The present manuscript is of the early part of the fourteenth century, and now consists of 202 folios with 35 lines on each page. Unfortunately both the beginning and the end are wanting, and it now commences with folio 51. Several leaves in the body of the volume are also missing. From certain marginal memoranda it would seem that in its original state the volume comprised about 300 leaves. The consuetudinary proper extends only to folio 257 of the original. The remainder of the MS. not being a part of the Augustinian consuetudinary, is not treated of in this notice. The contents of the book are not orderly in its arrangement, as will be seen from the list of contents, which it must be understood is that given on the basis of the original in the volumes of manuscript collection used by me (see preface) and which does not always render in full the headings of the sections as given in the rubrics of the orginal manuscript itself. Hence in the abstract [1] here given it has been

[1] The *primeur* of the text of the manuscript is thus reserved to the edition of abbat Ware's Westminster consuetudinary to be published by the *Henry Bradshaw Society*.

thought well to regroup them under certain distinctive heads. The picture obtained of the life at Canterbury in St. Augustine's is that of a fervent, well ordered, and exemplary convent.   E. L. T.]

CONTENTS

§ *De hospite petente concessionem capituli;*
§ *Petitio;*
§ *Concessio capituli;*
§ *De professione novitiorum;*
§ *Forma professionis;*
§ *Super* Jube dompne benedicere *et* Tu autem Domine *notitia;*
§ *Informatio novitiorum secundum usum istius ecclesiæ.*
§ *De vacatione abbatiæ per mortem abbatis Thomæ de Fyndon et de electione fratris Radulphi de Bourne in abbatem;*
§ *Litera obligatoria Guydonis Donati de præstanda pecunia procuratoribus monasterii in Curia Romana existentibus.*
§ *Mensura diversorum ædificiorum monasterii.*
§ *De ponderibus notula.*
§ *Reformatiuncula abbatis Nicholai de Spina anno ejusdem 2° facta.*
§ *De electione abbatis.*
§ *De observantiis abbatis.*
§ *De capellanis abbatis.*
§ *De officio camerarii abbatis.*
§ *De officio senescalli aulæ.*
§ *De officiis marscalli aulæ.*
§ *De officio servitoris cultelli abbatis.*
§ *De officio servitoris manutergii abbatis.*
§ *De officio panetarii abbatis.*
§ *De officio marscalli equorum.*
§ *De officio coci abbatis.*
§ *De officio valecti cameræ abbatis.*
§ *De officio subpincernæ abbatis.*
§ *De officio subhostiarii aulæ abbatis.*
§ *De officio coci aulæ et valecti ejus.*

APPENDIX

§ *De nuntio abbatis.*
§ *De palefridario abbatis.*
§ *De officio servientis elemosinariæ mensæ abbatis deputati.*
§ *De honestate aulæ.*
§ *Oblationes per obedientiarios familiæ abbatis tribuendæ.*
§ *Modus dandi munera familiæ abbatis quando vadit per maneria.*
§ *Ordinatio familiæ abbatis anno 2 abbatis Nicholai de Spina.*
§ *De iis quæ ad abbatis præsentiam et officium spectant; atque de fratre in abbatem electo qualiter se geret electionis tempore.*
§ *Qualiter se geret usque dum confirmetur.*
§ *De confirmatione electi alibi quam in monasterio proprio.*
§ *Ad installationem abbatis processus.*
§ *De benedictione abbatis non admittenda in conventu eo die quo confirmatur.*
§ *De priore.*
§ *Item de abbate.*
§ *De officio prioris seu præpositi.*
§ *De subpriore sive de priore claustri.*
§ *Quas licentias subprior dare poterit priore domi existente.*
§ *A quo petenda est licentia si custos ordinis in claustro non fuerit.*
§ *Explicatio brevis de fratribus ægritudinis causa extra chorum existentibus atque de minutis.*
§ *De tertio et quarto priore sive de exploratoribus claustri.*
§ *De officio cantoris et succentoris.*
§ *Quod juvenes qui noviter servitium reddiderunt nullum defectum in choro patiantur.*
§ *De officio precentoris in capitulo.*
§ *De cappis in choro portandis.*
§ *Quod nullus in cappa a choro recedat sine licentia precentoris.*
§ *Tria de quibus omnibus professis licitum est loqui in capitulo.*
§ *Præcentori in multis parcendum est.*
§ *De gestu præcentoris in festis solemnibus.*
§ *De succentoris officio.*
§ *De officiis sacristæ sociorumque ejus.*
§ *De candelis hospitibus liberandis.*
§ *Distributio ceræ per sacristam facta contra purificationem.*

§ *De luminaribus, claustro, capitulo, dormitorio, et locutorio accendendis.*
§ *De officio celerarii et subcelerario et granatoris.*
§ *Qualis debet esse celerarius.*
§ *De iis quæ ad hostiliarii spectant officium.*
§ *De magistro cryptarum.*
§ *Recapitulatio de officiariis.*
§ *Casus tangentes excommunicationem.*
§ *Definitio proprietarii.*
§ *Præcepta capituli et constitutionum.*
§ *De Refectorario socioque ejus et de observantiis refectorii.*
§ *De gesta fratrum in dormitorio atque in camera; de camerario et socio ejus; de more fratrum antiquo balneandi et sanguinem sibi minuendi.*
§ *De gestu fratrum in claustro; de mandato; de elemosinario et subelemosinario.*
§ *De capitulo fratrum quotidiano.*
§ *De excommunicatione et satisfactione culpæ levis.*
§ *Modus acrior aliquantulum de excommunicatione et satisfactione culparum.*
§ *De generali confessione a fratre qui ad laternam ponitur agenda.*
§ *Alius modus excommunicationis pro rebellione.*
§ *De sententia gravis culpæ.*
§ *De sententia et satisfactione fugitivorum.*
§ *Quæ sunt culpæ graviores.*
§ *Quæ leviores.*
§ *De sacerdote sive clerico sæculari postulante ut in hoc monasterio recipiatur.*
§ *Quod novitius non professus de infirmaria etc nihil est habiturus.*
§ *Quo ordine est agenda professio monachorum.*
§ *Quo ordine suscipiuntur laici conversi juxta consuetudinem istius monasterii.*
§ *De disciplina fratrum laicorum.*
§ *De negligentiis fortuitu ad missæ consecrationem contingentibus.*
§ *De concessione beneficii hujus monasterii alterius congregationis monacho.*

§ *De concessione fraternitatis personis sæcularibus et quid specialiter fiat audito obitu eorum vel obitu parentum eorum.*
§ *De fratribus ægritudinis causa extra chorum ; et de minutione.*
§ *Quod die tertia redire debent minuti vel ulterius morari licentiam postulare.*
§ *Nulli raucedinis causa extra chorum morandi licentiam concedatur.*
§ *De fratre qui medicinatur.*
§ *De fratre qui inungitur.*
§ *Regula de claustralibus infirmis.*
§ *De ordinato fratrum ingressu in chorum.*
§ *De gestu fratrum qui extra chorum fuerint in vigiliis festi principalis.*
§ *Quod fratres ad chorum reversi ad omnes horas eo die esse tenentur.*
§ *De gestu fratrum eodem die.*
§ *De minutione fratrum claustralium.*
§ *Tempora quibus fratres minui non debent.*
§ *De petenda licentia minuendi.*
§ *Quod tres collaterales simul minuere non debent.*
§ *De minutione fratrum in infirmario jacentium.*
§ *De minutione fratrum in quadragesima.*
§ *De minutione laicorum conversorum.*
§ *De minutione novitiorum minime professorum.*
§ *De gestu fratrum prima die minutionis.*
§ *De minutione unius fratris necessitate cogente.*
§ *Quod minuti et qui ægritudinis causa extra chorum existunt processionibus solemnibus interesse debent.*
§ *De gestu fratrum ad mandatum in capitulo si fiat prima die minutionis.*
§ *Quod stando dicetur completorium de Dei Genitrice.*
§ *Quod unusquisque fratrum quotidie primam et completorium de B. V. dicere debet.*
§ *De crasseto quod in locutorio intrinseco ardere debet.*
§ *A quibus dicendæ privatæ matutinæ.*
§ *De minutione domni abbatis.*
§ *De minutione juvenum sive novitiorum.*

APPENDIX

§ *Quod fratres minuti chorum intrare debent ad exorcismum salis et aquæ si secunda dies suæ minutionis dies dominica fuerit.*

§ *Quod fratres minuti extra chorum existentes ad missam matutinalem seu ad magnam missam indui non debent nisi ante missam agatur processio.*

§ *Quod fratres minuti aut qui ægritudinis causa extra chorum existunt missam cantare non debeant.*

§ *Quod nullus minuetur die quo alicujus fratris defuncti corpus in ecclesia jacet.*

§ *Quod nullus locutorium causa loquendi, ingredi debet die quo alicujus fratris defuncti corpus in ecclesia jacet.*

§ *Quod fratres minuti et de itinere reversi ad vigiliam et ad missam de principali anniversario esse teneantur.*

§ *Quod cantor aut alii fratres, cum sanguinati fuerint, nullum officium in conventu facient.*

§ *De refectorario et subrefectorario sive aliis duobus qui in una administratione conjunguntur, quod simul minuere non debeant.*

§ *Quod nullus causa raucedinis extra chorum permittatur.*

§ *De priore.*

§ *De cantore.*

§ *De gestu minutorum tertia die suæ minutionis.*

§ *De fratre cui domus infirmorum cura committitur et de iis quæ illius incumbunt officio.*

§ *Quod infirmarius quotidie dicet completorium infirmorum.*

§ *Quod sæculares personæ inter infirmos prandere nec bibere debent.*

§ *Quod prædicti famuli (sc. infirmariæ) aut unus eorum apud Cantuariam pro apotecharia quotiens opus fuerit incedere debent.*

§ *Quod omnes infirmi si fieri potest ad unam mensam prandere debeant.*

§ *Quod magnum altare infirmariæ nullo die per annum sine missa et matutinis esse debet.*

§ *De modo et ordine visitandi fratrem infirmum quando debet inungi.*

§ *Quod si infirmus loqui non valet ille qui officium facit in persona illius dicet confessionem.*

§ *Quo ordine sacerdos quæret Eukaristiam post fratris inunctionem.*
§ *Quo ordine fiet obsequium pro fratre inuncto in conventu usque in octavum diem.*
§ *Quod aliquis sacerdos de juvenibus vel ad minus diaconus, custodiæ fratris inuncti per priorem assignabitur quemcunque infirmus rogaverit.*
§ *De commendatione animæ exeuntis de corpore atque de cæteris omnibus seriatim quæ ad decedentium fratrum spectant officium.*
§ *Quod corpus defuncti nulla hora sine fratribus psallentibus remanebit.*
§ *De honestate et cura quas camerarius et subcamerarius circa corpus defuncti habebunt.*
§ *Quid sit faciendum si aliquis de fratribus obierit dum modo conventus fuerit ad missas vel ad horas vel in prandio vel in cena vel in completorio vel ad matutinas vel ad mandatum in sabbato vel alioquovis modo impeditus.*
§ *Qualiter fiet si aliquis obierit dum fratres ad missam vel ad horam fuerint regularem.*
§ *Quod si obierit dum fratres fuerint ad matutinas.*
§ *Quod si hora prandii aliquis moriatur.*
§ *Quod si obierit post quam sonatur cymbalum ad prandium aut ad cænam conventus vel dum fit mandatum in sabbato aut in V. feria.*
§ *Quod si obierit dum conventus sit in dormitorio in meridiana.*
§ *Quod si accederit incæpto completorio.*
§ *Qualiter fiet si in principali festo decesserit.*
§ *De vigiliis faciendis in decessu fratrum.*
§ *De vigiliis in obitu fratrum secundum diversa anni tempora rite distinguendis.*
§ *Si aliquis frater obierit post sonitum mane factum quod missam habebit matutinalem.*
§ *Consuetudo antiquitus de fratrum sepultura.*
§ *Quo ordine portabitur corpus in ecclesiam et ad sepulturam.*
§ *Qualiter fiet si aliquis obierit in nocte Paschæ vel Pentecostes.*
§ *De beneficiis fratrum quæ fiunt post obitum alicujus fratris.*

§ *Quod sit faciendum postquam corpus fuerit in ecclesiam delatum post commendationem.*
§ *Quod corpus defuncti nullo tempore sine psalmodia erit.*
§ *Quod nullus a monasterio egredietur donec fratris defuncti corpus sepeliatur.*
§ *Breviculum fratris qualiter scribi debeat.*
§ *Quod pro novitio non professo ad missam non fiet panis et vini oblatio.*
§ *De officio sacerdotis circa corpus post missam.*
§ *Qualiter revertetur processio in chorum post fratris sepulturam.*
§ *De balneo fratrum qui corpus defuncti tetigerunt.*
§ *De distribuendis fratris defuncti indumentis, aliisque rebus si quas habuerit.*
§ *Qualiter fiet obsequium pro eo cui conceditur habitus monachalis si ante professionem obierit.*
§ *De modo agendi obsequium in decessu fratris laici conversi.*
§ *Quo ordini fient exsequiæ fratris defuncti si feria quinta in Cæna Domini aut in die Parasceves vel in Sabbato Sancto aut in nocte vel in die Paschæ obierit.*
§ *Qualiter est agendum pro fratre de ecclesiæ gremio si extra monasterium qualicumque modo diem clauserit extremam.*
§ *Quo ordine fient tricennalia et cætera quæ agenda sunt pro fratribus istius monasterii professis de medio sublatis.*
§ *Quod nullus infra triginta dies post obitum fratris aliunde quam pro defunctis cantabit nisi fuerit in tabula de aliqua missa consueta.*
§ *De absolutione fratris defuncti trigesimo die post ejus obitum.*
§ *Quid fiet pro fratre defuncto in die anniversario obitus ipsius.*
§ *De consuetudine ecclesiæ quæ ad sacristam pertinet et de expensis ceræ per annum.*
§ *Quando servientes ecclesiæ habebunt cerevisiam in refectorio.*
§ *De stipendiis servientium ecclesiæ.*
§ *De diversitate sonitus in diversis festivitatibus.*
§ *De lucerna in festis Sancti Augustini, S. Adriani et S. Mildrethæ.*
§ *De lucerna in generali et in speciali.*
§ *De lucerna feria quarta ante Cænam Domini.*
§ *De lucerna in Cæna Domini.*

§ *De lucerna in Parasceve Domini.*
§ *De lucerna in Sabbato Sancto.*
§ *De lucerna in die Paschæ.*
§ *De processionibus.*
§ *De tabula argentea ante magnum altare.*
§ *De festis quæ habent matutinas de die.*
§ *De vigiliis principalium festorum.*
§ *De* Dirige *et* Placebo *per totum annum.*
§ *De Cæna.*
§ *De observantiis novitiorum in tempore professionis.*
§ *De festis habentibus octavas cum regimine chori.*
§ *De distributione bonorum fratris defuncti.*
§ *De modo minuendi et ejus observatione.*
§ *De infortunio ignis.*

I. ON THE ABBAT

The election of so important a prelate as that of the lord abbat of the exempt abbey of St. Augustine's and, as all documents have it, "belonging immediately to the Roman church," was a matter of great weight. The archbishop had nothing to do with it. But as the abbat was one of the great barons spiritual, the Crown had a great interest and made its power felt. In the case mentioned in the consuetudinary, that of Ralph Bourne in 1309 may be taken as a fairly typical example.

Even before abbat Thomas Fyndon[1] expired, the prior

[1] Abbat Thomas Fyndon (1283-1309) had been prior and succeeded upon the resignation of abbat Nicholas de Spina *or* Thorne, who became a carthusian near Paris. Fyndon was the great builder of the abbey, and his vast expenditure for a time impoverished the house. He was appointed by the pope without the royal licence. The king therefore seized the abbey, and only granted his favour after a fine of 400 marks had been paid. "In consequence of archbishop Winchesley's continual encroachments upon the privileges of this monastery, and the monks appealing to the see of Rome, pope Boniface VIII. granted a bull confirming all their privileges" (*Monasticon*, vol. i. p. 122). Among other things this abbat in 1293 gave a great banquet on the feast of St. Augustine to 4500 persons (*Chronologia Augustiniensis*).

and monks sent messengers with letters to influential men at court, such as the chancellor, the bishop of Chichester, and the treasurer; to ask them, in view of the injury done by a long vacancy, to obtain the royal licence for an immediate election on the demise of the abbat. As soon as Thomas Fyndon died, the royal subescheator took possession of the abbey and its revenues, according to the custom, in the king's name. The licence to elect was duly and speedily granted. The day appointed, the community assembled in the chapter-house, after the mass of the Holy Ghost had been sung; and their first business was to read the decrees of the general council concerning election. Then to safeguard the proceedings against irregularity, as some of the electors might be labouring under a hidden defect which would vitiate their right to an active voice, a public protest was made that any such illegitimate voting was wholly against the will and knowledge of the chapter. The manner of election had then to be discussed; and all agreed to proceed by way of compromise. Seven monks as electors were nominated out of the whole body; and were solemnly charged to choose one, either of the convent or from another house of the congregation, whom they should judge to be "good and benevolent, and useful to the welfare of this church and necessary for the observance of religion." They were warned not to choose any one or to pass over any one for human and personal motives; but to elect "him who knows how, who is able and desires to love his brethren in the fear of God and to observe to the utmost the estate and godly customs of this church." The commission to elect was signed by the common seal of the monastery, and the convent bound themselves to abide by the decision of the seven electors. The result was soon made known. Ralph de Bourne, one of the seven, was declared to be duly elected; and upon his assenting, he was led by the monks into the church with the singing of the *Te Deum*. There, prostrated

APPENDIX

before high altar, prayers appropriate to the occasion were chanted over him by the prior, and he was then led to pay his homage of devotion before the shrines of the saints which encircled the apse of the church. Meanwhile, the bells of the abbey in their joyous peals proclaimed the election to the town, and some "discrete person" from the pulpit made announcement to the people of the name of the newly elected abbat. A careful account of the whole day's proceeding was then drawn up by a public notary and duly witnessed.

The elect, after dinner, took up his abode in the buildings set aside for the use of the prior. There he was to remain humbly and not interfere more than any other of the convent in the affairs of the monastery. He was to be content with the attentions the monks paid him of their own free will, and was not to exact more. In the church chapter and refectory he took the first place on the right-hand choir; and had certain monks appointed to him as attendants and companions. But until the election was confirmed he could not enter upon his rights and dignities. After two days the elect with some of his monks began their journey to London to obtain the royal assent. They took with them all documents necessary to prove the validity of the election, together with the following letter from the prior and convent:—

> "To the most excellent prince and revered lord, Edward, by the grace of God, the illustrious king of England lord of Ireland and duke of Aquitaine, his humble and devoted prior and convent of the monastery of St. Augustine's at Canterbury, which belongs immediately to the Roman church, [give] all possible homage and honour in Him by whom kings reign and princes have their rule.

"The aforesaid our monastery being vacant by the death of Thomas of good memory, late our abbat, and licence having been called and obtained for us to elect another as abbat and pastor, we have observed the day of election and, after invoking the aid of the Holy Ghost, have elected unanimously our beloved fellow-monk, Ralph de Bourne, as our abbat and pastor. Him therefore, the brother Ralph our elect, we present to your royal majesty by our beloved fellow-monks William of Byhalt, Richard of Canterbury, and Solomon of Ripple, humbly and devoutly beseeching that you would deign to admit him, our aforesaid, as elect, and for ourselves to give your royal assent and favour to the election made by us. And further, asking, for the elect, whatever may be pleasing your royal will. In testimony whereof our common seal is appended to these presents. May the Most High keep you all.

"Given in our chapter at Canterbury, the viii of the ides of March in the year of the Lord 1309."

The affair at court was speedily settled; and by the seventeenth of the month the monks had returned to Canterbury with letters from the king and queen to the pope, to whom the elect had now to go in person for confirmation. They also had letters to recommend them to the king of France, through whose dominions they had to pass on their road to Avignon, where the pope (Clement V.) then was.

The king's letter to the pope is as follows:—

"To the most holy father in Christ, the lord Cl., by divine Providence, the high priest of the most holy Roman and Universal Church, Edward, by the same grace, king of England, &c., devoutly kissing the sacred feet.

"It becometh us, amidst the other cares which press upon us, with watchful care to take heed of the welfare of those monasteries of our kingdom which are in our patronage; that when widowed, they may be comforted by the solace of a pastor, and to frequently stir up your clemency for the relief of burthens. Since therefore the religious man, our right-well beloved in Christ, brother Ralph de Bourne, elect of the monastery of St. Augustine's at Canterbury in our patronage (to whose election we have given our royal assent and favour with the hope of obtaining confirmation of the same from your holiness), now approaches your presence: bearing in mind that the aforesaid monastery is greatly in debt,[1] and that the state of the house may, by the industry and circumspection of the elect, be in the future retained, we do specially commend to your holiness the elect as one who is provident, and circumspect in spiritual as well as in temporal affairs, and endowed with other kinds of virtue, asking with affectionate prayer that you would deign to admit the aforesaid elect, in those matters which he has to do with your holiness, to the favour of a hearing and to send him back to the aforesaid monastery with his business happily finished.

"Given at Westminster the xiii day of March in the third year of our reign."

The queen wrote in similar style commending the elect to the pope's favour. Together with their letters was a licence to Robert of Kendal, the constable of Dover Castle and warden of the Cinque Ports, to allow the elect to pass over to France.

At the kalends of April the elect set out for Avignon; but, before he started, money for the journey had to be obtained. The monastery paid over to one Guy Donatus, a Florentine merchant and member of the society of "Bards" of Florence, a sum of fifty pounds sterling and received back from him bills of exchange. Letters of procuration at the papal court were then made out, and a document from the monastery to the pope begging for his confirmation of their election was drawn up. In this latter, after recounting

[1] On account of Fyndon's building.

the royal licence and the result of the election, the prior and convent say: "We must humbly entreat your holiness to deign to confirm the above-mentioned election and to bestow on our elect the gift of the Blessing that having God as his authority he may rightly and profitably rule both us and others in those things which pertain to his abbacy."

The papers which had to be taken to Rome consisted of: (1) the royal licence to elect; (2) the formal appointment of the day of election; (3) all documents concerned with the preliminaries; (4) the letter to the pope asking for confirmation, signed by all the community and sealed with the common seal; (5) the decree of election signed and sealed in a similar way; (6) the royal letters of assent; (7) the notarial accounts of the election; (8) the protest against unlawful voting (this was only to be produced if any objection was made that some of the electors were suspended or excommunicated); (9) and finally a public testification of the date of the setting out from Canterbury to Avignon.

We learn nothing more from the consuetudinary about this election. But this formidable array of documents secured the confirmation after the dues had been paid. The abbat was blessed by the pope; and on his return to St. Augustine's, which he approached barefooted in all humility, he was received with great solemnity by the community and with chant and prayer, was duly installed. And while the *Te Deum* was being sung the monks, one by one, went up to pay their homage to their new pastor by kissing his hand, and then as to their father by kissing him on the mouth. The ceremony concluded by the solemn abbatical blessing.[1]

---

[1] Nor was a great feast forgotten on that festive occasion. The new abbat showed his hospitality by an enormous banquet which Thorne in his chronicle (*Decem Scriptores*, p. 2010) mentions "not that we may follow his example, but admire it." Among the articles consumed were 11 tons

Once installed, on high church festivals the abbat had to assist at matins[1] and lauds and terce, in alb and cope and mitre, gloves and ring; and with pastoral staff in hand stand at his seat amid his assistants, who were also clad in copes. After terce a solemn procession round the church took place. The community, vested in albs and copes, with the abbat would tarry before some statue or shrine, and make what is called a *station;* and there sing some special anthem with its proper versicles and prayers before continuing the procession. Afterwards, the abbat would prepare himself for pontifical mass, and would put on the tunic, the dalmatic, and sandals and buskins, besides the chasuble; and he would take his seat in a special *cathedra* which was placed near to the altar. Then he would sing mass according to the "use" of his own church, and employ a missal claiming to be identical with that brought by St. Augustine from Rome itself.[2] One striking feature was the solemn benediction given immediately after the *Pax Domini,* when turning to the people and using both mitre and staff, he chanted the formula of blessing contained in the *Benedictionale*, and which varied with the feast. At vespers, two of his assistant priests came in at the *Magnificat* with the thurifers, and when the abbat had put in the incense, they accompanied him for the thurification of the high altar, and the altar behind, and the shrine and altar of St. Augustine. One gave his thurible to the abbat, and held back the cope

of wine (at a value of £24); 30 oxen (£27); 34 swans (£7); 500 capons (£6); 1000 geese (£16); 200 sucking pigs (100 shillings); 9600 eggs (£4 10s.); 17 rolls of brawn (65 shillings); coals (48 shillings); wages of cooks and servants (£6)—total £287, 5s. Six thousand guests sat down to a banquet of three thousand dishes.

[1] At the great feasts the abbat, while the *Te Deum* was being sung, came in vested as for mass, and, having incensed the high altar, sang the gospel of the day.

[2] See Rule's most valuable and learned Introduction to the Missal of St. Augustine's, Canterbury.

while the prelate incensed the altars, the second assistant meanwhile incensing the altars together with the abbat. After the altar and shrine of St. Augustine had been honoured, the abbat and his chaplain remained before the shrine, while the two priests went with their smoking thuribles to incense all the other altars and shrines. They then all returned in procession to the choir, when the usual incensing took place, and the stately function ended with the abbatial blessing. On feast days, when he himself did not celebrate, he assisted at the function in cope, mitre, and gloves, with the staff, and took his place between the cantors; and at the end of the service proceeded to his throne, whence he gave the final benediction. Whenever he was present, even if only in his ordinary choral dress, the deacon always came to him for the blessing before the Gospel, and the holy text was carried to him to be kissed, and the incense to be blessed, and the pax brought from the altar. To him also fell the duty of blessing and distributing the ashes at the beginning of Lent, the candles on the feast of the Purification, and the palms on Palm-sunday.

If at home, he was bound to be present at all vespers of twelve-lesson feasts, and on all vigils; but he was not required to be at lauds, unless he officiated solemnly, save on the Wednesday before Christmas and on the eve of that feast. The other days in the year he was not bound to be at either vespers or lauds except the three days before Easter and the whole of the following week, and also Whitsuntide. At the office for the dead he was only present on [special anniversaries?] or for the funeral of a monk; and then only for matins.

The Household.—As befitted so high a prelate and so important a spiritual baron, in accordance with the requirements of the times, he was obliged to keep up a large household in the building set apart for his use, known as the abbat's lodging. He had to receive many visitors and keep up a state which would only bring disorder and discomfort into the monastery if the monks had to be subjected to these annoyances. But his intercourse with his monks was close and intimate, as his duty as pastor and father required.

The Chaplains.—Foremost in his household were the chaplains, two in number. The consuetudinary says: "The chaplains of the abbat ought to be courteous and discreet, and affable to all, and especially to strangers." They are bound to foster, as far as they can, the mutual love of abbat and convent. Both should say mass every day, and in turns take the office of assisting the abbat at his mass and attending upon him in the church and elsewhere. Whenever he went abroad they bore him company, and one of them carried a *diurnale*, in case the abbat wished to say office. They were in charge of his household, and ordered everything and corrected what was amiss. The elder had the charge of the abbatial cellars, the keys of which were taken to him every night. The prelatial jewels and money were in their care, and they had to have ten pounds in ready cash always in the house. To them belonged the duty of giving out the alms the abbat dispensed when he went abroad from the monastery. An account every year of all expenditure had to be given. They were also charged with the special care of the abbat's guests; and when he was at home, had to invite certain of the monks to eat at the abbatial board. The younger had also the duty of reading at the abbat's meal, unless for some reasonable cause another had the office.

The Chamberlain.—The chamberlain acted as a kind of secretary for documents which came under the seal. He took charge of the abbat's cup and napkin at meal times and saw that the guests were likewise provided, and that the wine was served in due course. "And it is to be borne in mind that from all who come to do homage to the abbat he has either half a mark or an outer garment, the which he should civilly and meekly ask for before they take their departure."

The Seneschal.—The seneschal, when the abbat was going to dine in the hall, had overnight (between vespers and compline), together with the cellarer and cook, to wait on the abbat and receive his orders for the morrow, and to inquire of the number of guests to be provided for. He had to see that the "commons" (*liberatio*) of the hall were duly provided. After grace, he set before the abbat the dishes which the servant brought up.

The Marshal of the Hall.—The marshal of the hall ministered the water for washing the abbat's hands before and after meals, and performed the same office for the chief guests. He arranged these latter in their proper places. "He is not to allow the servants to approach the tables too hastily. . . he is also not to allow a tumult of loose behaviour in the hall, especially among the waiters (*garciones*), and if he finds any one obstinate or rebellious, he shall presently cause him to be put without the hall, until humble satisfaction is made. If any one comes in after the first course, he is to take care that that course is served to the late comer. He shall punish those who throw their bones or beer-mugs on the ground."

The Carver.—The carver, who has always to have a clean napkin over his shoulder and at least two shining knives, is not to begin carving before the reading has begun.

The Waiter.—There was also a waiter who carried a napkin and handed the dishes to the seneschal. Everything he carried had to be covered with this napkin.

The Pantler.—The pantler had charge of the bread and the napery, and all other necessaries for the abbat's table.

The Master of the Horse.—The master of the horse had to see to the feeding of the horses, and have a special care of my lord abbat's palfrey. He had to buy the oats and corn and to see to the shoeing.

The Cook.—The cook had no small office. After he had received his instructions he had to provide all that was necessary; "and when the abbat was at home ought to go with the cellarer's buyers into the town to purchase better articles for the abbat and his guests." He had to prepare with his own hands whatever was for the abbat's own consumption, and was not to allow any one to help him. Every day he had to see that the kitchen utensils were scrupulously cleaned. He is never to be without some good seasonings (*salsamentis*), which he is himself to prepare, and is to take care that in the seasoning for the abbat he is not to use too much ginger. Immediately after every meal the cook has to collect the silver cooking utensils and return them to the chamberlain. He is always to keep the door of the kitchen shut.

The Valet.—The valet gave out the linen and plate necessary for the abbat's table to the pantler, and the wine and silver goblets when the chamberlain gave the order. He was the personal attendant of the abbat, and waited upon him in his private rooms.

The Cupboard-man.—The cupboard-man had to keep the cups dry and replace them after each meal.

The Porter.—The porter kept the door, and only allowed those to enter the hall who had a right. "He is not to allow ribald fellows to stand about the door of the house, nor upon the steps; he is to answer every one civilly and kindly, and is to take care that dogs do not remain in the hall."

The Hall Cook and Servant.—The hall had its own cook and servant. They should "so well and honestly prepare and see to the good of those who eat in the hall, that no complaint about them should reach the abbat's ear, if they desire to keep their position."

The Abbat's Messenger.—The abbat's messenger should be a prudent man, smooth-spoken, bold, and ever diligent (*impiger*) and trusty; always prompt and ready. He was not allowed to receive anything from outside without the abbat's leave. He had to know the gossip of the place about such travellers as were passing by or tarrying in the neighbourhood, so as to let the abbat or his chaplains know who to invite. He helped in the kitchen.

The Palfrey-man.—The attendant on the palfrey held the bridle when the abbat was mounted. He distributed also the alms given on a journey. He also helped the valet in the personal service.

The Almoner.—The almoner saw to the distribution among the poor of the daily leavings of the abbat's table. He too helped in the personal service, and in his instructions he is particularly warned to take heed, "under pain of dismissal, that he does not in any way reveal the secrets of the closet."

The Hall.—The cellarer was charged with the cleanliness of the hall and the respect due to the guests. A fire was provided during the meals from All Saints till the Purification; and during supper eleven candles were provided; but on fasting days only three, unless strangers were present. In this common hall all guests, monks or others, dined and supped unless they were specially bidden to the abbat's private apartments or arrived at hours too late for the common meal.

The Servants of the Household.—Such were the officers of the abbat's household. Each of them had, besides their duties, their own perquisites and salaries, and servants to attend upon them. In a list of the household of abbat Nicholas de Spina we read that the chamberlain had a companion, a squire, together with boys and horses at his disposal; the physician[1] was allowed a squire, two boys, and two horses; the seneschal had his squire and three boys, and as

---

[1] It is interesting to note that the physician was not one of the monks, but evidently a layman cunning in leechery.

many horses. And so with the others in less degree. The marshal of the hall had "one honest boy" and one horse, likewise the pantler; but his boy is described as not only "honest" but "trusty and discreet." The master of the horse had his boy, too, "one who knows how to shoe"; and the abbat's cook was only allowed "an honest and knowing boy," but no horse.

From the same list we learn that my lord abbat was served always with four courses, the household with three, and the servants with two.

The abbat's intercourse to his community was marked with the greatest deference on their part. Whenever he passed through the cloister or by any other place where the brethren were sitting, they rose and bowed whilst he passed. If they were standing they uncovered their heads and bowed. Should he in any place have occasion to rebuke a brother, at once the monk knelt before him and remained in that humble posture until bidden to rise. "But the abbat should wisely take care that he should not do this before seculars; neither should he allow this to be done for anything; for it is not becoming that he should by word of mouth sharply chide any brother before seculars."

Whenever he sat no one presumed, uninvited, to sit besides him; but according to the old custom, if so bidden, the brother should kneel and kiss the abbat's knees, if he allows, and then humbly take his seat. Whenever anything was handed to the abbat, or received from him, the prelate's hand was kissed, and if he were sitting the monk knelt before him. On the occasions that he dined in the refectory with the monks, the prior and two of the brethren served at the washing of his hands.

The ordering of the whole monastery depends upon his will; but nevertheless nothing is, as the Rule says, to be taught, commanded, or ordered (*quod absit*) beyond the precepts of the Lord. But also neither should anything be attempted against the approved customs of the monastery without consulting the seniors. If while he is absent something new has, by necessity or reason, to be arranged, on his return it is for him to decide, with the advice of the seniors, what has to be done. If he has been absent for some time (fifteen days), on his return he has to visit the sick, and with pity and paternal affection console them. If according to the old custom he sleeps in the dormitory, and remains in bed in the morning, no sound is to be made; but the master of novices, if he sees the hour is passed at which the prior is used to call them, is to rise as quickly as he can and call up the novices by touching them gently with a rod. When they are awakened, they go out of the dormitory, wash and comb their hair, and having said the usual prayer, go to their school, where in silence they wait until the abbat gets up, and then they go to prime.

When the abbat dies, all he has goes back to the monastery and he is buried like one of the other monks; except that, vested as a priest and clad in pontificals, with his staff on the right arm, he is laid out for the tomb. The schedule of absolution, a plate of lead bearing his inscription and date, a chalice and a paten, together with bread and wine, are buried with him, and the nearest abbat or bishop is invited to celebrate the funeral offices.

II. THE OFFICERS OF THE CONVENT

The Prior.—The prior was the chief of all the officers in the monastery, and was treated with a deference only less than that shown to the abbat himself. Like him he had a lodging apart, although he slept in the common dormitory. He was selected by the abbat out of three names elected by the convent. The precentor had the right of nominating one, the right side of the choir another, and the third by the left side. He is to be obeyed by all, and has to set an example of exactness in observing all rules. He is bidden to make himself be more loved than feared. Whenever he enters the chapter-house or the choir, all rise to salute him; but the monks don't rise when he passes by, only if he goes to sit in the cloister, those near his seat rise. It is his office, when the Rule is read in chapter, to comment on it *in French* for the sake of the more simple brethren; or to assign the duty to some one else. In the absence of the abbat he rules the monastery, and with the advice of the seniors can make what regulations are necessary. He holds chapter, and can inflict penances for breaches of the rule. "But according to modern usage, each obedientiary punishes his own servants, and removes those he considers ought to be removed and appoints others in their place, those only excepted who have received their appointments directly from the abbat and convent. The obedientiaries, if there chance to be anything negligent or slothful in their servants, shall sharply chide them if the prior so determines." The prior can withdraw from such of the household who are rebellious and incorrigible, their allowances until they make satisfaction, saving always the abbat's rights when he is at home. It pertains to the prior to give leave to the monks to be bled; and he also appoints the hours and days for baths. He can give dispensations from choir, even in the abbat's presence; and can also give leave to the weak, and those requiring it, to eat meat out of the refectory. He is always on duty; but when he is obliged to be absent, the sub-prior is appointed to take his place. In olden days, after the first prayer before matins, he used to take a lantern and go through the dormitory and other places to see lest any one, overcome by sloth, had remained behind. But in modern time this duty has been assigned to the *scrutatores ordinis*. At compline, having taken holy water from the hebdomadary, he used to remain until the monks had passed by, to see whether all had been present and whether they had observed due reverence and order, and whether, according to the custom, they had put up their hood on leaving the choir. But this office also is now done by the *scrutatores*. The prior sees that all go to the dormitory. Before the daily chapter he takes counsel with the other priors about the defects which call for correction; and the priors have to be unanimous in all things concerning reformation.

The Sub-prior or Claustral Prior.—The sub-prior or claustral prior was the officer who had the most direct relation with the monks. He was always with them and was responsible for the order and discipline of the house. In the absence of the prior he took his place, and had the same powers of dispensation. From time to time he had to go the rounds of the house, and had to know what every one was doing. It was an important part of his duty to visit the sick every day. Among his general powers of dispensation was that of leaving the cloister, but not of going into the town. He is not to give any one leave to stay outside the monastery for two days, unless the prior from ill health is away from the dormitory. All who with leave are going outside the monastery, and will not be back for the next meal, have to tell him. The claustral prior on certain days presided at the chapter, and on these days he could grant many other dispensations. When the prior was away or could not be found, the claustral prior could then give leave for the monks to go into the town or elsewhere, but not to take refreshments unless it was his day for holding chapter, or there was any reasonable cause. He also had to see that all were present at the office.

The third and fourth Priors.—The prior and the sub-prior appointed two guardians or *Exploratores ordinis*, who were a kind of domestic police. "As the choir, or the cloister, or the refectory, according to the right and ancient custom, should never be without two watchers of the order if it can be done; if one has to go out, the other remains." They are warned not to indulge in private malice in reporting a monk, nor from private friendship shut their eyes to any negligences. They cannot rebuke, but can only publicly "proclaim" or report the negligence at the next day's chapter. "If they find any one outside the cloister talking, the speaker has to rise and tell them that he is speaking with the leave of the prior or sub-prior. The guardians neither by sign nor word answer them, but modestly pass on, listening, however, with intent ears whether the conversation be useful. They go their rounds, one by one, not together. They are not allowed to go into the offices of the house, but can open the doors and look whether the brethren are properly engaged. They had certain fixed times for going round, but were free to do so whenever they thought fit. If a monk met them on their rounds, he had to stand still and uncover his head and wait till the guardian had seen him and passed by. But they are never allowed to go where the prior and sub-prior are, nor ever into the abbat's or prior's lodgings; nor into the infirmary nor the guest-house, unless there be some grave reason. "The guardians should be unanimous in all things and agree together, presuming upon nothing out of the spirit of contention, or a vain glory in their position." If the priors were all absent from the cloister, the monks had to get permission from the senior priest, but he could, as a rule, only give leave to go into the gardens; but even he, if there was any necessity, could give leave to go into the town, so wide and sensible was the rule in practice.

The Cantor.—The cantor or precentor not only had to take care that the offices in choir went smoothly and had to arrange for the distribution of the various parts, to set the pitch and correct mistakes, but he was also the librarian (*Armarius*) and had charge of the books, and had to keep a stock of parchment and other requisites for the use of the monks. In chapter he had publicly to accuse such as had been guilty of faults in psalmody. In his charge was one of the three keys of the chest which contained the common seal of the house. He was not to be treated too strictly in respect to absences from choir on account of his various duties, but he must not without manifest reason omit two successive hours, nor on the same day be absent from matins or vespers or compline. He has to arrange the *tabula* or list of masses and choral duties. During the *Benedictus* and *Magnificat* he goes from side to side of the choir, to encourage and give an example to the brethren of devout singing; but he has to be back in his place for the *Gloria Patri*. At processions he walks between the two choirs to keep them united in the chant. On great feasts he rules the choir with six companions in copes, and preintones the *Gloria* to the celebrant; and his is the duty of singing the choice portions of the Gradual and of the Tract. If necessary, during the singing he makes signs with his hands to modulate the chant according to his judgment. The importance of the precentor's office may be judged from the fact that he had the power to nominate one out of three for the post of prior, and had the same privilege in the appointments of sacrist and almoner.

The Succentor.—The succentor was in all things the aid of the precentor. But to him especially fell the duty of preparing the juniors for the parts they had to take in the office. He also had to arrange the collects and their order for the officiant. On him also was the duty of drawing up the mortuary notices (*Brevicula*) and despatching them to the various houses.

The Sacrist and his companions.—The sacrist was one of the obedientiaries that represented the choice of the convent. He had the care of the church, the plate, the vestments, and was responsible for the candles and the lighting not only of the church [1] but of the whole establishment. He also had to provide mats for the choir and those on the north side of the cloister "from the abbat's parlour as far as the dormitory door;" smaller ones for the novices, those for the chapter-house, and those before every altar. All these had to be renewed every year. On him depended the arrangements to be made for the burial of the *confratres*. Out of the funds set apart for his office, he had to keep the roofs of the church in order, besides those of the chapter-house and of that part of the cloister jutting on to the church. He was not to talk in the church "save for explaining some miracle or the power of some relic or some notice; and this, if necessary, not openly but briefly, that it may seem as though done in silence." The work of the sacrist was shared in by four other monks, viz. two sub-sacrists (they could not enter the sacristy without leave), a treasurer or *Revestiarius*, whose special care was the relics, and a companion. These and the sacrist himself slept in the precincts of the church itself, so as to be always on guard and ready for opening and closing the church. At the first sound of the bell the five get up and call the servants of the church; and it is laid down that if they are not at office or mass they are to be more sharply rebuked than those who sleep in the dormitory. After compline they have to prepare the candles for matins. Each novice and any one else who wished had one, and there was one for the readers of the lesson and one for the officiant. This last the sub-sacrist was to light, and to see that it was a taper so well made as to give plenty of light for the old monks and for those with weak sight. During the *Te Deum* the sacrist had to see that the bell-ringers did their duty and rang for lauds.[2] On Sundays the

[1] A note is made that the paschal candle is not removed until the day after Trinity Sunday.

[2] *Et tunc pulsandum est ad laudes.* The custom of ringing the bells during the *Te Deum* is not as a sign of joy during that hymn, but is solely with the view of giving notice that lauds, the original night office, is about to begin.

sub-sacrist has to get salt from the refectory-master for the blessing of the holy water, and what is over he returns to be distributed among all the salt-cellars in the refectory.

For the care of the altars special rules were laid down. After a feast day all the special ornaments had to be removed before prime of the next day. The high altar was always vested in a frontal (on great feasts there was a splendid silver frontal). The high altar should never be, *quod absit*, without the pyx, with the Eucharist and the book containing the four gospels and the name of our deceased brethren and benefactors written therein; so that the priest who celebrates there may have a special remembrance of them, for instance: "And of all our brethren and benefactors whose names are written in this book." In this spirit of reverence for the holy altar servants were never allowed to approach it or even to enter the sanctuary except to do some work the monks could not do themselves. When the treasurer put out the relics, he had to wear an alb and to say with his assistant the seven penitential psalms and the Litany of the saints; it was his duty, too, to assist the abbat in the sacristy when he washed his hands and combed his hair before pontificating. Before every Easter, and as often as necessary, the corporals were washed. They were not dried at a fire, nor in the sun, nor in the wind, for fear of smuts, but inside the house. After washing, the linen (albs included) had to be "reconciled" by the abbat or sacrist before use. The same ceremony had to be gone through if any of the sacred vestments fell on the ground. To the sacrist and his companions belonged the bells, and they had to instruct the servants when and how to ring them. The big bell was rung on the feasts of Christmas, Easter, Whitsuntide, St. Augustine, SS. Peter and Paul, and the Assumption. The clocks of the establishment were also under their care. When the abbat was present at a mass, the sub-sacrist had to prepare an offering of bread and wine which the abbat made, and assist him when he washed the priest's hands at the offertory and after the Communion. Once a year at least the sub-sacrist made the altar breads. Grain by grain the corn was chosen and placed in a clean bag, and then it was sent by a trusty servant to the abbey mill, which had to be specially cleaned for the occasion. When the breads themselves were to be made, the sub-sacrists, after washing their hands and faces, put on albs and covered their heads with amices and then made the paste. The servant who held the irons is ordered to wear gloves. While the work is going on (and the making of a large supply of altar breads to last perhaps for a year was necessarily a long business), the monks employed said the regular hours as well as those of our Lady and also the seven penitential psalms, together with the Litany. Otherwise it was all done in silence. A special note is made that the wood for the fire ought to be very dry and prepared many days previously.

The Cellarer, Sub-cellarer, and the Corn-master.—To the cellarer belongs all that concerns food, meat, fish, &c., "and ought to be, according to the Rule, the father of the whole congregation," and to have a special care to provide for the wants of the sick. On the day when the chapter in the Rule about his office (cap. xxxi.) is read, he had to give "an honest and festive service" to the monks in the refectory. He has to attend the daily chapter, high mass, and the collation, and at the offices for the dead and vespers and matins of twelve-lesson feasts, and at all processions; for the rest he was dispensed. He could not go out of the monastery without permission, and always had to leave word where he had gone to, in case he was wanted. When he did not attend choir, he said his matins in the chapel of St. Gregory, along with those who had been bled or were otherwise excused. He eat in the common refectory or at the abbat's lodging. Guests were to be received by him in a courteous (*curialiter*) manner, "and in all things he is to honourably minister to them." The servants of the household are under his care, and it is to him they take their oath of fidelity. Every day while the convent is at dinner he stands by the kitchen window to see that there is no defect in the service. It is part of his duty to dispense the extra dishes by way of pitance. For instance, the monk who sang the high mass always received on that day an extra pitance. The mill, the gardens and orchards were under his charge, and the general care of the buildings was part of his duty. He is told to be affable and pleasant in his dealings with the monks, and is never to send any one away annoyed by word of his. He has the power of punishing the servants, by rebukes, by ordering them to be flogged with a thin rod, or by fining them; which fines went to the poor, or for candles to be burnt before some shrine. Then, "all and each of the brethren, four times in the year, can receive from the sub-cellarer, without any condition, an *Exennium*[1] in honour of their friends who come to visit them, or can send it to them." The sub-cellarer had to see that "the convent bread is sufficiently white, and reasonably fermented and of good taste;" and also of the beer; that it is well purified (*defecata*), of good colour, bright, and well malted (*granata*) and of good flavour. The fish was to be in season and fresh, not kept for two or three days and stinking, for "that it should not be from the refuse of the people that the holy congregation be fed." The bill of fare had to be sometimes changed, lest disgust be generated, according to the saying, *Idemptitas parit fastidium*.[2] Concerning the pitance, the cellarer shall see that it is good, delicate, and well and decently (*curialiter*, a favourite term) prepared," with everything necessary. The food has to be ready and well cooked before the monks

---

[1] An *Exennium* was some little gift in the way of eatables or drinkables.
[2] *Toujour perdrix!*

enter the refectory, "for it is better that the cooks should wait to dish up than that the servants of God should be kept sitting and waiting without their food."

The Guest-master.—The guest-master represented the hospitality of the monastery. He is always to keep the guest-house supplied with beds, chairs, tables, towels, and everything else needed for the comfort of the guests.[1] When he hears of an arrival he goes to meet them, and, benignly receiving them, tells the guests whether it is a fast or feast day in the monastery. According to the Rule, they are taken to the church, and thence, after prayers, to the parlour, and saying *Benedicite,* he salutes them with a holy kiss. He then asks their names, residence, and country; and having ascertained these, leads them to the hospice, where, sitting down with them, he reads to them, as the Rule says, something from the divine page, and then speaks a few words salutary to their souls. If the guests are monks and strangers to this place, he then shows them the cloister and the dormitory, and, if time allows, the offices; and, for the sake of consoling them (*consolandi gratia,* another favourite phrase), he can take them over the whole monastery. The guests have to be treated especially well, and "all humanity and honour and welcome" shown to them by all. If the guest chances to be a conventual prior of some house, he is always to have the same allowances, both at dinner and supper, as the prior of St. Augustine's; and a stranger abbat is served in the refectory as the abbat of the monastery himself. A liberal allowance of four candles, according to the right and ancient custom (*ex recta et antiqua consuetudine,* another phrase of frequent occurrence) is made for each monk guest, and eight for a conventual prior. Should any guest wish to speak to the abbat or prior, or to one of the claustral brethren, he has to apply to the guest-master, who procures leave. If a

---

[1] For monk-guests *froccos eisdem per famulum suum continuo destinabit.*

stranger (a monk) behaves in an unseemly manner, so that his offence is great and known to all, the guest-master has to proclaim him at chapter, and there publicly he makes satisfaction. But if the fault is light he is not to be cited, but secretly rebuked and warned to behave himself better, "so that he may understand that in this house monastic observance flourishes." No monk-guest can go out of the enclosure without the guest-master's knowledge: neither ought he to leave when a brother is lying dead, until the funeral is over. If, *quod absit*, he should have any complaint about the food or drink supplied to himself or to his servants or horses, or any want of the usual necessaries, the guest-master has to mention it at the next chapter, and the president thereof proclaims "the brother who has thus brought discredit upon God and the Church." If any strangers (monks) come after the grace has been said, they are to take their meals in the refectory, and with the guest-master do penance for coming in late; and are then to be seated here and there among the seniors. If there are guests at the high table (*ad skillam*) they stay behind after dinner, and the guest-master remains also. But if they are invited to dine with the abbat or prior, the guest-master takes them there, and returns after the meal to conduct them back again. If they are not kept behind by the president, the guests have to go out with the rest of the monks to the church, but remain outside the choir, where with the guest-master they finish the grace. "But if they be monks of St. Edmund's, or from a monastery especially connected with ours," they enter the choir with the rest of the convent. If they remain behind with the president and guest-master, and such other monks as the superior chooses, behind the door of the refectory they are, as far as can be in silence, "exhilarated and consoled" by drinking; they are then, "according to the right and antient custom," taken to the guest-quarters, where doubtlessly they were duly "consoled." The guest-master has to warn his guests of the hours and places. He supplies all their wants, even to clothing if need be, and distributes to them what is wanted from the store of clothes belonging to the deceased monks of the house. Only a monk of the order is thus to be made as one of the family; all other guests, religious and secular, are entertained in the outer guest-house. According to the old custom, as long as a benedictine guest behaves "with probity and honesty," he can stay as long as he likes; but if he be found to be a wanderer (*gyrovagus*) and acting in an unseemly manner, he is to be corrected in chapter with both words and stripes, according to his fault, and then allowed to depart. A monk who comes on foot is only to be received in the outer guest-house, for he may be a truant (*trutannus*). He (and also poor chaplains and clerics) is to receive from the almoner only entertainment for the day, and is sent to sleep somewhere in the town. But any monk who comes as a guest of one of the convent is to be treated as one of the community. The parents and relatives of the monks are received in the outer guest-house, and are there to be most honourably and abundantly entertained.

The Master of the Crypts.—The master of the crypts had to provide there for the daily mass after prime, at which all the juniors assisted. It was a mass of our Lady, and used to be sung.

The Almoner.—The almoner had to visit the almonry two or three times a day, and see to the distribution of food to the poor which was made daily on behalf of the monastery. He also visited the sick poor of the neighbourhood and took them certain "consolations," and saw that they were properly provided with what was necessary. Anything they asked for was to be got if possible. The almoner did not personally visit sick women, but sent his servants in his place.

The Refectory-master.—The refectory-master has to see that the tables are properly prepared. On days when the convent take supper he has to lay five loaves before the president, viz. three "choyns" and two loaves of ordinary bread, one for dinner and one to be kept for supper. He has also to provide a loaf for the *mixtum*. On certain days the convent had a better bread; simnel bread (*siminella*), on some, and a species of gateau (*gastellum*) on others. He has to taste the drink provided for the refectory. He has to see to the lavatory outside the refectory being kept in a proper state. He provides mats for the benches and straw for the floor. At the beginning of each meal he "reverently" places a spoon before each monk, but five or six before the president on account of guests; and towards the end of the meal gathers them up again. Also when they have wine he himself lays out the silver wine-cups; and after the pitance, he carries honourably up through the refectory the cheese, and places it before the president and breaks it *curialiter*, and then passes it to the guests and to the monks. He must not speak "except for the sake of consoling, and then not openly but briefly." He has to see that the table-linen is changed whenever there is a general shaving of the convent, or oftener if necessary; also that six towels are placed in the cloister every Sunday morning before the procession. Of the five at the lavatory near the refectory one is kept for the sole use of the claustral prior, the other four being for general use. The sixth hangs at the smaller lavatory near the church door. At the high mass each day, as soon as the first *Agnus Dei* was sung, the three servers for the week, together with the reader, left the choir to take in the refectory the *mixtum* allowed by the Rule (cap. xxxviii.). It was, according to the day, bread and beer; or vegetables, or eggs, or fish, or cheese. The refectory-master had to serve them without delay, and with all care and honour. They ate sparsely, for they had to return to the choir for the next hour of the office.

III. THE CONVENTUS

1. THE RULES OF THE NOVITIATE

When a young man desired to enter the monastery of St. Augustine's, he had to remain for some time in the guest-house as a postulant. When the day was fixed for his admission, or as it was called "the shaving" of his head (*rastura*), the prior gave him notice that three days before he was to dine with the abbat. The abbat would then call the prior and two or three of the seniors, and they appointed the novice-master who was charged to instruct him in all necessary for his state, and to supply all his wants. The abbat then, after some kind words, left the youth in the hands of the master, who examined him and found out if he had everything he wanted for the time of his probation. The postulant was then warned to cleanse his soul by confession if necessary, and was instructed in the rudiments of monastic ceremonial. These instructions were spread over the intervening days, on one of which the postulant dined with the prior. On the day of the *rastura*, after prime, he attended the mass of our Lady and made an offering after the Gospel. His master then took him to the chapel of St. Bridget and there prepared him diligently for the ceremony. When the hour arrived he went with his master into the chapter-house where the convent was assembled, and having profoundly prostrated himself before the abbat, was asked by him what he desired, and replied in the customary form. He was then bidden to rise, and was told by the abbat how hard and trying was the life he desired. He was asked if he was free-born, in good health, and free from any incurable disease; if he was ready to accept hardships as well as pleasant things, to obey and bear ignominy for the love of Christ. To these he answered, "Yes, by the grace of God." Then pursuing the examination, the abbat asked if the postulant had ever been professed in any other stricter order; whether he was bound by any promise of marriage, free from debt and irregularity. On receiving an answer in the negative, the abbat granted his prayer; and he was forthwith taken by the novice-master to have his head shaved and be invested with the monastic habit. Now he was under tutelage, and remained a "novice" until he was ordained priest, although only for one year was he technically such.[1]

The life for novices was regulated in the greatest detail. For instance the ceremonial used in the refectory was minute and tended to secure regularity and recollection, together with courtesy one to another. They had to enter in due order, bow to each other, and while the others were coming in had to say silently a *De profundis* as a solace for the holy souls. After grace had been said they were to take their places at the table, but not to stir till the reading had begun; then they should uncover their loaves, put their cup in its place, and get their knives and spoon ready. They were taught not to drink until the signal was given. From the consuetudinary we learn that the novices communicated every Sunday and on the feasts of Christmas, Ascension day, the three last days of holy week, the three days of their profession, and the ember-days. They were taught to have great reverence for the abbat and for all bishops and prelates. If by chance the abbat came to give them a conference, they all humbly sat on the ground at his feet. During their year's probation the novices never eat meat except under most extraordinary circumstances. There are minute directions about changing their clothes and the times, places, and manner thereof; about the care of the

---

[1] The novice-master had an assistant "in that the most laborious and tiresome of all ministries."

lavatory and personal cleanliness; about blood-letting and the bath, &c.[1]

As the time for profession approached, the novices were instructed how to read and how to chant, how to serve in the church, and how to bear the thurible. Offices were distributed week by week, first to one side of the choir then to the other; so all had an opportunity of learning. Before the day came they had to write out the formula and then petition in chapter for the grace of profession, and pass through a public examination as upon entry. The ceremony was performed by the abbat during the mass, after the Gospel had been sung. For three days after their profession the hood was worn over the face (*usque ad medium nasi*), and they kept rigorous silence. At the following chapter, the newly professed took oath to preserve the secrets of the chapter; not to complain out of spite or wicked zeal against the priors and officers of the order; and, as far as in them lay, not to allow the monastery to be burthened with debt.

2. The Rules of the Cloister

The monk's life was largely spent in the cloister. There all sat in order and in fixed places. No one was allowed to go outside the cloister without leave. Silence was always

[1] It must be remembered that novices were, as a rule, but young men and had to be trained into habits of regularity and politeness, without which community life would be unbearable. And such rules as are laid down in the consuetudinary are, after all, only the expression of regulations which tacitly exist in every well-ordered family. They were inspired by the same thoughtfulness for the feelings of others which is the mark of a true gentleman wherever he is to be found. The rules were not left to the individual ideas of any one novice-master, but were the established and written rules of a house that had traditions of seven hundred years at its back when this consuetudinary was written, and was therefore able to stamp with an unmistakable character all who were educated within its walls.

observed save on certain days and times when conversation was allowed. At other times, they had to obtain leave to go into the parlour (*locutorium*) in order to speak. The abbat, according to his preference, sat at the top of the east cloister near the chapter-house door; the prior in the north cloister near the parlour door, the sub-prior in the eastern cloister near the smaller lavatory; the third prior on the western side. The novices and scholars used the southern cloister as their school. No one sat in the eastern cloister except the abbat and sub-prior and those appointed to hear confessions. Those brothers who were in penance also sat on this side. In the cloister they all sat one behind the other: but sideways when talking was allowed. On these occasions "Let no one dare to ask about the gossip of the world nor tell it, nor speak of trifles or frivolous subjects apt to cause laughter. No contentions are to be allowed. While talking is allowed, no brother should read a book or write anything unless he sits altogether apart." The monks were not allowed to go to the novices. These were not allowed to speak or to sit close to one another. They were always under the eye of a guardian, who while he was on duty was not allowed to read or write or do anything which would take his eyes away from watching. The monks seem to have always worn their hoods during the daytime. French was the general language of the monastery—Latin only occasionally. In the cloister took place the weekly washing of the feet, and while the monks were engaged in the process they wore their hoods drawn over their faces. Shaving took place here. The prior fixed the day (in the winter once in two weeks, in the summer twice in three weeks) and four barbers attended. The seniors were shaved first, "because in the beginning the razors are sharp and the towels dry," says the consuetudinary. The cloister was spread with straw in the winter and with green rushes in the summer.

3. THE RULES OF THE REFECTORY

In the refectory the monks preserved their respective places. They had to wash their hands before entry, and each say the *De profundis* while taking his place. At the sound of the *skilla*, which the president strikes, grace is begun, always by the precentor or succentor. The monks stand facing the east. At the end of the grace the reader approaches the step before the high table and asks the blessing. Until he has read the first sentence the monks sit quietly at the table. Should the reader, however, not be able to find the book at once he recites a short sentence from Scripture (*Deus caritas est*), so as not to keep them waiting unduly. The one who presides sits in the middle of the high table and has the little bell to give signals. The guests are placed on either of his sides. Should a bishop or abbat of some other order be present, out of respect he takes the chief place, but does not preside at the *skilla;* a benedictine abbat, however, presides as if at home. The various dishes are taken first to the superior and then in order round the community. The monk who sang the high mass that day is always served after the guests, and then the non-professed novices. No waiter (the monks, all but the novices, served week by week) is allowed to carry three dishes at once. The refectory being the common dining-hall, no singularity in eating or drinking is allowed. No noise to be made; for instance, if there are nuts, they are not to be cracked with the teeth, but a monk is privately to open them with his knife, so as not to disturb the reader. Should he spill anything, he has to go and do penance in the middle of the refectory if strangers are not present. He is not to make signs across the refectory, not to look about or watch what the others are doing; he is not to lean on the table; his tongue and eyes are to be kept in check, and the greatest modesty observed.

His ears, however, are always to be attentive to the reading and his heart fixed on his heavenly home. He eats with his head covered with the hood. "No one, whether in the refectory or outside, should drink without using both hands to the cup, unless weakness in one hand prevents him. . . . And this manner of drinking was common in England before the coming of the Normans." If the president sends any special dish to some one brother, the receiver rises in his place and bows his thanks. When the meal is finished each monk covers up the bread that has to serve for supper, and sets his knife and spoon and salt vessel in order. They then begin grace, and go out in procession to the church where it was finished. The reader and the servers have to go out also, but do not go into the choir; and as soon as they have privately finished their grace they return to the refectory for their meal, which is served precisely as the others. But they "as a reward of their labour ought to be served in the most honourable and best manner possible, both of the vegetables and pitance, and of the extra dish."

4. The Rules of the Chapter

One of the most important features in the government of the abbey was the daily chapter; it was the mainspring of discipline and the upholder of fraternal charity. Without such an institution it would have been impossible to govern the house. According to the old custom, every day before the chapter, the prior summoned the guardians of the order, some of the seniors and other discreet monks, if necessary, to consult with them about what should be treated of in the chapter or corrected; so that nothing should ever be done there on the spur of the moment or without advice. In chapter only those things which pertained to salvation were to be treated of, business matters being spoken about elsewhere; but any pressing business which required the knowledge and assent of the whole convent could be briefly gone into after the main business was completed. All in the house were bound to attend. The superior entered first and was followed in due order by the seniors; and when all had taken their places a junior read the martyrology for the day. The *tabula* or list of duties and notices was then read, and each monk on hearing his name bowed. Then followed a discourse if the superior thought fit, and at the end he said *Loquamur de ordine nostro*. At this point the non-professed novices rose and went out.[1]

There were "three voices" recognised in the chapter: the accuser, the answerer, and the judge; and another "five voices," to wit: he who presided; the guardians of the order; the precentor and succentor; the brothers charged with keeping the silence, "because silence is called the key of the whole order"; and then the almoner and sub-almoner. These five in their order were the first to "proclaim" any one whom through their respective offices they knew had infringed the rule. The monk so proclaimed had to go out into the centre of the chapter and, prostrating, made confession of his fault, and, saying *mea culpa* and promising amendment, then received penance and rebuke. Should he be accused falsely he could "sweetly" say that he has no recollection of the fault. Special severity was to be shown to the juniors, for then "order will much better flourish in the congregation." Every one who had ceased to be under ward had a right to speak in the chapter on three points; defects

---

[1] "The word *capitulum* can conveniently be said to mean *caput litium*, for in chapter all strife is put an end to and any discord or dissension there may have been among the brethren. The chapter-house is the workshop of the Holy Ghost, in which the sons of God are gathered together and reconciled to Him. And it is especially the house of confession, the house of obedience, mercy, and forgiveness; and the house of unity, peace, and tranquillity, in which whatever exterior offence committed to the knowledge of the brethren is confessed, and by satisfaction is mercifully forgiven."

in the public worship, the breaking of silence, and the distribution of the alms. On other subjects he must ask leave to speak. But the abbat's councillors, fourteen or sixteen seniors (*senpectes vel senes*), chosen from both choirs, have freedom of speech when any matters which concern observance and the increase of religion are discussed. Any one who speaks is to be heard by all, and is not to be rebuked for what he says unless he speaks disrespectfully. Any one disagreeing with what has been said, can with all modesty and reverence dispute the matter, "lest discordant contention finds place for overthrowing of the order." But disturbers of the chapter, the disobedient and those disrepectfully contending with their superiors, are to be sharply corrected by words, stripes, and fasts, that their bad example may not corrupt others. Provision is made against any insulting language to the president of chapter, and should such occur the guardians and all seniors are at once to proclaim him. Every fault confessed has to be punished. If in penance a monk is ordered to receive stripes, the president appoints one, never the proclaimer nor a junior, to execute the sentence; and the culprit, according to the old usage, prostrated and received on his bare shoulders the number of stripes ordained.[1] But according to the later custom he sits with his face and head enveloped in the hood. "While corporal discipline of this kind is being inflicted upon a brother all the rest sit with bowed and covered head, and with kind and brotherly affection should have compassion on him." In the meanwhile no one speaks, or even looks at him, except the president and the inflictor and some of the elders, especially the confessors of the house, who can intercede for him. The list of punishments is given, and is divided into those for *light faults*, such as: separation from the common table;

---

[1] According to the old custom a thick rod was used; but in later days a birch of "several lither twigs."

to take the meal three hours later than the community;[1] to take a lower place in choir and chapter; not to celebrate mass nor to assist ministerially; not to read in public, nor sing nor act as thurifer or acolyth; not to make the offertory, nor receive the *pax* or the holy communion; to prostrate during part of every office. For grave faults perpetual silence (in choir as well as elsewhere); bread and water every Wednesday and Thursday; the last place in the community. For the very grave crimes imprisonment according to the Rule. Such an one had also to lie prostrate in the doorway of the church at each hour, so that the monks passed over his body on entering or going out, and he had to sit outside the choir as one excommunicated.

If any one in chapter became altogether rebellious and would not be otherwise controlled, he was seized by the brethren, who took away his knife and girdle, lest he should in his madness do harm, and was then put into the prison.

Every one was liable to be proclaimed, even the abbat; but he, as a rule, had to be reverently spoken to by some of the seniors outside the chapter, should he have been guilty of any serious fault. But if his fault was notorious and it was judged useful, he could in a few words be proclaimed in the chapter. The prior, when proclaimed, stood in his place and bowed. If it was a serious offence, two of the seniors at his request go into the middle and do penance in his stead. The abbat is warned by the consuetudinary to have a great respect for his prior, and not to rebuke him publicly for an indiscreet word or so. The obedientiaries are not to be proclaimed by the names of their offices, but by their simple name and number—e.g. *Nonnus A quintus vel nonnus A decimus.* If by chance there are several of the same name, all of them have to rise until the proclaimer indicates which one he refers to. There are to be no mutual proclamations

[1] The time, while the others were eating, had to be spent in prayer in the church.

in the same chapter, nor is any one to proclaim after he has once sat down. The proclamations over, any monk who had a petition to make then went into the middle, and prostrating, in answer to the abbat's demand what he asked, replied, "I ask and beseech God's mercy and yours for—" according to his need. This was the occasion when a monk asked for prayers for his deceased parents and relations, for himself before ordination, for leave to give up some work imposed upon him, for mercy for others, for leave to go to the infirmary, or for the blessing before profession, &c. These petitions being heard and granted, if judged well, any laymen or others who desired confraternity were admitted by the chapter, and their petition was granted. The business being completed, prayers for the dead were said by the president, and upon the signal the blessing was given and all retired.

5. THE RULES OF THE DORMITORY

The dormitory was a place of perpetual silence. The monks wore their hoods drawn over the face, and walked with slow and grave footsteps and eyes cast down. After compline the convent go processionally to the dormitory, and according to ancient usage paused at the latrine for the common need. On entering the dormitory, each stood before his bed and said privately the compline of our Lady. They then prepared their beds for the night, and took off their upper garments according to a fixed rule [1] and got into bed. If any one was in the habit of calling out in his sleep, he slept elsewhere than in the common dormitory.

The monk rose at midnight for matins. Some, to stir up their fervour, used the words, *Ecce sponsus venit, exite obviam ei*; others, the words *Surgite mortui qui jacetis in sepulchris vestris et occurrite ad judicium*. The prayers used while

[1] "*Vestiti staminis, femoralibus et caligis atque cincti cingulis aut vestibus vel carrigiis dormire debent.*"

getting up were the *Ave Maria*, with special reference to the midnight hour at which Christ was born. After the office they went back to the dormitory. When they rose again before prime, they signed their foreheads with the cross and said, each one, the *Credo* and the prime of the little office of our Lady. According to the regulation, all had to have their feet out of bed before the sound of the caller has ceased; and he is instructed to sound slowly, as it were for the space of a *Miserere*. On rising they turn back their beds and go to the lavatory to wash and comb their hair; then to the church for prime; after which came the private masses.

In the olden days the monks changed their clothes on the occasion of the bath, which used to be taken four times a year. But since a stricter interpretation of the Rule was introduced, and the general bathing allowed only twice a year, the monks were allowed to change their clothes when they wished. They had a specified mode of making the change, which was always done after prime; and after putting on their clean clothes they were ordered to wash their hands before returning to the cloister.

There was a siesta in the middle of the day, for which they had to undress as for the night. Each bed-place had a shelf and a hook provided, but no other convenience except for the old and infirm. The bed-clothes were not to be of scarlet or any vivid colours. Great cleanliness was ordered in the dormitory, and no dirty or old boots were allowed to be kept in it. The chamberlain was responsible for the well-keeping of the dormitory, and had to have it thoroughly cleaned out, at least once a year. Hay, changed often, was strewn on the floor, and a large mat two and a half feet wide (which the guardian of the manor of Northburne had to provide) stretched the whole length of the dormitory. The beds were of straw, and had to be renewed every year. The chamberlain, besides the care of the dormitory, had to see to the monks' clothing, and had to make on stated days a distribution of various articles of clothing. Each monk had a new habit at least once a year, also one pilche,[1] one set of night wear, and one pair of slippers, &c. Boots were to be renewed once a year, and "no one could refuse to accept a pair of boots, if too large; but the chamberlain should do his best to get each one fitted." The old clothes were given to the poor, and therefore it is laid down that the monks' clothing is not to be mended too much.

6. The Rules of the Infirmary

The prior or guardians have to visit the infirmary every day after the private masses, after each meal, and after compline, to see the sick and make inquiries and receive complaints. If a brother is unwell, he has to get leave to go to the infirmary, and goes to the cellarer and gets for his consolation, doubtlessly, from him a good fat capon and some wine, from the sacrist a supply of candles, &c.; and thus supplied, is prepared for any contingency. He has to go to the infirmary for at least eight days, and during that time is not allowed, without special leave, to celebrate mass, but has to assist at the daily mass said in the infirmary. "In the infirmary no unseemly noise should at any time be made, nor should any sound of musical instruments be ever openly heard there. But if it is considered necessary for any one who is weak and ill, to have his spirit cheered up by the sound of music and harmony, the infirmarian can provide such relaxation. The sick brother is taken into the chapel and the door shut; then some brother or some honest and private servant can, without offence, play sweetly the music of the harp for his delectation. But great care must be taken lest any sound or melody of this kind should be

---

[1] These were of lamb's wool, cat or wolf's skin.

heard (*quod absit*) in the infirmary hall, or in the cells of the brethren." The sick are to have every attention and all that they want; and it is ordered that one of the servants of the infirmary has to go into the town to the apothecary when required to get the medicines, to collect herbs for decoctions, and, under the doctor's orders, to make the tisanes, &c.

Should these, together with the fat capon and other consolations, prove efficacious, the brother, when restored to health, had to present himself before chapter and ask absolution and penance for all the faults and infringements of the Rule he had been guilty of while ill. But if the sickness was unto death, the end was met and prepared for as became monks.

When it was announced that a brother was dying, the whole convent gathered together in the church, together with the abbat, and then went in procession to visit the sick, and to anoint him. The monks, headed by juniors bearing the holy water, cross, candles, and thurible, chanting the seven penitential psalms, set forth towards the infirmary. The sacrist followed bearing reverently the holy oil, and the abbat in alb, stole, and maniple humbly followed, accompanied by his chaplain bearing the ritual. Arrived at the place, the monks stand choirwise and continue their chanting while the sick man is aspersed and incensed. The public confession is made by the sick man himself if possible, and he is absolved by all his brethren, and absolves them in turn. Then, according to the old usage, after having kissed the cross he is anointed by the abbat. Meanwhile a priest goes with acolythes and candles to the church and brings the Sacrament of Christ's Body, borne on a paten, to the sick chamber, and on entering all kneel and adore. The mouth of the sick monk is rinsed out before he receives the sacred host, and immediately before communion he makes his profession of faith and receives the ablutions of the priest's fingers afterwards. For eight days after the anointing, special prayers are said for the sick man by the convent, at the end of each office and also at the morrow-mass. And now the sick man prepares himself for death by resuming the old ascetic practices. No longer does he take meat (unless he recovers), nor does he use a softer bed than usual. One of the monks, priest or deacon, whomsoever the sick man names, is assigned to him as tutor and friend, and special servants, who have special privileges, are appointed to wait on him. He is never left until death supervenes or he recovers. The brother is constantly to read the passion of our Lord to him as long as he can hear; and when unable to do so, the psalter is said to assist him in his agony. When death is at hand, according to the old custom, ashes were strewn on the floor in the shape of a cloth, and haircloth laid thereon; and on to this penitential bed the dying man was gently lifted, according to the example of St. Martin, who told his disciples that Christians ought only to die on ashes and sackcloth. But the more humane usage of later times modified this custom, and the ashes and haircloth were put upon the bed itself. As soon as the agony began the convent were summoned, and with thurible and cross, and singing *Credo* and penitential psalms, they assisted at the departure of their brother. The deceased, clad in his night garments (it was specified that the clothes had to be good, even new), with his face covered with a *sudarium*, was borne into the church, and there the office of the dead was sung, and vigil kept around the body, which was never left until the funeral. He was borne to the grave by his brethren, and laid therein by two monks vested in albs. In the chapter immediately after his death, the convent took the discipline *conventualiter* for the relief of his soul. For thirty days office was said for him, and the month's mind duly kept. Doles were made to the poor on his behalf; and each priest in the house said ten masses, and those not priests ten psalters. Notice of the death was sent to all religious houses in Great Britain, except to the mendicants, and a dirge and mass celebrated in each. In the houses specially connected with St. Augustine's, the name of the dead was inserted by the precentor in the Martyrology, and besides the public mass each priest said one, and the others read fifty psalms.

When news came of the death of a *confrater*, a dirge and solemn mass was sung as the official act of the convent, and each priest said a mass, and the other monks fifty psalms. The name of the *confrater* was entered in the Martyrology, and his anniversary kept as that of one of the monks. It was also inserted in the next *breviculum* which was sent out, and thus he shared in the prayers of every house.

7. Some General Rules

Among the regulations scattered throughout the consuetudinary are some of special interest. In the *Reformationcula* of abbat Nicholas Thorne it is laid down that on days when the convent assisted at a sermon they could say the usual penitential psalms privately; and this and the like dispensations were given, so that the office itself might be said more slowly and more devoutly. The eating of meat was allowed to the brethren who bore the weight of the office; but never in the refectory but in the *domus misericordiarum*, and always with the provision that never less than thirty monks were to be present at the ordinary meal in the refectory. No seculars were to be allowed in the *domus misericordiarum*, and the monks had to serve themselves. Obedientiaries and others whom business took abroad were not allowed to eat meat, especially in public; for, it is recognised "this is against the Rule, and altogether against canonical institution."

"Let the confessors discreetly do all that belongs to their office, viz. to know how to weigh and discern between sin and sin; between person and person; between manner and manner; and what circumstances aggravate a sin."

"Also let the brethren frequently confess, at least once a week; and not only once but twice or thrice, or daily if their conscience demands it, for it is said *the just man falls seven times a day*. And those who confess, let them be ready to receive and duly perform penance." The confessors have every month to give in, to the abbat or other superior, the names of those who confess to them, and whether they confess according to the above manner. Those who do not confess within the ordinary times are to be rebuked and publicly punished in the chapter.

No priest is to refrain from celebrating more than four days without the superior's consent; nor the others from weekly communion. Transgressors were to be put on lenten fare till they repented.

The monks were not allowed to write or receive letters without permission.

"That our Rule of our holy father Benet be held by all in great reverence. That the statutes of the popes, of the legates, and of the general chapter of our order are to be read in the chapter-house at fixed times, and are to be observed as far as they do not go against our privileges or reasonable customs."

That the monks all dress alike, the same cut, the same colour and material.

That in processions the monks should go orderly and gravely, and that there should be a distance of seven feet between each monk.

That no brother should become a guardian or have ward of seculars without special leave. No one is to take part in secular disputes unless for the convent or church.

The brethren were for the future forbidden, under pains provided for in the canons, to play at chess, dice, &c., or to use bows or slings, or run with poles, or throw stones, big or little, or to be present at fights or duels, or baiting, or cock-fighting, or to run in the woods, with shout and hounds, in the profane sport of the chase.

That behaviour is to be guarded between the monks and seculars as well as among themselves: and that no one gives ear to rumours or such like fatuities which profit not the soul.

That all wicked carnal affections and foolish consortings be repressed; and all giving of blows is forbidden.

That the younger monks, after they have finished their tutelage, should study Holy Scripture, for nothing is more hateful than not to know how to occupy oneself. Let them learn off by heart the epistles and gospels for the whole year. Before they venture to read them publicly, they must be diligently practised.

There are some who practise private acts of mortification and leave unobserved those prescribed by the Rule. Such as these are to be rebuked.

Since some of the monks get bled too often and without necessity, in order to get the *solatium* allowed at those times, it is ordered that bleeding is only allowed once in seven weeks.

Those who have leave to go outside the enclosure do not therefore get leave to eat and drink outside, or to go to the houses of seculars. On journeys, monks are to go to houses of our own order in preference to any other.

No one is to be promoted to the priesthood save by a special favour and by the advice of the seniors. If any youth of ability is sent to the university, he has to know by heart, before he is allowed to go, the psalter, the hymns, canticles, communion of saints, the ferial antiphons, and short responsories, and all the versicles of the whole antiphonary.

There are some who claim a general dispensation from compline. No such licence is ever to be given. Permission is only granted in individual cases from certain and reasonable causes. Those who are dispensed are to say their compline sitting near the chapter-house door, and not walking about the cloister. They, also, are to be in the dormitory before the curfew sounds.

"And let the brethren take heed that they fail not in these, for very perilous it is to fail in such laws until they have been revoked by the abbat, or with his permission by the prior or sub-prior in full chapter. There are some who attach little weight to the precepts of chapter, and say: 'We will do what is ordered for two or three days, so that we may seem to accept and obey them; but beyond this we don't care.' Such as these wickedly sin."

END OF VOL. I.

Printed by BALLANTYNE, HANSON & CO.
Edinburgh & London

www.ingramcontent.com/pod-product-compliance
Lightning Source LLC
Chambersburg PA
CBHW030011240426
43672CB00007B/902